Improving Productivity and the Quality of Work Life

Thomas G. Cummings
Edmond S. Molloy

The Praeger Special Studies program—utilizing the most modern and efficient book production techniques and a selective worldwide distribution network—makes available to the academic, government, and business communities significant, timely research in U.S. and international economic, social, and political development.

Improving Productivity and the Quality of Work Life

PRAEGER SPECIAL STUDIES IN U.S. ECONOMIC, SOCIAL, AND POLITICAL ISSUES

Praeger Publishers   New York   London

Library of Congress Cataloging in Publication Data

Cummings, Thomas G
    Improving productivity and the quality of work life.

    (Praeger special studies in U.S. economic, social,
and political issues)
    Bibliography: p. 292
    1. Personnel management.   2. Organizational
change.   3. Labor Productivity.   I. Molloy, Edmond S.,
joint author.   II. Title.
HF5549.C838   1977   658.3   76-24348
ISBN 0-275-56870-9
ISBN 0-03-022601-5 student ed.

PRAEGER SPECIAL STUDIES
200 Park Avenue, New York, N.Y., 10017, U.S.A.

Published in the United States of America in 1977
by Praeger Publishers,
A Division of Holt, Rinehart and Winston, CBS, Inc.

789   038   987654321

PREFACE

This volume is an outgrowth of a federally supported research project to review current literature related to productivity and job satisfaction. The major purpose of this study was to assess the current state of knowledge in this field to provide organizational members with a sound basis for improving the content and conditions of work. Among the literature evaluated were a number of promising approaches to enhancing productivity and the quality of work life. Referred to as "innovative work experiments," these studies represented most of the strategies used in organizations today to improve work. Upon close inspection, however, these experiments were often not reported in a way that would be beneficial to potential users. In most cases, the studies did not include thorough critiques of the validity of their results or information that might limit the general applicability of the findings. Furthermore, suggestions about how to implement the various strategies were rarely presented systematically, thus leaving the reader to cull the narratives of the experiments for such practical advice. Rather than despair over the inadequacy of this literature, the authors felt that a hard-nosed analysis of the experiments might provide the knowledge needed to improve productivity and human fulfillment. This book represents the fruits of this labor.

The book is aimed at managers, union officials, consultants, and researchers who are interested in enhancing both the economic and social sides of work. It is a major attempt to demystify the work-improvement literature, so that individuals can make decisions in this area based on scientific evidence and sound theory rather than rhetoric and vague metaphors. Each strategy reviewed includes a theoretical discussion of the concepts underlying the approach, a plan for implementation, a critique of the efficacy of the results, a discussion of possible limiting factors, and advice for carrying out organizational changes effectively. A representative experiment showing how the strategy works in a particular organization is also presented. The knowledge gained from a review of this type provides individuals with a comprehensive framework for choosing, implementing, and evaluating a work-improvement strategy relevant to their organizations.

The authors are highly indebted to their fellow researchers, whose support and advice contributed greatly to this book. Professors Suresh Srivastva and Paul Salipante from Case Western Reserve University in Cleveland, Ohio, were the principal investigators of the original research project, and their direction and administrative support were most valuable. Professor William Notz from the University of Manitoba in Winnipeg, Canada, provided a good deal of direction in assessing the validity of the different strategies. Roy Glen, a doctoral student at Case Western Reserve University, helped to review the work experiments and formulate relevant conclusions.

The authors wish to express their gratitude to the National Science Foundation, Research Applied to National Needs Division of Social Systems and Human Resources, whose financial assistance (NSF Grant no. G139455) made this work possible. Also, the aid provided by the University of Southern California, Los Angeles, Graduate School of Business Administration, and the Irish Management Institute, Dublin, is greatly appreciated, especially in the preparation of the manuscript.

CONTENTS

LIST OF TABLES, FIGURES, AND EXHIBITS

Improving Productivity and the Quality of Work Life

Organizations are rational instruments for achieving man's economic and social purposes. The pervasiveness of such complex structures as business firms, hospitals, educational institutions, and public service agencies lends a certain aura of truth to the feeling that most of us are merely organizational men or women. Indeed, it is difficult to imagine what life would be like without one of our most cherished yet ridiculed inventions, the modern organization. For it is in such complex social and technological settings that many of our fondest dreams are either consummated or thwarted. Most people would agree with the importance of organizations in their daily lives, yet few would dispute the statement that organizations are not as productive and humanly enriching as they should be. One need only go to work, read a newspaper, or talk with a neighbor to realize that problems of productivity and worker satisfaction abound in society. Poor-quality workmanship and productive inefficiency plague most sectors of our economy. Similarly, high rates of absenteeism, turnover, and counterproductive behavior are commonplace in both service and manufacturing industries. Solutions to these difficult problems are almost as plentiful as the organizations that devise them. Work-improvement programs, such as participative management, job enrichment, autonomous work groups, and flexitime, are receiving wide support and acclaim from a growing number of organizational members. Although advocates of these approaches are quite willing to extoll the benefits of their programs, there is underlying skepticism among many individuals as to the programs' validity and general applicability. Furthermore, adherents of specific work-improvement strategies are frequently remiss in reporting the details of their programs: many fail to include the theoretical basis of their strategy or the techniques used to change the organization. In the absence of

such information, prospective users are often left to their own wits to
devise an effective program. This knowledge gap, between what is
practiced in organizations and what is publicly known about such practice, impedes the accumulation of learning in this field and considerably reduces organizations' ability to improve productivity and the
quality of work life. This book is an attempt to rectify these problem
It brings together and critiques most of the major work-improvement
strategies used in organizations today. The book is a hard-nosed effort to understand and evaluate the efficacy of the approaches and to
provide individuals with sound advice for choosing, implementing,
and evaluating a strategy relevant to their organization.

As an introduction to this important topic, this chapter first
outlines the kinds of knowledge required to develop a work-improvement strategy. This provides a guide for reviewing the various approaches to see if they furnish the needed information. Second, the
original research report upon which this book is based—a federally
supported study of the policy implications of current research on job
satisfaction and productivity—is discussed. This provides a framework for how the various strategies were chosen and reviewed. Finally, the format of the book is presented, along with a review of its
major conclusions.

KNOWLEDGE REQUIRED TO IMPROVE
PRODUCTIVITY AND THE QUALITY
OF WORK LIFE

Given a decision to improve work, organizational members are
invariably faced with the issue of devising a strategy for implementing relevant organizational changes. To be effective, such strategies
must include information about what modifications lead to positive
outcomes and, also, how these results can be effected in a specific
organizational setting. Three kinds of knowledge appear to furnish
this information. The first involves the identification of action levers
organizational changes that lead to increases in productivity and the
quality of work life. For instance, increased task autonomy may result in greater worker satisfaction. Information that a specific change
does, in fact, lead to a positive outcome is the minimal condition for
successful change. Without cause and effect knowledge, it is impossible to formulate a rational work-improvement strategy.

The second kind of knowledge required for successful change
concerns the context of the organization and the way its members
react to work improvements. Referred to as "contingencies," this information includes those factors upon which desirable changes are
dependent. It may be, for example, that greater job autonomy is suc-

cessful only for workers with high needs for independence. To the extent that the effects of certain action levers are contingent upon such contextual variables as technology, organizational climate, and worker characteristics, it is necessary to take these factors into account when modifying the organization.

The third kind of necessary knowledge related to strategy formulation involves understanding of organizational change processes. Familiarity with the dynamics of change is essential for manipulating any action lever, especially those requiring new forms of organizational behavior. Information about change processes provides individuals with the practical knowledge to implement a change program and to respond to possible contingencies. Thus, for instance, it may be necessary to include first-level supervisors in planning the change program if the action lever of worker autonomy is to be implemented successfully. Whereas the identification of action levers informs the organization what to change, knowledge of change processes tells it how to change.

The three kinds of information discussed above provide a comprehensive framework for reviewing work-improvement strategies: identification of action levers furnishes a rational basis for making organizational changes; knowledge of contingencies points to those factors upon which successful results are dependent; and understanding change processes provides the know-how to implement a strategy effectively.

THE NATIONAL SCIENCE FOUNDATION STUDY

Much of the material presented in this book is based on an extensive evaluation of policy-related research on productivity, industrial organization, and job satisfaction supported by the Research Applied to National Needs (RANN) Program of the National Science Foundation (NSF) (Srivastva et al. 1975). The primary objective of the evaluation was to review current research in this field to help organizational members develop research-based policies for improving work. A major part of this study was an assessment of 58 work-improvement experiments (Cummings, Molloy, and Glenn in press). Since this critique (along with others added especially for this book) is the basis for the strategies reviewed in this volume, it is necessary to examine the methodology used to assess the different work-improvement studies. This furnishes a rationale for evaluating the innovative work experiments, as well as a comprehensive framework for further reviews of this kind. The methodology is presented in four parts. The first describes the choice of experiments and their classification into discrete change strategies; the remaining three parts correspond to the kinds of knowledge required for strategy formulation: action levers, contingencies, and change processes.

Choice of Experiments

A number of related criteria were used to select the work-improvement studies. First, organizational studies changing either the conditions or content of work and experimentally examining the results were the focus of study. Case studies, although they may record similar changes and are valuable sources of information, were excluded because they present only ex post facto analysis and, thus, do not permit adequate causal inference. For an almost opposite reason, laboratory experiments were also excluded. Generally, laboratory studies are good tests of causal inference; however, the gap between the laboratory and the organization is so great that it is difficult to apply laboratory findings to real world settings. Second only field studies reporting sufficient data to allow for an evaluation of their validity were chosen for review. This criterion deleted many experiments summarized in popular magazines, newspapers, and company brochures. Third, published articles or books presenting in detail the conduct of the studies were used whenever possible. In a few cases, unpublished reports restricted primarily to in-house circulation were obtained and included in the critique. Finally, experiments reported in 1959 or later were the primary focus of review, though a few pioneering studies conducted before this time were included. The choice of 1959 as a cutoff date provided a 15-year historical period, dating backward from the review's finishing date in 1974. It was felt that this time slice would include most of the major work-improvement strategies used in contemporary organizations.

Based on the above-mentioned criteria, 58 organizational experiments were chosen for the NSF study. Although it is difficult to tell how representative this sample is of the larger population of all work-improvement projects, it is decidedly biased toward published reports that tend to include only positive findings and a good deal of reconstructed logic (Kaplan 1964). On the other hand, published studies also provide the data and methodological rigor needed for a review of this kind.

Careful examination of the organizational studies revealed four relatively distinct theoretical and change strategies: autonomous work groups, job restructuring, participative management, and organization-wide change. The strategies represent sets of beliefs and findings about the causes of productivity and the quality of work life. Each orientation is guided by certain theories and empirical evidence, and each is associated with a particular method of organizational change. In practice, however, there is some overlap among the four strategies, as practitioners of one approach frequently select the best elements of the other perspectives. The four work-improvement strategies correspond to the first four parts of this book.

To make the NSF review more complete, 20 new work experiments have been added to this book. These studies comprise three additional theoretical and change strategies corresponding to the last three sections of the book: organizational behavior modification, flexible working hours (FWH) and the Scanlon Plan. Each of these approaches represents a relatively unique way of improving productivity and human enrichment. Their exclusion from the original NSF study was an unfortunate oversight rather than a judgment of their importance. When taken together, the 78 experiments, representing seven theoretical and change strategies, comprise most of the major work improvements used in organizations today.

Action Levers and Their Effects

Once studies were chosen for review, it was necessary to ascertain what specific organizational changes, or action levers, produce positive results. This was accomplished in two parts. First a general set of action levers and their effects was culled from the experimental reports. This resulted in nine identifiable action levers and five separate outcomes. Each study was then reviewed as to which action levers were changed and what results were obtained. Second, a method based on the experiments' research designs was used to assess the efficacy or internal validity of the findings. The research designs of all studies representing a particular work-improvement strategy were examined to see whether certain plausible explanations, other than the action levers, could have caused the results. This allowed for an assessment of the validity of both the performance and quality of work life outcomes for studies representing each of the change strategies.

Action levers are those factors that are manipulated or changed in the experiments. To arrive at a common list of action levers, each identifiable change was listed for each study. The total list from all experiments reviewed was then examined for categories common to related kinds of changes. This resulted in nine identifiable action levers.

1. Pay/reward systems: Most studies mentioning changes in pay or reward systems included this action lever as an inevitable side effect of the change program. Modifications in pay systems frequently supplemented the more preconceived parts of the work-im-

provement strategy. Thus, for instance, changes in financial rewards were tied to the higher skill levels required on the newly designed jobs, to the new hierarchical status conferred on the job occupant by the restructuring, or to productivity gains anticipated from the redesign. Given the supplemental nature of this action lever, it was difficult to determine the timing of payment changes. Most experiments did not specify at which point in the program the change in pay was granted. Sometimes it seemed to have come before the treatment, sometimes as part of it, and perhaps most often after the planned changes, when it was realized that the program was likely to be rejected or ineffective because workers saw themselves doing more demanding work without receiving requisite rewards. Two examples of changes in pay/reward systems included in the experiments are introduction of a marginal group bonus and replacement of individual piece rate with straight wage and periodic performance appraisals.

2. Autonomy/discretion: The most frequently changed of all organizational variables included in the experiments was the degree of autonomy or discretion that employees have over their work. In most cases, autonomy was increased directly for individual job holders or work groups. For example, the individual was allowed to pace himself, as opposed to being paced by the speed of the assembly line; permitted to sign letters that previously had to be passed on for signature; and allowed to determine his own work methods. Similarly, work groups were given influence over work methods, production layouts, and work schedules; some say over goal setting; and autonomy over assigning work roles. Whereas the above examples are concerned with the actual work individuals perform, changes in autonomy/discretion also involved control over the boundary conditions of work. Thus, job holders were given discretion over the inputs required to do their job, maintenance functions, quality control, and financial control. A final form of increased autonomy involved either direct participation or participation through representatives in the activities of higher groups, such as management and trade unions.

3. Support: The effectiveness of any organizational unit depends heavily on its relationships to other groups providing support services, such as raw materials, maintenance, and technical assistance. This action lever involves organizational changes aimed at improving the support services of the focal unit of change. Examples include additional support services, services on demand from technical groups, allocation of special repairmen to work groups, and integrated support functions.

4. Training: A primary outcome of many of the organizational changes reported in this book is that job holders are required to perform work that is more varied and skilled and that carries more re-

sponsibility than their previous jobs. Although it is likely that most of the experiments reviewed included some form of training to meet these new job demands, only those studies reporting specific training programs were included in this category. Training appears to have been used for at least three purposes. First, it was introduced prior to the change program to prepare a climate of acceptance for the proposed modifications and to familiarize supervisors and workers with the changes that would occur. Second, training programs were employed to equip employees with the necessary knowledge and skills required to perform their redesigned jobs. Third, training similar to that just mentioned was used to make rotation among different jobs possible. Given these three training objectives, typical programs ranged from direct skill learning—for example, sales training for branch managers—to more esoteric kinds of training, such as introduction to new theories of management and exposure to the concepts of job enrichment.

5. Organizational structure: This action lever refers to the formal organization as it would appear in a typical organization chart, including the grouping of job occupants from top management to shop floor operators. There is some reason to suspect that changes in organizational structure may be underreported in the studies. This conclusion is derived from the fact that in the majority of cases where technical or physical changes were made, there is no mention of modifications in organizational structure; yet, one might expect that technical changes would tend to be complemented by structural reorganizations. Typical changes in formal organizational structure were reduction in the number of hierarchical levels; increase in span of control; reorganization of discrete jobs into work groups; clearer management structure, with fewer individuals reporting to supervisors; and simpler, less formal, and better-integrated factory structure.

6. Technical/physical: Technical changes and modifications of the physical work setting were mentioned in many of the experiments. Clearly, many of the smaller-scale changes were conceived during the course of the work-improvement program, whereas most of the larger-scale designs were planned long beforehand, and their implementation provided the opportunity to study their impact on productivity and worker satisfaction. The costs of redesigning technology frequently prohibit its use as an action lever in change programs. The studies reviewed, however, reveal considerable scope for making minor but significant technical and physical modifications to improve work. Relatively minor changes in this action lever included installation of dust extractors, change in the color of decorations and wall paint to reduce glare, movement of an office to a side of the building where daylight could replace artificial light, and introduction of new tools. More costly modifications were a breakdown of a long assembly

line into smaller subunits, physical relocation of looms, increase in
the length of the unit work cycle, and new material-handling equipment.

7. Task variety: Changes in the degree of task variety were
reported explicitly in only a few of the experiments. This category
is not confined to explicit mention of task variety because it was clear
in several studies that increased variety was an inevitable outcome of
other changes, such as autonomy, reporting procedures, and structural modifications. In citing task variety as an action lever in this
latter group of experiments, there has been an attempt to avoid overlap that would occur by coding a change as "variety" and under some
other action lever as well. "Variety," where it was mentioned explicitly, was usually expressed as "task variety" or "job rotation."

8. Information/feedback: This action lever refers to the information or feedback that individuals receive about their work and organization. The range is from immediate knowledge about the quality
of a product or service to information about departmental or company
policy from a representative who attends periodic meetings. At least
four different kinds of information appeared in the experiments: (a)
information needed to perform a specific task; (b) feedback about one's
performance; (c) knowledge about other individuals or groups upon
which one's own performance is dependent; and (d) information about
the department, company, or environment, which is not necessarily
task related. Typical examples of this action lever were quicker feedback on quality of products, ready access to information on current
state of the department, routine daily feedback meetings, and better
communication procedures.

9. Interpersonal/group process: The final action lever represents changes in patterns of interaction or contact among individuals
and groups. As the reader is no doubt aware, changes in other action
levers, such as organizational structure and information/feedback,
frequently involve modifications in interpersonal relationships. Thus
there is some overlap between this category and others. Yet, many
studies focused explicitly on social interaction as a significant organizational change. These included increases in the amount of interaction among group members, provisions for increased teamwork, more
customer contact, and more interaction with staff members.

Like the action levers, it was necessary to cull the actual effects, or results, of the experiments from the narrative of the reports. Each identifiable finding was listed for each study. The total
list was then examined for categories common to most of the experiments. This resulted in five relatively discrete effects of the work-
improvement studies.

1. Costs: Many studies measured some aspect of cost to determine the effects of specific organizational changes. In most instances, cost data were taken directly from company records, where such information is readily available in most manufacturing and service industries. Typical examples of the costs recorded were clerical costs, overhead, direct labor costs per unit, and manufacturing costs.

2. Productivity: This category reflects how well people, machinery, or both together performed as a result of the experiments. While there was no standard definition or measure of productivity used in the studies, it was possible to discern a number of different referents. Some measures of productivity indicated that performance depended primarily on the behavior of the job holders themselves; other measures were explicit that gains or losses were determined by technology; still others reflected the combined efforts of man and machine; and a small number might best be interpreted as productivity effects resulting from a more logical organization of men, machines, and materials. Finally, a few productivity measures referred to the overall effectiveness of the organization or group studied. Some of the productivity measures included worker effectiveness, rate of operation, number of airline bookings, time spent on noncycle activity, and reduction in inspection time.

3. Quality: What constitutes high- or low-quality work depends on the industry and task. The following reflect some of the quality of performance measures reported in the studies: pulp quality, damage rate, waste rate, and number of customer complaints.

4. Withdrawal: The most commonly cited forms of withdrawal from work were labor turnover and absenteeism. Only a few experiments gave details about how the particular forms of withdrawal were recorded. Some of the distinctions made were between voluntary and involuntary withdrawal and between the frequency of absenteeism and the average length of time people were absent.

5. Attitudes: Attitudes represent people's relatively enduring perceptions of, and motivational dispositions toward, other persons, things, or events. Most of the studies assessed the attitudes of experimental subjects toward a variety of organizational events, persons, and objects, including the experiment itself. The following list indicates the range of attitudes measured: (a) general satisfaction; (b) intrinsic motivation; (c) job involvement; (d) job satisfaction; (e) morale; (f) satisfaction with pay, security, company, foreman, and work group; and (g) orientation to job.

Whereas the categories discussed above provide a scheme for determining which organizational changes were made and what results were obtained, the question inevitably rises: Are the claims made by the studies justified? To discover whether the action levers

did in fact produce the reported effects, it was necessary to assess
the internal validity of the experiments. When a study can be said to
have high internal validity, it is then reasonable to assume that the
relationship found in the experiment—for example, between level of
autonomy/discretion and amount of productivity—actually exists. In
evaluating the internal validity of any experiment, it is necessary to
check whether one or more factors, other than the action levers,
could have caused the results. The existence of any plausible alternative factor constitutes a threat to the efficacy of the findings. Campbell and Stanley (1966) have identified several threats to internal
validity. The following eight threats were judged relevant to the evaluation of the work-improvement studies.

1. History: If it could be reasonably argued that the outcome
of an experiment was not due to a particular action lever, such as increased task variety, but rather to some other specific event that
occurred during the experiment, then history would be considered a
threat. Organizational changes typically take from a few weeks to
several months to implement, and during this time, all kinds of extraneous events could influence the outcomes. Changes in the amount
of work available to a group, for instance, could affect productivity.
Similarly, fluctuations in the price of raw materials could influence
the costs of production. History also poses a threat to those experiments that are not easily isolated from other organizational units or
the wider work environment. Thus, for example, contact with workers not involved in the experiment could conceivably affect the attitudes of the experimental subjects.

2. Instability: Let us say that one of the effects being measured
before and after a work-improvement project is productivity. It is a
scientific fact that all measurements are subject to random fluctuations—in this case, random fluctuations in such factors as quality of
raw materials, machine speeds, and workers' behavior. To draw
valid conclusions about the outcomes of an experiment, it is necessary to show that the observed effect is likely to have exceeded the
random fluctuations that occur in any measurement process. The instability threat is usually dealt with by statistical tests, which provide
a precise measure of the probability that the differences between pre-
and posttest measures are not due merely to random fluctuations in
measurement.

3. Testing: This threat refers to the effects of taking a test on
the scores of the subsequent test. It is common in many of the studies
reviewed that individuals were asked to fill out a questionnaire about
their attitudes toward work both before and after the organizational
change. It is plausible that the mere act of filling out the questionnaire may affect individuals' subsequent attitudes. Thus, an improve-

ment in attitudes between the two testing periods may be a testing artifact rather than a true experimental effect. Recent research on the threat of testing shows that the plausibility of this threat is likely to be greatest in organizational settings where there is obtrusive measurement; where the purpose of measurement is readily apparent; where the study is important to the respondents; where individuals are publically identified with their scores; and where it is believed that powerful others have access to scores (Rosen and Sales 1966; Rosen 1970). Many of the work experiments included such factors.

4. Instrumentation: This factor refers to changes in the calibration of a measuring instrument or to changes in the observers that result in modifications in the obtained measures. This threat is likely to occur with subjective observational techniques, where different observers perceive different things, thus causing the data to change independent of the organizational changes. Modifications in record keeping are also sources of this threat.

5. Statistical regression: Whenever a group or organization is selected for experimentation because of its extreme score on some outcome variable, the results of the change program may be affected by statistical regression rather than the experimental changes. Extreme scores, whether high or low, are likely to regress either downward or upward toward their general trend lines. Thus, for example, when work groups are chosen for experimentation because they score extremely low on an outcome variable—for example, absenteeism, productivity, or quality—it is important to account for possible regression artifacts that could easily be mistaken for the effect of the experiment.

6. Selection: Selection biases may affect experimental outcomes whenever groups are selected for the change program because of some special characteristic, such as skill level or receptiveness to experimentation. Failure to control for selection could signify that the experimental and control groups might have differed anyway without the occurrence of the experiment. For instance, if a group of highly skilled workers was selected as the experimental group and then compared to a control group of averagely skilled workers in terms of productivity, the difference might be the result of preexisting differences in skills rather than the organizational changes.

7. Experimental mortality: This refers to differential loss of subjects from the comparison groups. Mortality is a threat not because of the differential loss of numbers of respondents but because of representativeness of respondents. That is, mortality is a problem when those who remain are systematically different from those who are left (which is often the case in work experiments).

8. Selection—history interaction, selection—testing interaction, and so on: These are defined as selection differences that result

in noncomparable responses to history, testing, and so on. This threat can operate even if the pretest scores of the comparison group: are equivalent. Consider, for example, an experimental group and a control group that were similar in all respects except seniority. The groups might differ in their responses to a common historical event, such as a change in company policy regarding the role of senio ity in layoffs and promotion. Thus, even though their preexperimenta scores had been equivalent, differences in the postexperimental scores could be a result of this selection-history interaction rather than of the experimental changes.

It should be noted that Campbell and Stanley (1966) identify another possible threat to the internal validity of an experiment's findings: maturation. This refers to those innate processes of maturation, such as growing hungrier and becoming more tired, which occur inevitably with the passage of time. Maturation was not considered a likely threat to the work experiments' findings for two reasons. The first is that many of the maturation processes are of such short duration that they are unlikely to have much impact on work experiments, which are usually longer-term projects. Growing hungrier or more tired are examples of short-term maturation processes The second reason is that the maturation processes that are specific to adults, the subjects of the experiments reviewed here, frequently take long periods of time to have a significant effect on behavior. Again, it was felt that such processes—for instance, growing less agile or becoming senile—would have little impact during the experimental period.

The extent to which the threats listed above reduce the validity of an experiment's findings is related to the study's experimental design. Those researchers who have complete control over the scheduling of treatments are able to control for most threats to internal validity. Typically, this is achieved by randomization of individuals to experimental and control conditions. In the studies reviewed here, the researchers did not have complete control over the scheduling of treatments. Rather, they were able to approximate such control through the expedient scheduling of data collection. Referred to as a "quasi-experiment," this kind of study allows the researchers to eliminate many of the threats to validity.

Given the relation between an experiment's research design and control over threats to internal validity, the method used to assess the efficacy of the work experiments' findings relied on evaluating their experimental designs. Using Campbell and Stanley (1966) as a guide, each study was classified initially according to its design. This made it possible to rule out immediately some threats to internal validity. In those cases where threats were not controlled by a

tudy's design, the experiment was examined in depth to see if the
hreats had been dealt with in some other manner. When the experi-
nents were classified according to experimental design, it was found
hat most studies used more than one research design, depending
pon the outcome measured. Productivity, for instance, was usually
aken from company records and reported as a time series; attitudes
vere frequently measured with questionnaires and reported as pre-
nd posttest comparisons with a control group. Because there was
nore than one experimental design for each study, it was decided to
ist and evaluate a separate design for each reported outcome. To
implify this procedure, it was also decided to evaluate the effects
.ssociated with costs, productivity, and quality as one grouping,
ermed performance. In those studies measuring more than one of
hese outcomes, the most representative experimental design was
aken as an index of this category.

Examination of threats to the internal validity of the experiments'
indings was carried out for each set of studies representing a partic-
lar theoretical and change orientation. By assessing whether the
hreats were similar or different over an entire set of studies, it was
ossible to judge the efficacy of the overall outcomes of each change
trategy. For example, if the threats to validity were different and
he set of studies reported similar conclusions, then one could have
easonable confidence in the strategy's findings, since the studies
aken as a whole would control for the various threats. Conversely,
f the threats were similar for an entire set of studies, one would not
ave much confidence in a strategy's conclusions, because the find-
ngs of all the experiments were subject to the same uncontrolled
hreats.

Because of the amount of detail used to assess each study's research designs, only the conclusions of this work are summarized
n this book. Similarly, the primary focus of the book is on strategies
or improving productivity and the quality of work life. Therefore,
ach strategy is evaluated only in reference to its performance and
ttitudinal findings. For the studies reviewed, the attitudinal out-
omes serve as indicators of quality of work life.

In summary, this section describes the identification of action
evers and their effects, as well as the evaluation of the efficacy or
nternal validity of the findings. Nine identifiable action levers and
ive separate effects were culled from the experiments. These provided a common set of categories to specify which organizational
changes were made and what results were obtained. The internal
validity of the experiments' outcomes was then assessed for each
change strategy using the studies' research designs to test whether
certain threats to validity were relatively controlled in the research.

Contingencies

After the studies were assessed in terms of action levers and the validity of their effects, it was necessary to determine what con tingencies limit the general applicability of the findings. In scientif terms, this concerns the external validity of the experiments' outcomes: To what specific populations, environments, and operation: definitions of the action levers and effects can the results be applie Logically, generalization of a study's findings to other populations, settings, and variables is never totally justified. This follows fron the simple fact that it is impossible to even define the numbers and kinds of people or the situations to which one would want to apply th findings or to determine exactly the experimental operations to be carried out. Although the external validity of a study's findings can never be assessed totally, it is important to determine as closely as possible the contingencies upon which positive outcomes are depe dent. This provides experimenters with some clues as to the gener applicability of the change strategies, and it provides knowledge abc what conditions may be required to obtain positive results.

Two kinds of information were used to assess the experiment: external validity. The first involved the identification of contextual variables, data about the research populations and settings of the studies. Each study was examined in depth as to characteristics of workers, type of work setting, and cultural environment. The expe riments provided sufficient data for seven contextual variables: (1) type of work performed by the experimental subjects, (2) sex of the participants, (3) blue or white collar job status, (4) number of individuals receiving the treatment, (5) union membership, (6) worker participation in the change process, and (7) country in which the experiment was conducted. Additional contextual variables that would have been of interest and for which there were insufficient data include age of workers, tenure in the organization, size of the organization, location of the organization (urban or rural), age of the organization, success of the organization, state of the economy, and rate of technological and product innovation.

The second kind of data used to evaluate external validity were the studies' research designs. Like the threats to internal validity, Campbell and Stanley (1966) have identified a number of threats to external validity that can be partially controlled by proper experime tal design. Three of these threats apply to the work-improvement studies.

1. Reactive effects of experimental arrangements: This refe to the artificiality of the experimental setting, which makes it atypic of settings in which the organizational change is to be applied regula

This threat suggests that positive outcomes are likely to emerge only in special experimental settings where subjects are treated in nonordinary ways. The well-known "Hawthorne effect," where workers are given added attention from outsiders and management, is a good example of the reactivity of many work experiments. The obvious control for this threat is to make the experimental changes and measures as unobtrusive as possible, thus reducing considerably the reactivity of the experiment.

2. Interaction effects of selection and treatment: This threat is defined as the unrepresentative responsiveness of the research population. Selection and treatment may interact when there is something special about the experimental subjects that makes them responsive to the organizational changes in a way that other groups would not be expected to react. In many work experiments, for example, volunteer subjects were chosen for experimentation. Such individuals are likely to be receptive to the work improvements, whereas nonvolunteers may not be as interested in such changes.

3. Interaction effects of testing: This refers to the effects of a pretest in sensitizing workers to the experimental changes, thus making generalization to unpretested populations precarious. Obviously, this threat applies only where individuals are given an obtrusive pretest that is easily tied to the subsequent change program. For example, a questionnaire asking workers how satisfied they are with different facets of their work may make workers more responsive to subsequent improvements in their work.

Campbell and Stanley (1966) also list another threat to external validity: miltiple-treatment interference. This refers to experiments where several treatments are given sequentially to the same individuals and the results are unrepresentative of the separate application of each treatment. This threat was not applied to the work studies because most of them made multiple, sequential changes, but the findings were applied to the whole set of changes taken as one treatment. Since the inability to differentiate the effects of separate changes was a problem in most of the experiments, it made little sense to differentially assess the studies for the presence of this threat.

Assessment of threats to external validity followed the same format as the evaluation of the internal validity of the experimental findings. The research designs of each set of studies representing a particular change strategy were examined as to whether they controlled for threats to external validity. This was carried out for both the performance and quality of work life findings, and the results were summarized for each theoretical and change orientation. When this evaluation was combined with data from the contextual variables, a number of contingencies that affect the general applicability of the work-improvement studies emerged.

Change Processes

The final kind of knowledge provided by the studies reviewed involved understanding of organizational change processes. Such information gives experimenters practical suggestions about how to change the action levers effectively in organizational settings. Unlike the data used to assess action levers and contingencies, knowledge about change processes was not reported systematically in the experiments. Rather, there was a good deal of anecdotal data concerning the techniques of experimental change. While this information was certainly interesting, it was not the focus of rigorous experimental testing in the studies. Thus, it was difficult to determine whether such practical advice is internally valid or generalizable to other situations. Furthermore, the studies differed widely in the amount of practical suggestions offered. This limited severely the data base for this kind of knowledge. Given these problems, the anecdotal data concerning change processes were summarized for each change strategy. This provides experimenters with some understanding of how to carry out organizational change effectively.

Summary

The NSF study provides much of the information used in this book. An assessment of 58 work experiments, in addition to 20 studie added to this book, furnishes three kinds of knowledge needed to formulate and implement a work-improvement program. Knowledge of action levers and their effects informs experimenters about what organizational changes produce increases in productivity and the quality of work life. Information about contingencies uncovers those factors upon which successful outcomes are dependent. Finally, understanding of change processes tells individuals about how to carry out organizational change successfully.

FORMAT OF THE BOOK

The book is organized primarily into seven parts corresponding to each of the theoretical and change orientations previously mentioned: autonomous work groups, job restructuring, participative management, organization-wide change, organizational behavior modification, flexible working hours, and Scanlon plans. Each section consists of three chapters. The first outlines the theoretical basis of the strategy and its method of organizational change. The second chapter reviews the experiments, representing each strategy in terms of action levers and the validity of their effects, contingencies, and change processes. The third chapter of each part presents one of the experiments reviewed to provide the reader with a detailed example of the change strategy in action. The book ends with implications of the various strategies for the management of organizational change. A strong argument is made for the development of tailor-made or situation-relevant approaches for improving work. Put differently, it is simply not feasible to transplant carbon copies of the various experiments into one's organization. Rather, the studies reviewed in this book serve as guides for generating specific strategies on site. This experimental approach involves an interest in solving important organizational problems rather than defending specific solutions, data gathering as an integral part of the change program, and a concern for possible contingencies and their effects on the experiment. A practical guide for organizational change is also presented, as well as suggestions for the conduct of organizational experiments.

I

AUTONOMOUS
WORK GROUPS

2

AUTONOMOUS WORK GROUPS:
THEORY AND CHANGE STRATEGY

Autonomous work groups are work structures where members regulate their behavior around relatively whole tasks. This work design has at least two features that distinguish it from more traditional task structures: the focus of design is interdependent task groupings rather than individual tasks, and task control is located within the work group rather than external to it. Both of these characteristics offer important advantages for task performance and worker satisfaction. Grouping interdependent tasks within a single work system allows for overall task integration. Internal control permits expedient responses to variances from goal achievement. Task integration and control, in turn, are powerful sources of satisfaction, meeting workers' needs to master their work environment. Given these advantages, autonomous work groups are effective structures for achieving both productivity and human satisfaction.

Autonomous work groups derive from sociotechnical systems theory. This body of theoretical and empirical work has been developed over the past 25 years by social scientists from the Tavistock Institute of Human Relations in London (Rice 1958; Emery 1959; Trist et al. 1963). Their research represents the most extensive application of the systems approach to organizations today. Indeed, the design of autonomous work groups is based on certain systemic properties that provide these units with their self-regulating capacity. This chapter describes the theory behind autonomous work groups and discusses a change strategy for implementing them in organizations.

THEORETICAL FOUNDATION

Autonomous group theory dates formally from a coal mine study carried out 25 years ago by Trist and Bamforth (1951) of the Tavistock

Institute of Human Relations. The major impetus behind the study
was a change in the technology and method of coal mining from non-
mechanized to mechanized mining./Prior to the change, miners
worked under a single-placed task structure, where small groups of
workers—two or three individuals—performed all of the tasks needed
to complete a whole cycle of coal getting. Since workers regulated
their task performance with little external supervision, their behavior
was adaptive to the changing conditions of the underground situation.
This task design also provided individuals with task variety and
autonomy congruent with their social-psychological needs. The introduction of a new form of mining, involving mechanized coal cutters
and a conveyor method of transporting coal, drastically altered the
single-placed tradition. Designed according to mass production
methods, the newer form of mining, referred to as "the conventional
long-wall method," separated the tasks required to complete a whole
cycle of coal getting into three sequential groups covering three shifts
Since the primary impact of this innovation was to isolate groups of
workers performing interdependent tasks, external supervision was
needed to integrate the separate groups into a whole cycle of operation
    Contrary to expectation, the conventional long-wall method re-
sulted in both reduced productivity and satisfaction. Its major flaw
was the separation of workers performing interdependent tasks. Specifically, miners were unable to adjust their task performance across
work groups. This made it almost impossible to adapt the whole cycl
of operations to the changing conditions at the coal face. External
supervision was ineffective in providing the necessary integration,
since the underground situation precluded external forms of control.
Workers reacted to this situation by developing norms of low productivity. The frustration resulting from a lack of overall task control
also led to hostility among workers and between workers and supervisors.
    Against this background, the Tavistock researchers studied
other coal fields, where groups of miners had developed adaptive
work structures aimed at reducing the problems inherent in the conventional long-wall method (Trist et al. 1963). Referred to as "the
composite long-wall method," relatively autonomous groups of workers took responsibility for a whole cycle of mining. Based on self-
selection and a common pay note, group members adapted their task
behavior to match changes at the coal face. This resulted in increase
productivity and reduced conflict and tension. In many ways, the com
posite method resembled the earlier single-placed task structure; engineers and managers had failed to recognize its applicability to mech
anized forms of mining.
    The coal mine studies were a major development in the study
and design of work. They demonstrated empirically the subtle yet

powerful relationship that exists between the social and technical dimensions of work. Trist and Bamforth (1951, p. 11) summarize this point: "So close is the relationship between the various aspects that the social and psychological can be understood only in terms of the detailed engineering facts and of the way the technological system as a whole behaves in the environment of the underground situation." The research also provided a viable alternative to traditional forms of mass production—composite or autonomous work groups. The success of the composite work teams showed clearly that more than one form of work design can operate the same technology effectively. In other words, there is considerable choice in structuring the relationship between the technical and social parts of work for goal achievement.

Under the name sociotechnical systems, the Tavistock approach to studying and designing work has spread to Asian, European, North American, and Scandinavian countries. Additional field experiments using autonomous group methods have added to the general applicability of sociotechnical theory and practice. This continuing development has led to two fundamental premises about work. First, in any purposive work situation where individuals are required to perform tasks, there is a joint system operating, a sociotechnical system. Second, a sociotechnical system is open to its environment; hence, it must maintain environmental relationships to function and develop. Both premises point to two key relationships that must be managed if work is to be productive and satisfying: the social and technical, and the systemic and environmental.

The Social and Technical Relationship

The notion of work as a sociotechnical system follows from the simple fact that task performance requires both a technology—tools, techniques, and methods—and a social structure that relates people to the technology and to each other. The relationship between the technology and the social structure results in a combined, social-plus-technological system. To make the system work, it is necessary to organize the interface between the social and technical parts so that the best match can be obtained between both. This requires an understanding of sociotechnical systems as comprised of two independent yet correlative elements: social and technical. Both components are independent by virtue of the different laws that govern their behavior. The social system is animate, operating according to biological and social-psychological laws. The technical system, on the other hand, is inanimate, following physical laws. Both systems are also correlative, since they must relate to each other for task achievement.

Therefore, the essential issue is how to structure the independent but correlative social and technical parts into an integrated system for effective task performance. Emery (1969) has coined the term joint optimization to refer to this social and technological structure. Specifically, "where the achievement of an objective is dependent upon independent but correlative systems, then it is impossible to optimize for overall performance without seeking to jointly optimize these correlative systems" (p. 119). Joint optimization represents a match between the social and technical systems such that each functions optimally, according to its own laws, without interfering with the other. Pragmatically, a sociotechnical system operates optimally when the task requirements of its technical part and the biological and social-psychological needs of its social part are both satisfied.

Designing jointly optimized work systems requires knowledge of their social and technical components and how they operate together in the actual work situation. Certain technological characteristics place demands and set limits on the type of social structure possible, while the social structure itself has social and psychological features that exert an influence on workers. The spatial and temporal character of the technology, for example, may influence the physical arrange ment of jobs. This arrangement, in turn, may either facilitate or thwart workers' needs for social interaction. Given this interdependence between the social and technical aspects, work design starts from an understanding of each component and its interaction with other then proceeds to specification of a work structure response to both systems. This may require modifications in the technology, in the social structure, or in both systems, and it may often lead beyond the work system to include changes in the related managerial, support, and control structures of the organization.

The System and Environment Relationship

Sociotechnical systems relate to an environment that both influences and is influenced by the system. This follows from the observation that work systems exchange materials and information with their environment to function and develop. This exchange represents an import-conversion-export cycle. The system imports materials and information from its environment, converts them to products or services, and exports these back to the environment for continued imports. Given this system and environment interdependence, sociotechnical systems must maintain environmental relationships to exist. Therefore, beyond designing the social and technological interface to form a jointly optimized work system, one must also structure its relationship to its environment.

Structuring the system and environment interface requires knowledge of open-system properties needed to relate to an environment. These properties represent certain structural characteristcs that provide the system with both the independence necessary to function as an entity and the interdependence needed to exchange with the environment. The first property relates to the system's import-conversion-export cycle. In most sociotechnical systems, there are several such cycles operating. Many hospitals, for example, process food and linen in addition to patients. If the system is to organize its resources around a common objective, it must specify clearly its dominant import-conversion-export cycle. This allows the system to sort out from among the variety of activities it performs the essential process needed to exist in its environment. The term primary task is used for this conversion process; it is "the task the system must perform if it is to survive" (Miller and Rice 1967, p. 25). The determination of primary task allows the system to order its multiple import-conversion-export cycles. This identifies both the predominate social and technical resources required for task performance and the environmental exchanges needed to exist.

The second property needed for environmental relationships involves the system's boundary. The boundary serves two primary functions: it differentiaties the system from its environment, and it regulates environmental exchanges. These functions permit the system to operate as an independent entity while relating to an environment. Without a clear boundary, it is not possible to distinguish between system and environment. Miller (1959) has proposed that sociotechnical systems differentiate themselves according to three criteria: technology, territory, and time. Boundaries located in reference to these criteria provide the system with clear points of differentiation, which serve as regions for environmental control. Returning to the concept of primary task, the boundary regulates imports and exports needed for task achievement. Therefore, the primary task determines, to a large extent, the boundary conditions of the system.

The third open-system property concerns regulation of the system's behavior. Sociotechnical systems, like all open systems, maintain themselves in relatively steady states while doing work and exchanging with their environment. They perform this function by keeping an orderly balance among their components and between themselves and their environment. Forces that tend to disrupt this steady state—whether from within or without the system—are countered by regulatory processes that restore as closely as possible the system's organized condition. The maintenance of a steady state implies that exchange and conversion processes are operating within limits necessary for system survival. These limits may be considered standards against which the system regulates its behavior. In other words, the standards, related to exchange and conversion processes, represent goals, and the system regulates its behavior to reduce deviations from these goals. This regulatory behavior constitutes a negative feedback process, whereby information about deviations from goals is fed back to the system so that it can take regulatory action to negate such deviations. Specifically, system regulation requires four characteristics: (1) a set of goals, (2) information as to the actual state of these goals, (3) a repertoire of regulatory behavior to correct for any deviations from the goals, and (4) a decision-making capacity, which enables the system to enact a corrective response before the cause of the disturbance changes.

The final property required for environmental exchanges involves the system's ability to achieve a particular steady state from a variety of initial conditions and in different ways. Referred to as "equifinality," this allows the system, by moving from one steady state to another, to adapt continually to environmental changes while keeping its basic form intact. It is this succession of steady states, each standing in a particular relation to an environment, which represents the growth or development of the system. Development toward greater levels of complexity and size enables the system to relate to a wider range of environmental conditions. This provides the system with a certain stability and constancy of direction in spite of fluctuations in its environment. For sociotechnical systems, equifinality suggests that there is no one right way to design the system. Given certain social and technical components, a specific task, and a particular environment, there is choice in organizing the components for goal achievement.

Autonomous Group Design

Autonomous work groups are an attempt to structure the social and technical components of work into a jointly optimized system and to provide this unit with the open-system properties needed for self-regulation. When designed according to these principles, autonomous groups are able to control variance from goal achievement while performing work and relating to an environment. Thus, they are a major step toward managing both the social and technological and the systemic and environmental relationships.

Autonomous work groups offer at least two advantages over more traditional task designs at the individual job level. First, many production processes require interdependent tasks that exceed the capacity of single man-machine systems. Designing individual task structures does not account for necessary interactions across separate jobs. Rather, grouping interdependent jobs into relatively whole task groups provides the interaction needed for goal achievement. Second, the traditional method of decomposing production processes into their simplest, elementary parts and then specifying in detail the behavior of these parts results in task designs that are not responsive to internal control or to workers' needs for autonomy. These task structures, usually at the man-machine level, require an external control apparatus to coordinate the separate parts and to counter variances that arise both within and across parts. This additional control structure requires coordination and produces its own variances, which leads to a next higher-level control system, and so on. An effective method to counter this segregative tendency is to stop the decomposition and task specification process at the group, rather than the individual, job level. This allows for the selection and linkage of individual operational units into relatively whole task groups. It also leaves the specification of individual jobs free to vary with the control and task needs of the system. Thus, the group is provided with the necessary freedom to respond to variances from goal achievement, and workers are given sufficient autonomy to master their task environment. Given these advantages, autonomous work groups are a viable alternative to traditional methods of successive decomposition and complete-specification task design.

The design of autonomous groups proceeds from a specification of the minimal set of conditions needed to create self-regulating work systems. Referred to as "developmental system design" (Herbst 1966), only those conditions required for self-regulation are implemented, and the remaining variables are left free to vary with the control needs of the system. This provides the work group with some degree of potential variability to respond to variances from goal achievement. The minimal conditions for self-control derive from an analysis of the task requirements of the system. Although these vary from one situation to another, there are a minimal set of self-regulating properties applicable to all autonomous groups. Herbst (1966, pp. 10-11) describes these as follows:

1. The unit should have a clearly definable and easily measurable outcome state which will generally be in the form of quantity and quality of a product, and also an easily measurable set of relevant import states. This provides the necessary information to management for performance evaluation of the system and the necessary information for internal process maintenance and adjustment;

2. The unit should contain all the functions required for process control, maintenance and adjustment;

3. A single social unit is responsible for the total production unit. It must contain all the required technical
skills and be capable itself of self-maintenance and adjustment;

4. Given that the functional elements of the production process are interdependent with respect to the achievement
of the outcome state, the social organization should be
such that individual members (in the case of a work
group) do not establish primary commitment to any
part function, that is, do not lay claim to or force
others to accept ownership or preferential access to
any task or equipment but are jointly committed to op-
timizing the functioning of the unit with respect to the
outcome state as a primary focal goal.

Given these initial conditions, autonomous work groups are able
to adjust their task behavior to cope with both internal and external
sources of variance. Since group members can structure themselves
in a variety of ways to respond to emergent conditions, they are able
to take full advantage of the system property of equifinality. That is,
autonomous groups can reorganize themselves, through a series of
growth stages, to more fully developed conditions. This allows the
group to respond to environmental changes while performing work and
keeping its basic form intact. This freedom to cope with change contrasts sharply with more conventional forms of task design, which tend
to constrain workers' behavior to a narrow range of prescribed tasks.
The function of management also shifts from internal system control
to support in relating the group to its environment. Thus, management focuses on those boundary conditions needed to relate the work
system to a succession of suitable environments that enable it to survive and develop.

Summary

Autonomous work groups are based on sociotechnical systems
theory. They are an attempt to structure the social and technical
parts of work into a jointly optimized work system and to relate this
system to its environment. The design of autonomous groups proceeds
from a specification of the minimal conditions required for self-regulation. After these conditions are implemented, the remaining variables are left free to vary with the control and task needs of the system
This freedom allows group members to organize themselves to cope
with emergent conditions. The function of management changes from
system control to one of support in relating the group to its environment.

CHANGE STRATEGY

Autonomous work groups have been implemented in a variety of organizational settings. Although the specific implementation strategy tends to be tailored to the situation, a common method of change underlies these experiments. This change strategy applies primarily to organizations where existing work structures are modified to autonomous group structures. With minor changes, the strategy seems relevant to the design of new work systems. It is important to note that sociotechnical experimenters do not enter organizations with the specific goal of implementing autonomous work groups. Rather, their change strategy proceeds from organizational support for experimentation to a thorough analysis of the system's design needs. Autonomous groups are one of several designs that may follow from this analysis.

The change strategy is based on work of the Tavistock Institute of Human Relations, London, England (Rice 1958; Trist et al. 1963), the Work Research Institute, Oslo, Norway (Thorsrud 1966), and the Organizational Behavior Department at Case Western Reserve University, Cleveland, Ohio (Cummings in press). The strategy derives from three assumptions about effective sociotechnical change. First, operational experiments are carried out in selected parts of the organization as a means of introducing this approach to the total organization. By experimenting with autonomous groups under relatively protected conditions, organizations may gain a clearer understanding of their consequences. This knowledge is then disseminated to other parts of the organization for purposes of wider, systemic change. Second, sociotechnical experimentation requires an organizational climate responsive to innovation and change. This implies that organizational members who are interpersonally open, experimental, and high in trust and risk-taking behavior are better able to cope with this form of change than those who are not. Furthermore, changes in both the social and technological parts of work often require effective interpersonal and group processes if they are to be implemented. Third, sociotechnical experimentation involves organizational members directly in the change process. Since autonomous groups are usually implemented on the shop floor, those engaged in the tasks of the production system collaborate in the experiment. This increases the likelihood that changes will be relevant, and it minimizes workers' resistance to change. Although worker collaboration suggests a "bottom-up" approach to change, the support required from all organizational levels is best typified by a strategy that gains sanction from the top and middle of the organization to engage with the bottom.

The autonomous group change strategy consists of eight sequential steps: (1) defining the experimental system, (2) sanctioning the experiment, (3) forming an action group, (4) analyzing the system, (5) generating hypotheses for redesign, (6) implementing and evaluating hypotheses, (7) making the transition to normal operating conditions, and (8) disseminating results. Each stage is presented separately for ease of understanding, although in an actual experiment, they may overlap considerably.

Defining the Experimental System

The purpose of this step is to define, or bound, a work system for sociotechnical experimentation. Ideally, the unit should have the following characteristics:

1. clearly differentiated social and technical components
2. clearly defined and easily measured inputs and outputs
3. high probability for success
4. high potential for dissemination of results
5. members who are interested in experimentation

The need for clearly differentiated social and technical component can be understood in terms of separating the work system from its environment. Those units whose components form a relatively self-contained whole are easily bounded from the rest of the organization. This increases the likelihood that the design problem will be located within the system rather than external to it. It also provides the unit with sufficient protection from external forces. Without a clearly differentiated system, experimental activities tend to disrupt related parts of the organization, and these parts, in turn, are likely to intrude on the change process.

Sociotechnical experimentation requires a thorough analysis of the work system's functioning. Clearly defined and easily measured inputs and outputs help to provide this knowledge. They enable the experimenter to discover the rationality of the system's behavior. By tracing inputs through actions to outputs, the task effectiveness of the unit may be analyzed. Then, the question of whether the task is performed in the least costly manner can be addressed. In the absence of clear measures, it is almost impossible to analyze the operation of a work system.

Choosing a unit with a high probability of success is important if the experiment is to serve as an initiating condition for wider, organizational change. One strategy is to pick a low-performing system. Successful changes may produce rather dramatic results. On the other hand, such units may not have the productive slack or health to engage in experimentation. The converse strategy of choosing a high-performing system also has its pros and cons. On the positive side, members of such units tend to seek challenges that are likely to improve their successful image; they are also likely to be secure enough to experiment with change. On the negative side, high-performing systems may be an experimental risk. Existing work relationships may be disrupted; productivity can decrease; and members may resent the implication that they should improve. The important point is to realize that any change has both intended and unintended consequences. Thus, there is no way to guarantee positive results; rather, one can examine explicitly the advantages and disadvantages of one site versus another and proceed accordingly.

Since a major purpose of experimentation is to generate knowledge applicable to other organizational units, it is important to choose a unit with a high potential for dissemination of results. In scientific terms, this implies high generalizability; in reference to organizational change, it suggests a "leading edge" for innovation. The issue of generalizability means that the work system should have characteristics similar to those of other systems to which one wishes to transfer results. Controlling for technology, workers' characteristics, environmental conditions, and leadership styles is likely to increase the probability that results will be applicable to other settings. Judging the extent to which a unit is a leading edge for innovation requires knowledge of the dissemination process in organizations. Current theory on diffusion of innovations suggests that individuals must both actively seek new ideas and be influential if innovations are to be accepted and disseminated (Rogers 1962). Examination of workers' interest in experimentation and their influence in the organization provides this information.

Finally, workers' interest in experimentation is crucial for successful sociotechnical change. Since this change strategy is predicated on worker collaboration and involvement, organizational members are given the opportunity to accept or reject experimentation. Without this opportunity, true collaboration is impossible.

Sanctioning the Experiment

Sociotechnical experiments require considerable protection to generate and implement new work designs. Experimental sanction furnishes this security. It provides a protective umbrella under which experimentation takes place free from normal organizational demands. The primary means of protection is by official sanction from the highest organizational levels directly affecting the work system. Both workers and management agree to the terms of the experiment. These may include exemption from normal production schedules, as well as suspension of contractual arrangements, such as job classifications, payment systems, and company policies. Since workers are often afraid to experiment if they feel they will lose money or a job, they are given some wage and job security. These sanctions provide the freedom, both organizational and psychological, to experiment with new task structures.

Sanctioning requires three forms of protection, corresponding to different phases of the experimental process (Herbst 1957). Conceptual protection is needed during the analysis and design stages. This allows workers complete freedom to explore all dimensions of their work system and to design new ways of working. Experimental protection is required during the implementation and evaluation phase. It provides the unit with substantial exemption from normal operating demands, so that redesigns may be examined without undue requests for productivity. Finally, operational protection is needed during the transition stage to normal operating conditions. Here, workers must be given sufficient time to bring new task structures on line. The amount and length of time of operational protection varies, depending upon the magnitude of the change and the adaptive capacity of workers.

Forming an Action Group

Sociotechnical experiments are frequently carried out under the direction of an action group comprised of workers and first-level supervisors from the experimental unit. The purpose of the action group is to analyze the work system and to generate proposals for redesign. Action groups are required whenever the size of the experimental system is too large to involve all members directly in the analysis and hypotheses-generation phases. To expedite the experimental process, action groups are limited in size from three to six members—first-level supervision and a few committed workers. These individuals spend considerable time analyzing the work system and generating proposals for change. This requires knowledge of the sociotechnical approach, as well as analytical and design skills. A sociotechnical consultant often helps members to acquire such competence.

Analyzing the System

Sociotechnical analysis provides knowledge of the design needs of the experimental system. It involves the collection and interpretation of social, technological, and environmental data. Although Chase (1975) has identified several sociotechnical, analytical methods, the variance control model developed by Foster (1967) and his colleagues from the Tavistock Institute appears to receive the most use. Briefly, this model attempts to identify key variances from goal achievement and to redesign the system for greater variance control. By examining both the social and technical parts of work and how these parts operate in the work environment, Foster's model also generates jointly optimized designs that are responsive to external conditions. The model has the following six steps:

1. Initial scanning: The main characteristics of the work system and its environment are identified to determine where the primary focus of the analysis should be placed.

2. Identification of unit operations: The separate phases of the production process are located, and each is viewed as a unit operation with its own identifiable transformation process.

3. Identification of key process variances and their interdependencies: Variances that arise from the production process or from the nature of the throughput are located in reference to the unit operations. A variance refers to any deviation from some standard on specification, and a variance is "key" if it significantly affects production, operating, or social costs.

4. Analysis of the social system: The main features of the social system are examined, and a variance control table is constructed to determine whether key variances are controlled. Ancillary activities, spatiotemporal relationships, job mobility, and payment systems are also analyzed, and work roles are tested against a list of basic psychological needs.

5. Workers' perception of their work roles: Workers are asked about their perceptions of their work roles in reference to the basic psychological needs.

6. Environmental analysis: The impact of various environmental units on the work system is examined. Specifically, the supply and user systems, the maintenance system, and the larger organization are considered.

The application of Foster's analytical model is based on certain practical guidelines. First, the experimental system is examined as it is currently being operated. This provides a base line for change. Second, data are collected from a variety of sources, to prevent biased reporting. Third, only key information is examined. This prevents overelaboration of data, which tends to slow the analysis and confuse the design problem. Finally, redesign hypotheses generated during the analysis are carried forward into the next stage of the experiment.

Generating Hypotheses for Redesign

The analytical data are used to generate redesign proposals.
Once individuals are aware of the problems of the work system, its
objectives, and its available resources and organizational constraints,
they can begin to evolve alternative redesigns. Depending upon the
design problem, the focus may be on the social system, the technology, or both; it may also include relevant segments of the environment. Regardless of the focus, each proposal is tailored to the needs
and situation of the experimental unit. This increases the likelihood
that redesigns will be relevant to the system and responsive to situational factors that affect its performance.

Typically, sociotechnical redesigns attempt to jointly optimize
the social and technical components and to match the system with its
environment. These designs may be either at the individual job, the
work group, or the departmental level. Often, however, they include
requisite changes in larger organizational variables, such as managerial structures, reward systems, control procedures, and company
policy. Although specific proposals are tailored to the situation,
guidelines for sociotechnical redesign appear in the work of Davis
(1957), Rice (1958), Emery (1963), Herbst (1966), and Cummings and
Srivastva (1976).

Implementing and Evaluating Hypotheses

Hypotheses for redesign represent specific changes intended to
improve the work system's functioning. Since their actual effects
must be demonstrated in the work situation, redesigns are implemente
under experimental conditions. This allows for a thorough critique
of the hypotheses, and it permits system members to experiment
with changes under relatively protected circumstances. The implementation and evaluation phase of the experiment comprises four
steps:

1. reducing the hypotheses to a more manageable set
2. devising an action program
3. implementing the action program
4. evaluating results

Since a variety of redesigns are often generated, it is necessary
to choose those worthy of experimental testing. This involves judgment as to their effects and costs. Each proposal is stated clearly
in terms of its intended effects—both economic and social. Once
these effects are identified, an assessment as to their probability of

achievement is made. Although this is essentially a subjective process, three criteria appear useful. First, examination of potential spillover effects of a proposal may reveal some unintended consequences to the wider organization. Second, assessment of workers' perceptions of the redesign may uncover subtle flaws and implementation problems. Third, evaluation of whether the redesign is simple or precise in its solution to a complex problem shows how elegant, or parsimonious, is the change. Once the likelihood of achieving intended results has been determined, the relative cost of different designs is assessed. In assessing costs, both short- and long-term consequences are projected. Here, economic as well as social costs are examined. Although the final choice of an experimental redesign is relatively subjective, an explicit assessment of effects and costs is likely to improve this decision-making process.

Given the choice to experiment with a specific redesign, an action program for implementation is needed. This serves as a plan for introducing the change so that it may be evaluated properly. The action program specifies the following:

1. a detailed listing of the proposed changes
2. a timetable for introducing changes
3. conditions for experimental protection
4. an inventory of services, tools, and materials needed for experimentation
5. a timetable for evaluation—instrumentation, analyses, and feedback
6. training needs
7. supervisory responsibilities

Implementing the action program requires knowledge of organizational change. There are at least three issues relevant to sociotechnical experiments. First, timing the change is critical if workers are to experience their existing tasks as coming to closure before starting something new. Naturally occurring disjunctions, such as the end of an accounting period, the close of a project, and the change to a new product, provide individuals with clear boundaries for discontinuing the old and starting the new design. Second, the speed of social change often lags behind that of technological change. Members must not only learn new tasks and role relationships but must often forget parts of the old structure. The change program must account for this learning process by providing workers with sufficient time to develop appropriate task structures. Third, changes in existing work systems frequently disrupt existing sources of worker satisfaction and security. To the extent that the redesign provides new ways for obtaining these social rewards, it is likely to reduce individuals' resistance to change.

Evaluating the results of a redesign provides knowledge of whether the change did, indeed, improve the work system. This is referred to as internal validity: Did the redesign produce the observed effects In assessing the internal validity of a particular change program, the authors are, in fact, rejecting alternative explanations for the results Campbell and Stanley (1966) have identified several extraneous variables that, if not controlled in the experiment, may produce confounding results. The best way to control for these rival hypotheses is to randomize those who are exposed to the change. Randomization is no usually possible in experiments with natural task groups. Rather, there are alternative methods, quasi-experimental designs, for evaluating work experiments. Quasi-experiments control for extraneous variables through the expedient scheduling of data gathering. Althoug they are not as strong as randomized experiments, they reduce the likelihood that rival explanations account for the results. Sociotechnical experiments employ a variety of quasi-experimental designs to evaluate the effects of change proposals. Typically, these involve the use of control groups and pre- and posttest measures relevant to worl system performance. Since evaluation is critical for successful work improvement, it is among the first issues addressed in sociotechnical experimentation.

Making the Transition to Normal
Operating Conditions

The transition from experimental testing to normal operating conditions involves a gradual handing-over process. Once a particular redesign has been shown to be effective, experimental protection is reduced until the work system is operating under normal conditions The length of the transition process varies, depending on the magnitude and type of change—larger deviations from the traditional and social change taking longer. Since the transition phase takes place only after the unit has been operating successfully, evaluative activities continue during this period. This provides information about the system's ability to sustain progress, and it provides an ongoing feedback process for sociotechnical functioning. In other words, continued evaluation provides individuals with built-in indicators of system performance. These enable members to monitor their behavior and to make appropriate modifications if needed.

Disseminating Results

The last stage of the change strategy involves dissemination of results to the wider organization. Current knowledge of sociotechni-

cal diffusion is rather limited. Walton (1975), however, has studied
eight work experiments' dissemination experience. He concludes
that even if these projects offer relative advantages over existing work
designs, they have a number of self-limiting characteristics: their
character and results are difficult to communicate; they are not congruent with existing norms and values; their results are pervasive
rather than fractionated; they are not readily reversed; and too many
affected individuals serve as decision makers for effective implementation. Although these problems are difficult to overcome, Walton
suggests a number of solutions to increase their wider acceptance.
First, introducing a number of experiments at the same time may increase their generalizability. This makes it more difficult to attribute their results to special circumstances, and it provides more
focal points for wider change. Second, avoiding overexposure and
glorification of particular change projects may promote their acceptance in other work systems. Others are less threatened by less publicized efforts. Finally, having the experiment identified with top
management at its initial stages may provide the sustained support
needed for wider diffusion. Walton's suggestions, when combined
with early concern for dissemination problems, appear to increase
the likelihood that sociotechnical experiments will receive wider organizational support and acceptance.

Summary

The change strategy for introducing autonomous work groups into
organizations is based on an experimental approach. Work designs
are implemented in limited parts of the organization as demonstration
projects for wider organizational change. The strategy is predicated
on top-level sanction and support and, at the bottom level, on worker
collaboration. Each stage of the experiment represents a logical sequence: from sanction to analysis and redesign, to implementation,
evaluation, and dissemination.

3

AUTONOMOUS WORK GROUPS:
16 SELECTED EXPERIMENTS

Autonomous work groups have been implemented in a variety of organizations with different technologies, workers, and cultural settings. Existing evidence suggests that autonomous groups are both productive and humanly satisfying. Indeed, current literature presen overwhelming support for the positive effects of these task structures The purpose of this chapter is to review 16 selected experiments that follow, in large part, the theory and change strategy underlying auton omous work groups. The review provides empirical knowledge of these work designs and critiques their results. The chapter is divide into three sections. The first examines action levers or organization changes implemented for autonomous groups. The results of these changes are evaluated in terms of their validity. The second section presents contingencies upon which successful results may be dependent. Finally, the third section discusses the implementation of autonomous group strategies.

ACTION LEVERS AND THEIR EFFECTS

The 16 experiments representing autonomous groups changed a variety of action levers to form self-regulating work groups. Table 1 identifies these studies by author and lists data about contextual variables, as well as action levers and their effects. The contextual variables reveal a considerable amount of information about the organizational settings of these experiments. Since these data bear directly on the issue of contingencies, those factors upon which successful results are dependent, they are examined in the next section of this chapter. Turning to action levers and their effects, Table 2 shows that each study made from two to nine specific changes to design autonomous groups. Rather than review each experiment separately, the set of studies provides a comprehensive illustration of those action levers producing positive outcomes. The most prevalent action lever involved the amount of autonomy/ discretion given to workers. Some 88 percent of the studies manipulated this action lever by providing individuals with greater control over such areas as task assignment, production schedules, and job rotation. This was followed closely by changes in interpersonal/ group process (75 percent), information/feedback (63 percent), task variety (63 percent), technical/physical (63 percent), and pay/reward (56 percent). Less than half of the experiments changed action levers of training (44 percent), support (31 percent), or organizational structure (19 percent). Since the action levers were intended to provide conditions necessary for autonomous group functioning, a closer examination of the changes reveals their purpose. Table 2 presents the minimal conditions required for self-regulating groups (Herbst 1966). Those action levers manipulated in over half of the studies are listed next to the condition they were intended to provide. Table 2 shows clearly the number of related changes needed to form autonomous groups. In many cases, these action levers represent changes from individual task structures to group redesigns. Typically, technical/ physical modifications involved the relocation of equipment and materials to facilitate group formation. This was followed by information systems aimed at group rather than individual performance. Workers were also given more discretion over their task assignments, with attendant increases in task variety. Finally, attention to interpersonal and group process helped members to interrelate around a whole task, while group reward systems reinforced members' commitment to group goals. It is interesting to note that those action levers changed in less than half of the studies—training, support, and organizational structure—also facilitated group formation. Training provided workers with requisite task skills; support services gave the work groups needed resources; and organizational structure arranged managerial assignments to correspond with natural task groupings.

Examination of the action levers' effects in Table 1 shows a large number of positive outcomes. Counting only those experiments that measure a particular result, the data reveal totally positive effects for productivity (93 percent), costs (88 percent), quality (86 percent), withdrawal (73 percent), and attitudes (70 percent). These results attest to the impact of autonomous work groups on important organizational outcomes. They also suggest that when conditions for autonomous group functioning are not implemented fully, negative results may follow. This may seem by examining the four experiments reporting that the treatment, the action levers, did not take, or only

TABLE 1

Autonomous Work Groups: Contextual Variables and Action Levers and Their Effects

		Contextual Variables						
Authors	Type of Work	Sex	Occupa-tional Sta-tus	Num-ber Treated	Union-ized	Partici-pation in Change	Coun-try	Treat-ment Took Effect
Anonymous	Assembly line in slipper plant	?	Blue	350	?	?	United States	?
Bregard, A., et al., 1968	Chemical process in fertilizer plant	?	Blue	40	Yes	Yes	Nor-way	Yes
Cummings, T. G. (a), 1976	Assembly line in forging plant	Male	Blue	43	Yes	Yes	United States	Partial
Cummings, T. G. (b), 1976	Die designing and es-timating in forging plant	Male/female	White	28	No	Yes	United States	No
Emery, F., et al., 1970	Wire drawing	Male	Blue	12	Yes	Yes	Nor-way	Partial
Englestad, P. H., 1970	Chemical process	Male	Blue	28	Yes	Yes	Nor-way	?
Gorman, L., Molloy, E. S. (a) 1972	Clerical in a bank	Female	White	19	?	Yes	Ire-land	Yes
Prestat, C., 1971	Weaving in textile plant	Male	Blue	100	?	Yes	France	?
Rice, A. K. (a), 1958	Automatic weaving in textile plant	Male	Blue	28	Yes	Yes	India	Yes
Rice, A. K. (b), 1958	Nonautomatic weav-ing in textile plant	Male	Blue	66	Yes	Yes	India	Yes
Trist, E. L., et al. (a), 1963	Coal mining (conven-tional versus com-posite methods)	Male	Blue	41	Yes	Yes	Great Brit-ain	Yes
Trist, E. L., et al. (b), 1963	Coal mining (compo-site versus compo-site methods)	Male	Blue	41	Yes	Yes	Great Brit-ain	Yes
Van Gils, M. R., 1969	Key punching	Female	White	66	?	Yes	Nether-lands	Yes
Van Liet, A., 1970	Assembly line	Male/female	Blue	7	?	Yes	Nether-lands	?
Vossen, H. P., 1974	Assembly line	?	Blue	20	?	Yes	Nether-lands	Partial
Walton, R. E., 1972	Assembly line in dog-food plant	?	Blue	70	?	Yes	United States	Yes

Action Levers									Effects				
Pay/ Reward Systems	Autonomy/ Discretion	Support	Training	Organizational Structure	Technical/ Physical	Task Variety	Information/ Feedback	Interpersonal/ Group Process	Costs	Productivity	Quality	Withdrawal	Attitudes
x	x			x		x			−	+			−
x	x	x	x			x	x	x	−	+		−	+
x	x	x		x		x		x	0	−		+	±
x				x		x		x		+	−		−
x	x	x	x			x	x	x		+			+
x	x	x	x	x		x	x	x	−	+	+		
x						x	x	x	−	+			+
x	x	x		x			x	x		+	+	−	
x	x		x				x	x		+	+		+
x				x			x			+	+		
x	x	x					x	x	−	+	+		−
						x	x			+	+	0	
x		x		x		x	x						+
x						x	x		−	+			+
x						x	x						±
x	x	x	x	x	x	x	x	x	−	+		−	+

Code: blank = not relevant; x = variable manipulated; ? = insufficient data; + = variable increased; − = variable decreased; 0 = variable static.

Source: Srivastva et al. 1975, pp. 93-94.

TABLE 2

Conditions for Autonomous Group Functioning: Action Levers
and Their Intent

Conditions for Group Functioning	Action Levers	Intent
Necessary information for process maintenance and adjustment	Information/feedback	Provide workers with relevant and timely information about inputs and outputs
All functions required for process control, maintenance, and adjustment	Technical/physical	Provide workers with a relatively whole task, including maintenance and control functions
A social unit with all the required skills for self-maintenance and adjustment	Autonomy/discretion and task variety	Provide individuals with the control and skills necessary to cope with variance from goal achievement
A social unit where individuals are jointly committed to the functioning and goals of the whole group	Interpersonal/group process and pay/reward systems	Provide group members with cohesion around the unit's primary task; align reward system around group rather than individual participation

Source: Compiled by the authors.

partially took, effect. Three of these studies (Cummings [a] and [b]
1976; Vossen 1974) show negative results on one or more of the outcomes. This points to a possible risk in implementing autonomous
group designs: if the action levers are not changed effectively, the
work system may be worse off than if no changes are made.

    Given the overwhelming number of positive results attributed to
autonomous work groups, the question of internal validity arises:
Did the action levers produce the positive outcomes? To assess internal validity, each experiment was examined as to whether one or

more alternative factors, other than the action levers, could have accounted for the positive effects. The existence of rival explanations constitutes a threat to the efficacy of the findings. Rather than review the validity of each experiment separately, the set of studies was evaluated in terms of various threats to their overall validity (Campbell and Stanley 1966). If a particular threat runs through most of the studies, then the internal validity of the overall results is questionable. On the other hand, if a threat is present in only a few of the experiments, it is unlikely to account for the findings. Although the method of evaluating the validity of the experiments was discussed at length in Chapter 1, two important points are worthy of review. First, the primary method of evaluation was to assess whether a study's research design controlled for threats to validity. When this was done, it was discovered that most experiments used a different research design for each outcome measured. Thus, the results were evaluated separately for each of the outcomes. Second, since this book is concerned primarily with the outcomes of productivity and the quality of work life, only these findings are reported here.

Validity of Performance Results

Fifteen of the experiments measured some aspect of performance—costs, productivity, or quality. When taken as a whole, these studies show a large number of positive outcomes for this variable. In fact, performance findings are the most positive outcome for autonomous group experiments. Examination of the research designs associated with performance measures reveals that two threats to validity were relatively uncontrolled in this set of studies—instability and mortality. The remaining threats to validity—history, testing, instrumentation, statistical regression, selection, and selection interaction —were controlled in over half of the experiments. Thus, they do not appear to distract from the positive performance findings. Most of the studies measuring performance failed to account for instability because of a lack of statistical tests. Without such tests, it is possible that increases in performance may be caused by measurement errors—random fluctuations that occur in any measurement process. All studies in this set failed to control for mortality—differential loss of subjects from the comparison groups. It was difficult to assess the extent of this threat because most of the experiments did not provide withdrawal data, information needed to evaluate differential loss of individuals from the comparison groups.

Normally, the existence of any threats to validity uncontrolled in a set of studies demonstrating similar results places the findings in serious question. This is not totally the case for these results.

Although most of the autonomous group experiments did not control
for instability by the use of proper statistical tests, many of the positive performance results were of such a large magnitude that it is unlikely that they were solely random measurement errors. In regard
to mortality, about one-half of the studies did not report withdrawal
data—turnover and absenteeism, for example—to allow for adequate
assessment. In the absence of such information, the performance
findings remain questionable but not altogether inplausible. Therefore, the efficacy of the performance findings appears to be justifiab
.

Validity of Quality of Work Life Results

The findings pertaining to quality of work life are represented
by the attitudinal measures—for example, job satisfaction, involvement, and morale. The autonomous group experiments reveal positi
attitudinal effects for about 75 percent of the studies. The validity of
these results does not appear to be as strong as that for the performance findings. Five threats to validity were present in over half of
these experiments—history, statistical regression, selection, mortality, and selection interaction. Failure to use control groups resulted in history threats—some event other than the action levers
could have caused the results. Statistical regression was uncontrolle
because of a lack of time series data. Thus, it is possible that increases in attitudes were merely regressions upward toward the
groups' general trends. Selection was a threat to validity, either because comparison groups were not used to equate subjects on the pretests or repeated measures were not obtained from experimental subjects. Like the performance results, mortality was difficult to asses
because of a lack of withdrawal data. Finally, selection interaction
was uncontrolled in this set of studies because of a lack of time serie
data. Thus, for example, the comparison groups might have differec
in their responses to a common historical event, such as changes in
company policy.

The efficacy of the quality of work life findings seems to be que
tionable. Several threats to validity were uncontrolled in more than
half of the experiments. In fact, statistical regression and mortality
were not accounted for in any of the studies. Although it seems im-
plausible to attribute all of the positive attitudinal effects to these
rival explanations, the general weakness of the experiments' researc
designs makes these findings doubtful. Before dismissing these results entirely, however, it is worth noting that several of the studies
reported anecdotal data about workers' positive attitudes toward
autonomous group membership. These data, from researchers, man
gers, and workers, suggest improvements in the quality of work life

as a result of the experiments. Although these reports do not have
high internal validity, they do support the attitudinal claims of autonomous work groups.

CONTINGENCIES

Although the internal validity of the autonomous group findings
is not totally acceptable, the results are plausible enough to warrant
examining contingencies upon which these effects may be dependent.
In scientific terms, contingencies represent the external validity or
generalizability of the experiments. In other words, they are those
factors, such as situations, population treatment variables, and
measurements, which limit the general applicability of the results.
Information about contingencies was obtained from two sources.
First, the contextual variables in Table 1 include data about the organizational contexts and subjects of the autonomous group studies.
This information suggests a number of contingent factors. Second,
certain threats to the generalizability of the findings were assessed
by examining the experiments' research designs (Campbell and
Stanley 1966). Like internal validity, the studies' research designs
determine, to a large extent, the presence or absence of threats to
external validity. Both kinds of data, contextual variables and research designs, provide important clues as to those factors upon
which successful results are contingent.
        Thirteen studies reported totally positive increases in perfor-
mance (Bregard et al. 1968; Emery, Thorsrud, and Lange 1970;
Englestad 1970; Gorman and Molloy [a] 1972; Prestat 1971; Rice [a]
1958 and [b] 1958; Trist et al. [a] 1963 and [b] 1963; Van Gils 1969;
Van Liet 1970; Walton 1972; and Anonymous). Examination of the
contextual variables in Table 1 suggests that these findings are applicable to different forms of work, types of workers, and cultural settings. Closer scrutiny of these data, however, reveals possible contingent factors. The types of work included in the autonomous group
designs seem to be weighted toward material-processing technologies,
such as coal mining, assembly lines, and weaving, rather than infor-
mation-processing tasks. Perhaps, autonomous groups demonstrate
greater performance effects in the former work settings because they
facilitate the formation of physically discrete task groupings. Information technologies, on the other hand, are not as likely to afford
such clear task boundaries. The characteristics of workers involved
in these experiments show a preponderance of male, blue collar,
unionized workers. Although this could be interpreted as a limiting
factor, it seems more plausible that such characteristics coincide
with material-processing types of work. Furthermore, such workers

appear to be the focus of most work-improvement experiments, a fate possibly attributed to their low position in the organizational hie archy. The number of subjects involved in autonomous group design ranges from 7 to 350, with a median of 41.5. Although there is prob ably an upper limit to the number of the individuals who can be in volved directly in this form of experimentation, there appears to be a wide latitude. Worker involvement in the change process seems to be the most predominate contingency factor in the studies. All expe ments reporting data on this dimension revealed that workers were involved directly in the change process. The formation of task groups may require such involvement if workers are to develop appropriate task relationships. Thus, the performance results appear to depend on high worker involvement. Finally, the countries in which the experiments were carried out are mostly industrialized— France, Great Britain, India, Ireland, the Netherlands, Norway, and the United States. Although the variety of cultures implies that this is not a limiting factor, generalization to nonindustrialized coun tries may not be warranted.

Only seven experiments reported totally positive attitudinal re sults (Bregard et al. 1968; Emery, Thorsrud, and Lange 1970; Gorman and Molloy [a] 1972; Rice [a] 1958; Van Gils 1969; Van Liet 1970; and Walton 1972). Examination of Table 1 shows data similar to those of the experiments reporting performance improvements. Thus, the quality of work life effects of autonomous groups appear to be contingent upon the same factors as the performance results— types of work, number of subjects, worker involvement in the change process, and culture.

Examination of the research designs of the autonomous group experiments revealed additional factors upon which the results are contingent. The first contingency refers to experimental arrangements, the inability to apply findings from experimental settings to nonexperimental situations. Both the performance and quality of work life effects were limited by this factor. Since most of these studies were sanctioned experiments, carried out by workers and managers collaboratively, the atypical conditions of this arrangement make generalizations to other settings questionable. A second contingency involves the interaction effects of selection and treatmen This refers to the inability to apply findings beyond the population from which the subjects were drawn because of the interaction of selection biases and the experimental changes. Autonomous group results may be contingent upon the selection of volunteer subjects. Specifically, several of the studies reported that volunteers were in volved in the changes. Since it is plausible that such individuals are more responsive to autonomous groups than nonvolunteers, the findi appear to be limited to subjects who volunteer freely for such experi ments. The final contingency concerns testing/ treatment interactions, the effects of a pretest on generalizability to nonpretested populations. This threat to external validity increases the possibility that reactive measurements may sensitize workers to subsequent changes, thus increasing their responsiveness to such changes. The performance findings were not susceptible to this factor because they involved nonreactive data taken from company records. The attitudinal results, on the other hand, appear to be limited to pretested subjects. Questionnaires and interviews were the primary means of collecting these data. Since over half of the studies employed pretests, it is likely that these instruments sensitized workers to the autonomous group changes.

In summary, several contingencies appear to limit the general applicability of the autonomous group effects. These factors may increase the likelihood that positive results are obtained. Material-processing technologies—coal mining and weaving, for instance—seem to facilitate the formation of physically discrete task groupings. This provides group members with clear task boundaries and concrete measures of performance, two conditions necessary for self-regulation. The number of workers who can be involved directly in this form of experimentation ranges from 7 to 350. Since workers are directly involved in the change process, another contingent factor, numbers of workers toward the lower end of this range, may promote successful results. Although cultural settings do not appear to limit the applicability of this approach, conditions associated with industrialized countries—positive work ethic, technological innovation, and economic development—may facilitate positive results. The experimental setting of autonomous group studies also appears to be a limiting factor. Worker and management collaboration may be necessary to implement this approach. Similarly, volunteer subjects seem to be more susceptible to this strategy than those who are made to participate. Again, the collaborative nature of this change strategy appears to affect the type of workers who are likely to participate in autonomous groups. Finally, pretests, such as questionnaires and interviews, may sensitize workers to subsequent organizational changes. Thus, pretests may be necessary to produce maximal results, especially quality of work life effects.

IMPLEMENTATION OF AUTONOMOUS GROUPS

The autonomous group experiments provided a rich array of anecdotal data about implementing this strategy. While this information was not systematically examined under rigorous conditions, it points to several rules of thumb for designing successful work groups.

First, the organizational sanction and support needed for experimentation appears to be pervasive. This suggests that much prework must be done to assure a supportive organizational climate, as well as top-level approval. Second, operating mechanisms and company policy need to be consistent with a group approach. Payment and reward systems, information systems, training programs, and the like must be congruent with group membership and performance. Third, the tasks of the organization should fall naturally into whole task groupings. When this does not occur, technical and physical changes may be required to provide such boundaries. Fourth, provisions may have to be made to provide workers with alternative forms of wor if they do not like group tasks. Fifth, special training programs, involving group dynamics as well as multiple skills, may be needed to provide workers with the knowledge and ability to operate autonomous. Sixth, autonomous groups are responsive to complex and changing wo environments. Thus, when group environments are simple and static this approach may be too sophisticated for the demands of the task. Seventh, the implementation of autonomous groups requires considerable direction, as well as attention to self-regulating properties. Rather than underspecify these initial conditions, it is better to overspecify during the start-up period. Eighth, managing the boundary conditions of the group demands a supportive style of management. This may require special selection and training of autonomous group leaders. The above-mentioned conditions appear to facilitate the formation of autonomous work groups. Although they have not been studied extensively in the field, they are the result of a good deal of experience and common sense. Therefore, attention to such factors appears warranted by those implementing this strategy in contempora organizations.

SUMMARY

Autonomous group experiments have been carried out in a varie of organizational settings. A review of 16 of these studies reveals a considerable amount of empirical knowledge of this approach to work design. Specifically, the implementation of certain action lever —autonomy/discretion, interpersonal/group process, information/ feedback, task variety, technical/physical, and pay-reward systems —appears to lead to improved performance and human satisfaction. Although the efficacy of these results is less than ideal, existing evidence supports the positive effects attributed to autonomous work gro These results, however, may be contingent upon certain organization factors, such as type of work, number of workers, worker involvement, culture, special experimental arrangements, volunteer subject and sensitizing pretests. When these contingencies are combined with certain rules of thumb and good common sense, organizational members should be able to implement this strategy with successful results.

Managers do not need anyone to tell them that employee alienation exists. Terms such as "blue collar blues" and "salaried drop-
outs" are all too familiar. But are they willing to undertake the majo
innovations necessary for redesigning work organizations to deal effectively with the root causes of alienation? The purpose of this cha
ter is to urge them to do so, for two reasons:

1. The current alienation is not merely a phase that will pass
in due time.
2. The innovations needed to correct the problem can simultaneously enhance the quality of work life (thereby lessening alienation) and improve productivity.

In the first part of the article, there shall be a risk of covering
terrain already familiar to some readers in order to establish that
alienation is a basic, long-term, and mounting problem. Then some
examples of the comprehensive redesign that is required will be presented.

It is also hoped that today's managers will be provided with a
glimpse at what may be the industrial work environment of the future
as illustrated by a pet-food plant that opened in January 1971.

In this facility, management set out to incorporate features tha
would provide a high quality of work life, enlist unusual human invol\

---

ment, and result in high productivity. The positive results of the
experiment to data are impressive, and the difficulties encountered
in implementing it are instructive. Moreover, similar possibilities
for comprehensive innovations exist in a wide variety of settings and
industries.

The word "comprehensive" is important, because my argument
is that each technique in the standard fare of personnel and organizational development programs (for example, job enrichment, management by objectives, sensitivity training, confrontation and team-building sessions, participative decision making) has grasped only a limited
truth and has fallen far short of producing meaningful change. In
short, more radical, comprehensive, and systemic redesign of organizations is necessary.

ANATOMY OF ALIENATION

There are two parts to the problem of employee alienation: (1)
the productivity output of work systems, and (2) the social costs associated with employee inputs. Regarding the first, U.S. productivity
is not adequate to the challenges posed by international competition
and inflation; it cannot sustain impressive economic growth. (Economic growth is not referred to here as something to be valued merely
for its own sake—it is politically a precondition for the income redis-
tribution that will make equality of opportunity possible in the United
States.) Regarding the second, the social and psychological costs of
work systems are excessive, as evidenced by their effects on the mental and physical health of employees and on the social health of families
and communities.

Employee alienation affects productivity and reflects social
costs incurred in the workplace. Increasingly, blue and white collar
employees and, to some extent, middle managers tend to dislike their
jobs and resent their bosses. Workers tend to rebel against their
union leaders. They are becoming less concerned about the quality
of the product of their labor and more angered about the quality of
the context in which they labor.

In some cases, alienation is expressed by passive withdrawal—
tardiness, absenteeism and turnover, and inattention on the job. In
other cases, it is expressed by active attacks—pilferage, sabotage,
deliberate waste, assaults, bomb threats, and other disruptions of
work routines. Demonstrations have taken place and underground
newspapers have appeared in large organizations in recent years to
protest company policies. Even more recently, employees have co-
operated with newsmen, congressional committees, regulatory agencies, and protest groups in exposing objectionable practices.

These trends all have been mentioned in the media, but one expression of alienation has been underreported: pilferage and violence against property and persons. Such acts are less likely to be revealed to the police and the media when they occur in a private company than when they occur in a high school, a ghetto business district, or a suburban town. Moreover, dramatic increases in these forms of violence are taking place at the plant level. This trend is not reported in local newspapers, and there is little or no appreciation of it at corporate headquarters. Local management keeps quiet because violence is felt to reflect unfavorably both on its effectiveness and on its plant as a place to work.

Roots of Conflict

The acts of sabotage and other forms of protest are overt manifestations of a conflict between changing employee attitudes and organizational inertia. Increasingly, what employees expect from their jobs is different from what organizations are prepared to offer them. These evolving expectations of workers conflict with the demands, conditions, and rewards of employing organizations in at least six important ways:

1. Employees want challenge and personal growth, but work tends to be simplified and specialties tend to be used repeatedly in work assignments. This pattern exploits the narrow skills of a worker while limiting his or her opportunities to broaden or develop.
2. Employees want to be included in patterns of mutual influence; they want egalitarian treatment. But organizations are characterized by tall hierarchies, status differentials, and chains of command.
3. Employee commitment to an organization is increasingly influenced by the intrinsic interest of the work itself, the human dignity afforded by management, and the social responsibility reflected in the organization's products. Yet organization practices still emphasize material rewards and employment security and neglect other employee concerns.
4. What employees want from careers, they are apt to want right now. But when organizations design job hierarchies and career paths, they continue to assume that today's workers are as willing to postpone gratifications as were yesterday's workers.
5. Employees want more attention to the emotional aspects of organization life, such as individual self-esteem, openness between people, and expressions of warmth. Yet organizations emphasize rationality and seldom legitimize the emotional part of the organization experience.

6. Employees are becoming less driven by competitive urges, less likely to identify competition as the "American way." Nevertheless, managers continue to plan career patterns, organize work, and design reward systems as if employees valued competition as highly as they used to.

Pervasive Social Forces

The foregoing needs and desires that employees bring to their work are but a local reflection of more basic, and not readily reversible, trends in U.S. society. These trends are fueled by family and social experience, as well as by social institutions, especially schools. Among the most significant are:

The rising level of education: Employees bring to the workplace more abilities and, correspondingly, higher expectations than in the past.

The rising level of wealth and security: Vast segments of today's society never have wanted for the tangible essentials of life; thus they are decreasingly motivated by pay and security, which are taken for granted.

The decreased emphasis given by churches, schools, and families to obedience to authority: These socialization agencies have promoted individual initiative, self-responsibility and -control, the relativity of values, and other social patterns that make subordinacy in traditional organizations an increasingly bitter pill to swallow for each successive wave of entrants to the U.S. work force.

The decline in achievement motivation: For example, whereas the books my parents read in primary school taught them the virtues of hard work and competition, my children's books emphasize self-expression and actualizing one's potential. The workplace has not yet fully recognized this change in employee values.

The shifting emphasis from individualism to social commitment: This shift is driven, in part, by a need for the direct gratifications of human connectedness (for example, as provided by commune living experiments). It also results from a growing appreciation of our interdependence, and it renders obsolete many traditional workplace concepts regarding the division of labor and work incentives.

These basic societal forces underlie, and contribute to, the problem of alienation and also sums up the discussion thus far. Actually, protests in the workplace will probably mount even more rapidly than is indicated by the contributing trends postulated here. The latent dissatisfaction of workers will be activated as the issues receive public attention, and as some examples of attempted solutions

serve to raise expectations (just as the blacks' expressions of dissatisfaction with social and economic inequities were triggered in the
1950s, and women's discontent expanded late in the 1960s).

Revitalization and Reform

It seems clear that employee expectations are not likely to revert to those of an earlier day. The conflicts between these expectations and traditional organizations result in alienation. This alienation, in turn, exacts a deplorable psychological and social cost, as
well as causing worker behavior that depresses productivity and con-
strains growth. In short, we need major innovative efforts to redesign work organizations, efforts that take employee expectations into
account.

Over the past two decades, we have witnessed a parade of organizational development, personnel, and labor relations programs
that promised to revitalize organizations:

Job enrichment would provide more varied and challenging content in the work.

Participative decision making would enable the information,
judgments, and concerns of subordinates to influence the decisions
that affect them.

Management by objectives would enable subordinates to understand and shape the objectives toward which they strive and against
which they are evaluated.

Sensitivity training or encounter groups would enable people to
relate to each other as human beings with feelings and psychological
needs.

Productivity bargaining would revise work rules and increase
management's flexibility with a quid pro quo whereby the union ensures that workers share in the fruits of the resulting productivity
increases. Each of the preceding programs by itself is an inadequate
reform of the workplace and has typically failed in its more limited
objectives. While application is often based on a correct diagnosis,
each approach is only a partial remedy; therefore, the organizational
system soon returns to an earlier equilibrium.

The lesson that must be learned in the area of work reform is
similar to one learned in another area of national concern. It is now
recognized that a health program, a welfare program, a housing program, or an employment program alone is unable to make a lasting
impact on the urban-poor syndrome. Poor health, unemployment,
and other interdependent aspects of poverty must be attacked in a coordinated or systemic way.

So it is with meaningful reform of the workplace: we must think "systemically" when approaching the problem. We must coordinate the redesign of the way tasks are packaged into jobs, the way workers are required to relate to each other, the way performance is measured and rewards are made available, the way positions of authority and status symbols are structured, and the way career paths are conceived. Moreover, because these types of changes in work organizations imply new employee skills and different organizational cultures, transitional programs must be established.

A PROTOTYPE OF CHANGE

A number of major organization design efforts meet the requirements of being systemic and comprehensive. One experience in which I have been deeply involved is particularly instructive. As a recent and radical effort, it generally encompasses and goes beyond what has been done elsewhere.

During 1968, a large pet-food manufacturer was planning an additional plant at a new location. The existing manufacturing facility was then experiencing many of the symptoms of alienation already outlined. There were frequent instances of employee indifference and inattention that, because of the continuous-process technology, led to plant shutdowns, product waste, and costly recycling. Employees effectively worked only a modest number of hours per day, and they resisted changes toward fuller utilization of manpower. A series of acts of sabotage and violence occurred.

Because of these pressures and the fact that it was not difficult to link substantial manufacturing costs to worker alienation, management was receptive to basic innovations in the new plant. It decided to design the plant to both accommodate changes in the expectations of employees and utilize knowledge developed by the behavior sciences.

Key Design Features

The early development of the plant took more than two years. This involved planning, education, skill training, and building the nucleus of the new organization into a team.

During this early period, four newly selected managers and their superior met with behavioral science experts and visited other industrial plants that were experimenting with innovative organizational methods. Thus, they were stimulated to think about departures from traditional work organizations and given reassurance that other organizational modes were not only possible but also more viable in the current social context. While the consultations and plant visits provided some raw material for designing the new organization, the theretofore latent knowledge of the five managers played the largest role. Their insights into the aspirations of people and basically optimistic assumptions about the capacities of human beings were particularly instrumental in the design of the innovative plant. In the remainder of this section, nine key features of this design will be presented.

Autonomous Work Groups

Self-managed work teams are given collective responsibility for large segments of the production process. The total work force of approximately 70 employees is organized into six teams. A processing team and a packaging team operate during each shift. The processing team's jurisdiction includes unloading, storage of materials, drawing ingredients from storage, mixing, and then performing the series of steps that transform ingredients into a pet-food product. The packaging team's responsibilities include the finishing stages of product manufacturing—packaging operations, warehousing, and shipping.

A team is comprised of from 7 to 14 members (called operators) and a team leader. Its size is large enough to include a natural set of highly interdependent tasks, yet small enough to allow effective face-to-face meetings for decision making and coordination. Assignments of individuals to sets of tasks are subject to team consensus. Although at any given time, one operator has primary responsibility for a set of tasks within the team's jurisdiction, some tasks can be shared by several operators. Moreover, tasks can be redefined by the team in light of individual capabilities and interests. In contrast, individuals in the old plant were permanently assigned to specific jobs.

Other matters that fall within the scope of team deliberation, recommendation, or decision making include: coping with manufacturing problems that occur within or between the teams' areas of responsibilities; temporarily redistributing tasks to cover for absent employees; selecting team operators to serve on plant-wide committees or task forces; screening and selecting employees to replace departing operators; and counseling those who do not meet team standards (for example, regarding absences or giving assistance to others

Integrated Support Functions

Staff units and job specialties are avoided. Activities typically performed by maintenance, quality control, custodial, industrial engineering, and personnel units are built into an operating team's responsibilities. For example, each team member maintains the equipment he operates (except for complicated electrical maintenance) and housekeeps the area in which he works. Each team has responsibility for performing quality tests and ensuring quality standards. In addition, team members perform what is normally a personnel function when they screen job applicants.

Challenging Job Assignments

While the designers understood that job assignments would undergo redefinition in light of experience and the varying interests and abilities on the work teams, the initial job assignments established an important design principle. Every set of tasks is designed to include functions requiring higher-order human abilities and responsibilities, such as planning, diagnosing mechanical or process problems, and liaison work.

The integrated support functions just discussed provide one important source of tasks to enrich jobs. In addition, the basic technology employed in the plant is designed to eliminate dull or routine jobs as much as possible. But some nonchallenging, yet basic, tasks still have to be compensated for. The forklift truck operation, for example, is not technically challenging. Therefore, the team member responsible for it is assigned other, more mentally demanding tasks (for example, planning warehouse space utilization and shipping activities).

Housekeeping duties are also included in every assignment, despite, the fact that they contribute nothing to enriching the work, in order to avoid having members of the plant community who do nothing but menial cleaning.

Job Mobility and Rewards for Learning

Because all sets of tasks (jobs) are designed to be equally challenging (although each set comprises unique skill demands), it is possible to have a single job classification for all operators. Pay increases are geared to an employee mastering an increasing proportion of jobs, first in the team and then in the total plant. In effect, team members are payed for learning more and more apsects of the total manufacturing system. Because there are no limits on the number of operators that can qualify for higher pay brackets, employees are also encouraged to teach each other. The old plant, in contrast, featured large numbers of differentiated jobs and numerous job classifications, with pay increases based on progress up the job hierarchy.

Facilitative Leadership

Team leaders are chosen from foreman-level talent and are largely responsible for team development and group decision making. This contrasts with the old plant's use of supervisors to plan, direct, and control the work of subordinates. Management feels that, in time the teams will be self-directed and so the formal team leader position might not be required.

"Managerial" Decision Information for Operators

The design of the new plant provides operators with economic information and managerial decision rules. Thus production decisions ordinarily made by supervisors can now be made at the operator level

Self-Government for the Plant Community

The management group that developed the basic organization plan before the plant was manned refrained from specifying in advance any plant rules. Rather, it is committed to letting these rules evolve from collective experience.

Congruent Physical and Social Context

The differential status symbols that characterize traditional work organizations are minimized in the new plant. There is an open parking lot, a single entrance for both the office and plant, and a common decor throughout the reception area, offices, locker rooms, and cafeteria.

The architecture facilitates the congregating of team members during working hours. For example, rather than following the plan that made the air-conditioned control room in the process tower so small that employees could not congregate there, management decided to enlarge it so that process team operators could use it when not on duty elsewhere. The assumption here is that rooms which encourage ad hoc gatherings provide opportunities not only for enjoyable human exchanges but also for work coordination and learning about others' jobs.

Learning and Evolution

The most basic feature of the new plant system is management's commitment to continually assess both the plant's productivity and its relevance to employee concerns in light of experience.

I believe pressures will mount in this system with two apparently opposite implications for automation: On the one hand, people will

consider ways of automating the highly repetitive tasks. (There are
still back-breaking routine tasks in this plant; for example, as 50-
pound bags pile up at the end of the production line, someone must
grab them and throw them on a pallet.) On the other hand, some processes may be slightly deautomated. The original design featured
fully automated or "goof-proof" systems to monitor and adjust several
segments of the manufacturing process; yet some employees have become confident that they can improve on the systems if they are allowed
to intervene with their own judgments. These employees suggest that
organizations may benefit more from operators who are alert and
who care than from goof-proof systems.

Implementation Difficulties

Since the plant start-up in January 1971, a number of difficulties
have created at least temporary, and in some cases enduring, gaps
between ideal expectations and reality.

The matter of compensation, for example, has been an important source of tension within this work community. There are four
basic pay rates: starting rate, single job rate (for mastering the
first job assignment), team rate (for mastering all jobs within the
team's jurisdiction), and plant rate. In addition, an employee can
qualify for a "specialty" add-on if he has particular strengths—for example, in electrical maintenance.

Employees who comprised the initial work force were all hired
at the same time, a circumstance that enabled them to directly compare their experiences. With one or two exceptions on each team,
operators all received their single job rates at the same time, about
six weeks after the plant started. Five months later, however, about
one-third of the members of each team had been awarded the team
rate.

The evaluative implications of awarding different rates of pay
have stirred strong emotions in people who work so closely with each
other. The individual pay decisions had been largely those of the
team leaders who, however, were also aware of operators' assessments of each other. In fact, pay rates and member contributions
were discussed openly between team leaders and their operators, as
well as among operators themselves. Questions naturally arose:
Were the judgments about job mastery appropriate? Did everyone
have an equal opportunity to learn other jobs? Did team leaders depart from job mastery criteria and include additional considerations
in their promotions to team rate?

Thus, the basic concepts of pay progression are not easy to
treat operationally. Moreover, two underlying orientations compete

with each other and create ambivalences for team leaders and operators alike: a desire for more equality, which tends to enhance cohesiveness; and a desire for more differential rewards for individual
merit, which may be more equitable but can be divisive.

Similar team and operator problems have also occurred in othe⸱
areas. Four of these are particularly instructive and are listed on
page 61.

Management, too, has been a source of difficulty. For example, acceptance and support from superiors and influential staff
groups at corporate headquarters did not always come easily, thus
creating anxiety and uncertainty within the new plant community.

Management resistance to innovative efforts of this type has a
variety of explanations apart from natural and healthy skepticism.
Some staff departments feel threatened by an experiment in which
their functions no longer require separate units at the plant level.
Other headquarters staff who are not basically threatened may nevertheless resist an innovation that deviates from otherwise uniform pra
tives in quality control, accounting, engineering, or personnel. Mor
over, many managers resent radical change, presuming that it implie
they have been doing their jobs poorly.

Evidence of Success

While the productivity and the human benefits of this innovative
organization cannot be calculated precisely, there have nevertheless
been some impressive results. Using standard principles, industrial
engineers originally estimated that 110 employees should man the
plant. Yet the team concept, coupled with the integration of support
activities into team responsibilities, has resulted in a manpower leve⸱
of slightly less than 70 people.

After 18 months, the new plant's fixed overhead rate was 33
percent lower than in the old plant. Reductions in variable manufacturing costs (for example, 92 percent fewer quality rejects and an
absenteeism rate 9 percent below the industry norm) resulted in annual savings of $600,000. The safety record was one of the best in
the company, and the turnover was far below average. New equipmen⸱
is responsible for some of these results, but more than one-half
of them derive from the innovative human organization.

Operators, team leaders, and managers alike have become
more involved in their work and, also, have derived high satisfaction
from it. For example, when asked what work is like in the plant and
how it differs from other places they have worked, employees typicall⸱
replied: "I never get bored." "I can make my own decisions." "People will help you; even the operations manager will pitch in to help you⸱

Implementation Problems in the Pet-Food Plant

Here are four team and operator problems encountered in the design of the innovative plant:

1. The expectations of a small minority of employees did not coincide with the demands placed on them by the new plant community. These employees did not get involved in the spirit of the plant organization, participate in the spontaneous mutual-help patterns, feel comfortable in group meetings, or appear ready to accept broader responsibilities. For example, one employee refused to work in the government-regulated product-testing laboratory because of the high level of responsibility inherent in that assignment.

2. Some team leaders have had considerable difficulty not behaving like traditional authority figures. Similarly, some employees have tried to elicit and reinforce more traditional supervisory patterns. In brief, the actual expectations and preferences of employees in this plant fall on a spectrum running from practices idealized by the system planners to practices that are typical of traditional industrial plants. They do, however, cluster toward the idealized end of the spectrum.

3. The self-managing work teams were expected to evolve norms covering various aspects of work, including responsible patterns of behavior (such as mutual help and notification regarding absences). On a few occasions, however, there was excessive peer group pressure for an individual to conform to group norms. Scapegoating by a powerful peer group is as devastating as scapegoating by a boss. The same is true of making arbitrary judgments. Groups, however, contain more potential for checks and balances, understanding and compassion, and reason and justice. Hence it is important for team leaders to facilitate the development of these qualities in work groups.

4. Team members have been given assignments that were usually limited to supervisors, managers, or professionals: heading the plant safety committee, dealing with outside vendors, screening and selecting new employees, and traveling to learn how a production problem is handled in another plant or to troubleshoot a shipping problem. These assignments have been heady experiences for the operators, but have also generated mixed feelings among others. For example, a vendor was at least initially disappointed to be dealing with a worker because he judged himself in part by his ability to get to higher organizational levels of the potential customer (since, typically, that is where decisions are made). In another case, a plant worker attended a corporationwide meeting of safety officials where all other representatives were from management. The presence and implied equal status of the articulate, knowledgeable worker was at least potentially threatening to the status and self-esteem of other representatives. Overall, however, the workers' seriousness, competence, and self-confidence usually have earned them respect.

clean up a mess—he doesn't act like he is better than you are." Especially impressive was the diversity of employees who made such responses. Different operators emphasized different aspects of the work culture, indicating that the new system had unique meaning for each member. This fact confirms the importance of systemwide innovation. A program of job enrichment, for example, will meet the priority psychological needs of one worker but not another. Other single efforts are similarly limited.

Positive assessments of team members and team leaders in the new plant are typically reciprocal. Operators report favorably on th greater influence that they enjoy and the open relations which they experience between superiors and themselves; superiors report favorably on the capacities and sense of responsibility that operators have developed.

While the plant is not without the occasional rumor that reflects some distrust and cynicism, such symptomatic occurrences are both shorter lived and less frequent than are those that characterize other work organizations with which I am familiar. Similarly, although the plant work force is not without evidence of individual prejudice towar racial groups and women, I believe that the manifestations of these social ills can be handled more effectively in the innovative environment.

Team leaders and other plant managers have been unusually active in civic affairs (more active than employees of other plants in the same community). This fact lends support to the theory that participatory democracy introduced in the plant will spread to other institutional settings. Some social scientists, notably Carole Pateman, argue that this will indeed be the case.[1]

The apparent effectiveness of the new plant organization has caught the attention of top management and encouraged it to create a new corporate-level unit to transfer the organizational and manageria innovations to other work environments. The line manager responsib for manufacturing, who initiated the design of the innovative system, was chosen to head this corporate diffusion effort. He can now repor significant successes in the organizational experiments under way in several units of the old pet-food plant.

What It Costs

It has already been suggested what the pet-food manufacturer expected to gain from the new plant system: a more reliable, more flexible, and lower-cost manufacturing plant; a healthier work climate; and learning that could be transferred to other corporate units. What did it invest? To my knowledge, no one has calculated the extra costs incurred prior to and during start-up that were specif cally related to the innovative character of the organization. (This is probably because such costs were relatively minor compared with the amounts involved in other decisions made during the same time period.) However, some areas of extra cost can be cited:

Four managers and six team leaders were brought on board several months earlier than they otherwise would have been. The cost of outside plant visits, training, and consulting was directly related to the innovative effort. And a few plant layout and equipment design changes, which slightly increased the initial cost of the new plant, were justified primarily in terms of the organizational requirements.

During the start-up of the new plant, there was a greater than usual commitment to learning from doing. Operators were allowed to make more decisions on their own and to learn from their own experience, including mistakes. From knowledge of the situation, it is inferred that there was a short-term—first quarter—sacrifice of volume, but that it was recouped during the third quarter, when the more indelible experiences began to pay off. In fact, it would not be surprising if the pay-back period for the company's entire extra investment was greater than the first year of operation.

Why It Works

Listed in the insert on page 64 are eight factors that influenced the success of the new pet-food plant. It should be stressed, however, that these are merely facilitating factors and are not preconditions for success.

For example, while a new plant clearly facilitates the planning for comprehensive plantwide change (factor 3), such change is also possible in ongoing plants. In the latter case, the change effort must focus on a limited part of the plant—say, one department or section at a time. Thus, in the ongoing facility, one must be satisfied with a longer time horizon for plantwide innovation.

Similarly, the presence of a labor union (factor 6) does not preclude innovation, although it can complicate the process of introducing change. To avoid this, management can enter into a dialogue with the union about the changing expectations of workers, the need for change, and the nature and intent of the changes contemplated. Out of such dialogue can come an agreement between management and union representatives on principles for sharing the fruits of any productivity increases.

One factor that is essential, however, is that the management group immediately involved must be committed to innovation and able to reach consensus about the guiding philosophy for the organization.

Conditions Favorable to the Pet-Food Experiment

Listed below are eight factors that facilitated the success of the new plant.

1. The particular technology and manufacturing processes in this business provided significant room for human attitudes and motivation to affect cost; therefore, by more fully utilizing the human potential of employees, the organization was able to both enhance the quality of work life and reduce costs.

2. It was technically and economically feasible to eliminate some (but not all) of the routinized, inherently boring work and some (but not all) of the physically disagreeable tasks.

3. The system was introduced in a new plant. It is easier to change employees' deeply ingrained expectations about work and management in a new plant culture. Also, when the initial work force is hired at one time, teams can be formed without having to worry about cliques.

4. The physical isolation of the pet-food plant from other parts of the company facilitated the development of unique organization patterns.

5. The small size of the work force made individual recognition and identification easy.

6. The absence of a labor union at the outset gave plant management greater freedom to experiment.

7. The technology called for and permitted communication among and between members of the work teams.

8. Pet foods are socially positive products, and the company has a good image; therefore, employees were able to form a positive attitude toward the product and the company.

A higher-level executive who has sufficient confidence in the innovative effort is another essential. He or she will act to protect the experiment from premature evaluations and from the inevitable, reactive pressures to bring it into line with existing corporate policies and practices.

Management and supervisors must work hard to make such a system succeed—harder than in a more traditional system. In the case of the pet-food group, more work was required than in the traditional plant, but the human satisfactions were also much greater.

THE OTHER INNOVATORS

While the pet-food plant has a unique character and identity, it also has much in common with innovative plants of such U.S. corporations as Procter & Gamble and TRW Systems. Moreover, innovative efforts have been mounted by many foreign-based companies—for example, Shell Refining Co., Ltd. (England), Northern Electric Co., Ltd. (Canada), Alcan Aluminium (smelting plants in Quebec Province, Canada), and Norsk-Hydro (a Norwegian manufacturer of fertilizers and chemicals). Related experiments have been made in the shipping industry in Scandinavia and the textile industry in Ahmedabad, India. Productivity increases or benefits for these organizations are reported in the range of 20 percent to 40 percent and higher, although all evidence on this score involves judgment and interpretation.

All of these experiments have been influenced by the pioneering effort made in 1950 in the British coal mining industry by Eric Trist and his Tavistock Institute colleagues.[2]

Procter & Gamble has been a particularly noteworthy innovator. One of its newer plants includes many design features also employed in the pet-food plant. High emphasis has been placed on the development of "business teams," in which organization and employee identification coincides with a particular product family. Moreover, the designers were perhaps even more ambitious than their pet-food predecessors in eliminating first-line supervision. In terms of performance, results are reportedly extraordinary, although they have not been publicized. In addition, employees have been unusually active in working for social change in the outside community.[3]

Progressive Assembly Lines

Critics often argue that experiments like those discussed are not transferable to other work settings, especially ones that debase human dignity. The automobile assembly line is usually cited as a case in point.

I agree that different work technologies create different opportunities and different levels of constraint. I also agree that the automotive assembly plant represents a difficult challenge to those who wish to redesign work to decrease human and social costs and increase productivity. Yet serious experimental efforts to meet these challenges are now under way both in the United States and overseas.

To my knowledge, the most advanced projects are taking place in the Saab-Scandia automotive plants in Södertälje, Sweden. Consider, for example, these major design features of a truck assembly plant:

Production workers have been included as members of development groups that discuss such matters as new tool and machine designs before they are approved for construction.

Workers leave their stations on the assembly line for temporary assignments (for example, to work with a team of production engineer "rebalancing" jobs on the line).

Responsibility for in-process inspection has been shifted from a separate quality-inspection unit to individual production workers. The separate quality section instead devotes all its efforts to checking and testing completed trucks.

Work tasks have been expanded to include maintenance care of equipment, which was previously the responsibility of special mechanics.

Individuals have been encouraged to learn several jobs. In some cases, a worker has proved capable of assembling a complete engine.

Encouraged by the results of these limited innovations, the company is applying them in a new factory for the manufacture and assembly of car engines, which was opened in January 1972. In the new plant, seven assembly groups have replaced the continuous production line; assembly work within each group is not controlled mechanically; and eventually, the degree of specialization, methods of instruction, and work supervision will vary widely among the assembly groups.

In effect, the seven groups fall along a spectrum of decreasing specialization. At one end is a group of workers with little or no experience in engine assembly; at the other end is a group of workers with extensive experience in total engine assembly. It is hoped that, ultimately, each group member will have the opportunity to assemble an entire engine.[4]

In addition to the improvements that have made jobs more interesting and challenging for workers, management anticipates business gains that include: (1) a work system less sensitive to disruption than is the production line (a factor of considerable significance in the company's recent experience); and (2) the twofold ability to recruit workers and reduce absenteeism and turnover. (The company has encountered difficulty in recruiting labor and has experienced high turnover and absenteeism.)

Another Swedish company, Volvo, also has ambitious programs for new forms of work systems and organization. Especially interesting is a new type of car assembly plant being built at Kalmar. Here are its major features:

Instead of the traditional assembly line, work teams of 15-25 men will be assigned responsibility for particular sections of a car (for example, the electrical system, brakes and wheels, steering and controls).
Within teams, members will decide how work should be divided and distributed.
Car bodies will be carried on self-propelled carriages controlled by the teams.
Buffer stocks between work regions will allow variations in the rate of work and "stock piling" for short pauses in the work flow.
The unique design of the building will provide more outside windows, many small workshops to reinforce the team atmosphere, and individual team entrances, changing rooms, and relaxation areas.

The plant, scheduled to open in 1974, will cost 10 percent more than a comparable conventional car plant, or an estimated premium of $2 million. It will employ 600 people and have a capacity to produce 30,000 cars each year. Acknowledging the additional capital investment per employee, with its implication for fixed costs, Volvo nevertheless justifies this experiment as "another stage in the company's general attempt to create greater satisfaction at work."[5]

Question of Values

The designers of the Procter & Gamble and pet-food plants were able to create organizational systems that both improved productivity and enhanced the quality of work life for employees. It is hard to say, however, whether the new Saab-Scandia and Volvo plants will result in comparable improvements in both areas. (As mentioned earlier, the assembly line presents a particularly difficult challenge.)
In any event, managers who concern themselves with these two values will find points at which they must make trade-offs—that is, that they can only enhance the quality of work life at the expense of productivity or vice versa. Since it is easier to measure productivity than to measure the quality of work life, it is possible that this will bias how trade-off situations are resolved.
Productivity may not be susceptible to a single definition or to precise measurement, but business managers do have ways of gauging changes in it over time and comparing it from one plant to the next. They certainly can tell whether their productivity is adequate for their competitive situation.
But we do not have equally effective means for assessing the quality of work life or measuring the associated psychological and social costs and gains for workers.[6] We need such measurements if this value is to take its appropriate place in work organizations.

CONCLUSION

The emerging obligation of employers in our society is a twin one: to use effectively the capacities of a major natural resource—namely, the manpower they employ, and to take steps to both minimize the social costs associated with utilizing that manpower and enhance the work environment for those they employ. Fulfillment of this obligation requires major reform and innovation in work organizations. The initiative will eventually come from many quarters, but professional managers and professional schools are urged to take leadership roles. There are ample behavioral science findings and a number of specific experiences from which to learn and on which to build.

Furthermore, the nature of the problem and the accumulating knowledge about solutions indicate that organizational redesign should be systemic; it should embrace the division of labor, authority and status structures, control procedures, career paths, allocation of the economic fruits of work, and the nature of social contacts among workers. Obviously, the revisions in these many elements must be coordinated and must result in a new, internally consistent whole.

This call for widespread innovation does not mean general application of a particular work system, such as the one devised for the pet-food plant. There are important differences within work forces and between organizations. Regional variances, education, age, sex, ethnic background, attitudes developed from earlier work experiences, and the urban-rural nature of the population all will influence the salient expectations in the workplace. Moreover, there are inherent differences in the nature of primary task technologies, differences that create opportunities for, and impose constraints on, the way work can be redesigned.

NOTES

1. Participation and Democratic Theory (Cambridge, England: Cambridge University Press, 1970).
2. See E. L. Trist et al., Organizational Choice (London: Tavistock Publications, 1963).
3. Personal correspondence with Charles Krone, Internal Consultant, Procter & Gamble
4. For a more complete description of this plant, see Jan-Peter Norstedt, Work Organization and Job Design at Saab-Scandia in Södertälje (Stockholm: Technical Department, Swedish Employers' Confederation, December 1970).

5. Press release from Volvo offices, Gothenburg, Sweden, June 29, 1972.

6. For the beginning of a remedy to this operational deficiency, see Louis E. Davis and Eric L. Trist, Improving the Quality of Work Life: Experience of the Socio-Technical Approach (Washington, D.C.: Upjohn Institute, 1973).

5

JOB RESTRUCTURING:
THEORY AND CHANGE STRATEGY

Job restructuring denotes a closely related group of techniques for redesigning jobs. The best known of these methods, and probably the most widely used, is job enrichment. Job enrichment is often distinguished from job enlargement; the essential difference is that the latter involves adding to a job more tasks of the same kind, whereas to enrich a job, tasks from a higher level, such as supervisory or quality control tasks, are added. A third kind of restructuring, job rotation, consists of moving the individual between different tasks, usually on a regular basis. Since job enrichment has the most thoroughly developed theory of these three kinds of restructuring, and in most respects embodies the main elements of the other two, it is unnecessary to retain the distinction between the different techniques. This chapter discusses the theory behind job enrichment and a strategy for implementing it in organizations.

HERZBERG'S TWO-FACTOR THEORY OF
MOTIVATION

The originator of the theory that underlies job enrichment is Frederick Herzberg, one of the best-known figures in the field covered in this book. Herzberg's theory has given rise to several years of debate, but whatever its weaknesses, it has stood the test of time. Indeed, criticism and research have helped to refine this approach and make it a widely used management technique.

According to Herzberg (Herzberg, Mausner, and Snyderman 1959; Herzberg 1966, 1968), satisfaction and dissatisfaction are not opposite poles of one and the same human feeling. A person who is not dissatisfied is not necessarily satisfied or motivated, he simply has no reason to complain. Because someone is not complaining abou his job does not necessarily mean that he is motivated to do it well. To reduce dissatisfaction among employees is not the same as to increase their motivation.

The causes or determinants of dissatisfaction are quite distinct from the causes of satisfaction. Dissatisfaction is determined by what is called <u>hygiene factors</u>, such as working conditions, pay, tech nical supervision, status of the job, company policy and administration, and interpersonal relations. These are all aspects of the situation or context within which a person works, a fact that is captured by the word <u>hygiene</u>.

The sources of motivation in a person's job are a quite different set of factors, termed <u>motivators</u>. Motivators include significant achievement, recognition for work, the nature of the work itself, the exercise of responsibility, opportunities for growth in competence, and advancement on the job. Motivators have more to do with the actual work itself than with the situation. Hence, motivators can be thought of as aspects of job content, and hygiene (or maintenance) fac tors can be considered as aspects of job context. To reduce dissatisfaction, improve the context or hygiene. To increase motivation, improve the motivators or content of the job. This latter strategy is the essence of job enrichment.

The research technique used by Herzberg (1966) in developing his theory is of interest, and can easily be repeated by a manager as part of an introduction to the motivator-hygiene theory. Briefly, sub jects were asked to recall and relate in some detail an actual time or occasion when they had felt exceptionally good or happy in their jobs, and to do the same for a bad or unhappy experience. When these two sets of stories were examined, it was found that the causes of dissatisfaction were predominantly the hygiene factors, while the sources of satisfaction were the motivators. This simple experiment can be verified by asking almost any group of people to write out details of a bad and a good experience at work and, when they have done so, to code their stories according to Herzberg's categories. The same pattern usually emerges: dissatisfaction is associated with hygience problems, and the good experiences are predominantly related to achievement, responsibility, or to the other motivators. It follows that to provide for improved hygiene is no substitute for improving the factors that really motivate, and vice versa. This simple insight is perhaps one of the reasons for the impact of the two-factor theory, since managers have typically expected high motivation to result from better hygiene, often only to be disappointed at the short-lived effects of increased pay or improved working conditions.

Before leaving the matter of Herzberg's research methodology, a note of caution is in order: several studies have sought to test the

theory, and among the weaknesses that have been identified is that
the methodology used by Herzberg tends to elicit socially desirable
responses. In other words, when other methods are used to test the
theory, the two-factor theory is not often validated. This somewhat
technical point is discussed, along with several other related matters,
by Wall and Stephenson (1970) in a comprehensive evaluation of the
relevant literature.

On a more practical note, there has been some concern that
the theory tends to assume that the presence of the motivators in a
job will motivate all employees. An important study by Hulin and
Blood (1968), however, has shown the presence of individual differences in reactions to job restructuring. Also, it has been noted that
the theory does not specify how the presence or absence of the motivating conditions can be measured for existing jobs (Porter, Lawler,
and Hackman 1975). These two difficulties have been largely resolved
by a group of researchers whose refinements of Herzberg's theory
and technique are worth mentioning. In a series of studies (Hackman
and Lawler 1971; Hackman et al. 1975), a questionnaire was developed
for measuring the motivating potential of a job on five core dimensions
—skill variety, wholeness of the task, significance of the task, personal responsibility, and knowledge of results—and for measuring each
person's degree of satisfaction with these five aspects of his job.
With the same instrument, it was also possible to extract a score
that would indicate the subject's growth needs. This latter measure
is a useful refinement because a person's growth need, the degree to
which the individual is desirous of obtaining higher-order need satisfaction from his work, has been found to determine the degree of acceptance or resistance to job enrichment (Hackman and Lawler 1971).

Hackman and his colleagues (Hackman et al. 1975) argue that
the five core dimensions of a job create three critical psychological
states: experienced meaningfulness of the work, experienced responsibility for the outcome of the work, and knowledge of the actual results of work activities. The first three core dimensions—skill variety,
wholeness, and significance—create a sense of meaning; scope for
autonomy on the job results in the experience of exercising responsibility; and knowledge of results comes from the feedback dimension
of the job.

To summarize the motivator-hygiene theory of job satisfaction:
good hygiene reduces dissatisfaction but does not motivate the person, except, perhaps, for a relatively short period. To sustain high
motivation, a job must embody motivators to a sufficient degree. The
degree to which a job has motivating potential can be assessed, as
can the likelihood of job occupants being receptive to an enriched job.

THE STRATEGY OF JOB RESTRUCTURING

The motivator–hygiene theory (Herzberg 1966) is probably the best-known theory of motivation among managers. The reason for its popularity is its simplicity and, what is more important, its demonstrated applicability to real organizational problems. Over the last decade, scores, and perhaps hundreds, of job-restructuring projects based on this theory have been published. The term job enrichment is most commonly used to denote the intervention strategy. In the earlier projects, a good deal of trial and error was involved in carrying out job enrichment, but in more recent years, there have been a number of attempts to formulate a comprehensive strategy (Hackman et al. 1975; Mumford 1976; Reif and Tinnell 1973; Ford 1969).

The strategy of job-restructuring involves six distinguishable steps: general diagnosis, building commitment, detailed diagnosis of the job and job occupants, generating ideas for change and evaluating ideas, implementation, and project evaluation.

General Diagnosis

The identification of jobs that need restructuring should be approached systematically. The fact that a particular group has low morale or that a certain line manager is eager to try it out are not sufficient bases for inaugurating a project in that section or department, although these have been fairly typical reasons for attempting job restructuring. In order to increase the probability of success, the process of selecting jobs for enrichment should begin with a general assessment of several factors (Reif and Tinnell 1973).

1. The job itself: Related job criteria that have been found most relevant are cost, quality, flexibility, coordination, specialization, wage-payment plan, and man-machine relationship. Indications that job enrichment is appropriate would be where costs can be reduced; where quality is attributable to the workers; where the work force is flexible, at least in the sense that they can be retrained; where the benefits of task specialization are not indispensible; or where the project is unlikely to be seen as jeopardizing aspects of the wage system that are favored by the people concerned.

2. Technology: A major constraint on job enrichment is the technology involved in the operations. As a rule of thumb, the more closely the individual is anchored to a piece of technology, the less scope there is for enrichment, unless massive technological change is to be carried out. With regard to this point, it is worth noting that when a company is contemplating technological change for other

reasons, an opportunity is provided for enrichment of jobs. The opportunism of managers in situations like this has played a big part in
the success of many job-enrichment projects.

3. The worker: It has already been indicated that people vary
in their willingness and ability to respond positively to enriched jobs.
The human factors that need to be taken into account are the level of
knowledge or skill, education, previous work experience, background,
job security, present level of job satisfaction, and unionization. Thus,
the prospects of a successful project would tend to be enhanced where,
for example, a job was not already sufficiently enriched (or even too
much so), where people were not so "numbed" by years in a routine
job as to reject any increase in responsibility, where job security
was not threatened by the proposed changes, and where the unions
were likely to cooperate rather than resist.

4. Management: Without the support of relevant managers,
job-restructuring projects are unlikely to succeed. This has been
the experience of most practitioners, and the failure to get the necessary commitment has been commonly cited as the main reason for the
failure of a project. By relevant managers, we mean any manager
who is likely to be affected by the changes or held accountable for the
eventual outcomes.

Reif and Tinnell (1973) have produced a short (two-page) questionnaire that managers can use to guide their examination of the
situation and selection of the best target area. Additional questions
could readily be added where necessary to ensure that all relevant
factors have been taken into account in the early stages.

Building Commitment

People will usually be more accepting of change if they have
been consulted beforehand in order to gain their commitment. Job
enrichment rarely creates major disruption of the work, but it does
affect many people—those in the target group, their boss, people in
other departments, and senior management. It can occur, for instance, that for a period immediately after jobs have been enriched,
there is a drop in productivity, which can be attributed to people's
lack of familiarity with the new situation. Unless top managers are
fully committed to the enrichment program and fully understand it,
they are likely to put a stop to it at the first sign of a downturn in
production, thereby losing out on the possibility of better results in
the longer term. Line managers and supervisors must also be committed, since these are the people who must implement the enrichment program. Where the members of the target group belong to a

trade union, it is necessary to consult the union and seek its comm
ment to the job restructuring. One approach to building commitme
from the outset has been to form a working group or committee tha
supervises the program from beginning to end and also takes respo
sibility for disseminating results throughout the organization. In
Europe, such committees are common and may involve unions, ma
agement, and even government representatives. The Phillips orga
zation, with headquarters in Holland, is an outstanding example of
cooperative approach to job restructuring, and several other examp
can be found in Sweden (Petersen 1976).

Whether or not a formal structure is set up to carry out the p
gram, considerable education in this strategy is needed. Managers
and supervisors must be introduced to the theory and techniques of
job enrichment. Case studies based on similar situations can be us
as part of this process.

Detailed Diagnosis of the Job and Job Occupants

When a decision has been taken regarding which jobs are to be
restructured, detailed diagnosis is recommended. Essentially, the
job is analyzed to see where the leverage for change exists. The
satisfactions and needs of the job occupants are also assessed to as
certain which changes would most likely be valued and which ones
would be rejected. A number of questionnaire–type instruments hav
been developed for this diagnosis. The one that seems most related
to motivator–hygiene theory is that developed by Hackman and Lawl
(1971), the job diagnostic survey (JDS). (Walters and Associates
[1975] give several examples of the use of the JDS.)

The JDS appears to be particularly useful because it answers
the following critical questions:

1. Are motivation and satisfaction central to the problem, or is
   something else causing the difficulty?
2. What is the motivating potential of the job?
3. Which particular aspects of the job are causing the problems?
4. To what degree does the target group have a need for the kinds
   satisfaction that follow job enrichment?

Certain categories of people tend to resist job changes more
than others, as Collins and Raubolt (1975) have shown in a study of
employee resistance to job enrichment. A summary of their finding
was that "approximately 62% of workers studied (i.e., engineers,
engineering associates and draughtsmen in a large manufacturing
company) are non-resistent to job enrichment." They continue: "W

is the profile of the non-resistent worker? First, he has more education than the resistent worker. Second, he is younger; the resistent worker tends to be older. Third, he will likely work in a department doing similar tasks" (p. 235). While these findings may vary somewhat for other groups of workers, they seem to coincide with the experience of many practitioners, some of whom would probably add to this profile: "Has spent a long time at the same level of job."

A further diagnostic question is suggested by Mumford (1972, 1976), where she proposes a method of assessing the best fit between the individual, the job, and the company's requirements. It can happen, for instance, that there is considerable scope in the job for restructuring and enthusiasm for the changes among the work force but, at the same time, such changes could be at odds with the requirements of the company.

While the main focus of the detailed diagnosis is the job itself and the job occupant, there is considerable merit in widening the investigation to look at jobs or functions that border on the target group's work. Examination of these closely related functions frequently reveals additional scope for enrichment, as noted by Whitsett (1975). He pinpoints a number of structural clues that indicate the room for maneuver that is necessary for significant enrichment to take place. The clues listed include: the existence of communication units or jobs, checking functions or jobs, trouble-shooting jobs, supergurus, job title elephantiasis, one-to-one reporting relationships, dual reporting relationships, unclear division of responsibility, over-complicated work flow, duplication of functions, and labor pools. Where these phenomena occur, they would suggest that, over time, jobs have been impoverished or stripped of motivators. For example, the responsibility for checking one's own work may have been passed on to a quality control supervisor.

In brief, by means of questionnaire, observations, or interview, the scope for enriching a given set of jobs should be assessed in detail; the attitude of the job occupants to possible changes should also be ascertained.

Generating and Evaluating Ideas for Change

One of the more striking aspects of the job-enrichment process is the common discovery that considerably more scope exists for enrichment than anyone would have guessed at the outset. Many possible changes will have come to light by this stage, but many more can be added by conducting sessions that have the specific purpose of collecting ideas for change. It is a matter of judgment as to who should participate in these sessions, but certainly all immediate supervisors of the target group should be involved.

The name given to these creative meetings is <u>greenlighting</u> sessions (Ford 1969; Walters and Associates 1975). Greenlighting, or <u>brainstorming</u> as it is sometimes called, is a process that helps to facilitate creative or ingenious thinking. The principle rule is that there should be absolutely no evaluation or judgment of the ideas at this stage. Every idea, including apparently impractical or crazy ones, must be written down; it is quantity of ideas that is required, as people are encouraged to build on each other's ideas. As an aid to thinking, the participants may be presented with the full list of motivators and asked to think of concrete ideas for building more of these factors into the job.

A good brainstorming session typically produces scores of ideas These suggestions must be evaluated and sorted. There are no fixed criteria for sorting ideas, because in each case, the needs will be different. It is useful, however, to begin by separating what are obviously useless ideas from those that seem plausible; a third category of questionable ones might be included. Several ideas will be related to hygiene factors, and these should also be set aside. Other categories that might be used are ideas that can be implemented quickly and without cost, ideas that involve risk, ideas that can be implement only over a long period of time, ideas that will require retraining, ideas that will have industrial relations implications, and so on.

Once an agreed list of proposals for change has been compiled, it may be necessary to carry out more detailed evaluation and problem solving. For instance, it might be necessary to ascertain the union's attitude to a certain change or to obtain detailed information on the cost of another. Some thought should also be given to the likely "ripple effect" of the job restructuring. If changes are made in a given set of jobs, there will often be an effect on surrounding jobs. The supervisor, for instance, may be left with less to do if several of his duties have been delegated to subordinates. Where this happen the supervisor's job may also need to be enriched.

There are both intended and unintended consequences to job enrichment. It is worth emphasizing, however, that some of the mos effective projects have involved simple changes. Part of the success of this approach to improving productivity and quality of work life is that it typically involves relatively little disruption of the work.

Implementation

As for any set of change proposals, implementation needs to be planned carefully. Responsibilities for the changes should be defined clearly, and all relevant parties should be aware of the timing of the changes. It is not necessary to announce the changes publicly and

make a big event of them; the best way, in many cases, is to introduce the changes in a matter-of-fact way as part of the day's work.
Where the target group has been involved in the earlier stages of the
process, it is useful to keep a chart to document the progress of the
implementation strategy.

The proposed changes can be grouped together under a small
number of implementing concepts, which help to put order or logic to
the diverse aspects of the restructuring. Hackman et al. (1975) list
five implementing concepts or basic forms of restructuring.

1. Form natural work units: This involves organizing the individual's or group's tasks according to a logic that can be seen and
made sense of. For example, Gorman and Molloy (1972) report a
case where the card-punching requirements of user departments
were met by a small group of punch card operators, whereas previously the punching work was distributed randomly to a large pool
of operators. A Hackman et al. (1975, p. 63) note: "The principle
underlying natural units of work . . . is 'ownership'—a worker's
sense of continuing responsibility for an identifiable body of work."

2. Combine tasks: Combining tasks goes directly against the
well-known principle that the breakdown of tasks into simpler units
is the most efficient way to organize work. Where possible, tasks
should be regrouped to form larger, more coherent units of work.
Wild (1974) gives several examples of task combinations, and he
shows how the cycle time of the tasks carried out by the individual is
thereby increased—in one case from 30 seconds to 6.5 minutes.
Obviously, such changes reduce the boredom associated with short-
cycle, repetitive work. Scope for task combination will frequently be
constrained by the layout and flexibility of the technology. It is worth
emphasizing, however, that many of the functions listed by Whitsett
(1975), such as communications, checking, and trouble shooting, can
be regrafted onto assembly line jobs, at least for a work group if not
for the individual. It is also worth noting that the same kind of restructuring could be carried out for supervisory and managerial jobs
where important functions, like staff development, have been given
to separate departments.

3. Establishing client relationships: It will greatly increase
the significance of a person's work if he has more direct contact with
the client, either face-to-face, by phone, or by mail. When the
client or user can convey to the worker his pleasure or displeasure
with the product, the latter gets more direct feedback. The other
benefit of such direct contact, of course, is that the "frontline" worker
(for example, the counter clerk or the waiter) does not have to take
the brunt of complaints about work performed by the "backroom"
worker (for example, the accounts clerk or the cook).

4. Vertical loading: Vertical loading refers to delegation of responsibilities from higher levels of management to lower ones. For each job, the details of vertical loading will vary greatly, but some general distinctions can be made. For instance, delegation may be to an individual or to a group. Increased discretion or control over the boundaries of work is often possible, as noted by the present authors in an earlier publication (Srivastva et al. 1975). Examples cited were "discretion over (a) inputs required to do their job adequately; (b) maintenance functions; (c) quality control; (d) financial control; and (e) other functions on which productivity depended" (p. 74). Another category of autonomy has to do with day-to-day aspects of supervision, such as authority to excuse lateness or allow time off. Increased discretion may also be given regarding work methods, pacing, rotating between jobs, priorities of work, the management of one's time, and the handling of complaints or problems. A final category of increased responsibility is that of training new employees.

5. Open information and feedback channels: The fifth implementing concept includes information feedback. At least four categories of information may be considered when restructuring jobs: (a) information needed to do the job; (b) information about one's performance; (c) information about other individuals, groups, or departments upon which one's own performance is partly dependent; and (d) information about the department, company, or environment that is not necessarily of direct relevance to task performance but which people nevertheless want to have. Feedback enables the person to learn how well (or badly) he is doing; it also has a motivational impact. Knowledge of performance can come directly from the work itself, especially if very clear standards have been set and if a method of monitoring performance has been attached to the job. Feedback that is directly available is preferable to that given by the supervisor, since the latter may involve relatively arbitrary judgment, interruptions, and other disruptive interpersonal problems.

To conclude this discussion of the implementation stage, other possible implementing concepts involve bringing together spatially separated jobs; building staff development into day-to-day operations; making the hierarchy more flat; bringing staff functions into the line operations; standardizing titles; and breaking down rigid job demarcation. There are probably many other such concepts that the practitioner may use when organizing the diverse items that are to be included in the restructuring.

Project Evaluation

The last step in the strategy of job restructuring is to evaluate the project. Evaluation serves to find out whether the whole exercise was worthwhile and whether further intervention is needed. Insofar as systematic evaluations have been carried out, or rather insofar as they have been published, they have tended to concentrate on the successful aspects of job restructuring. Total failures have rarely been published, and unsatisfactory aspects of successful projects have been discussed only minimally. Far more rigor is required, therefore, if job restructuring is to become a useful management tool.

Project evaluation should be built into the program from the outset. Those involved with the supervision of the project need to agree on the outcomes that will be monitored and on the selection of comparison or control groups. Criteria will vary according to each situation and the particular concerns of management. Typical categories include: (1) costs—for example, clerical costs, direct labor costs, manufacturing costs, cost of downtime; (2) productivity—for example, reduction in inspection time, worker effectiveness, initiative in seeking new business, machine efficiency as a percentage of standard; (3) quality—for example, quality of maintenance, average rate of rejects; (4) withdrawal—for example, tardiness, early departures, absenteeism, employee trips to the health center; and (5) attitudes—for example, employee satisfaction, other departments wanting to carry out job restructuring, satisfaction with the new arrangement, good reaction from the job-restructuring committee, satisfaction of growth needs.

SUMMARY

Job restructuring has its origin in Herzberg's (1966) motivator-hygiene theory of motivation and his early work on job enrichment. Later refinements of the theory and the experience of practitioners in restructuring jobs have led to the evolution of a well-integrated strategy for improving productivity and quality work life. Job restructuring has been popular among managers, but has tended to be "oversold" in literature on the topic. More rigorous adherence to a comprehensive strategy, such as that outlined in this chapter, should see the retention of this technique as a widely used tool for the management of human resources. Readers who wish to assess the relevance of job restructuring for their own situation will find it worthwhile to read a number of articles that raise, and in some cases deal with, possible weaknesses of the theory and strategy. The articles in question are by Hackman (1975), Schappe (1974), Wall and Stephenson (1970), and Shepard (1974).

CHAPTER

6

JOB RESTRUCTURING:
A REVIEW OF 28
SELECTED EXPERIMENTS

A notable feature of published reports of job restructuring has been their total concentration on successful outcomes and a corresponding failure to report failures. Reviewers of the job-restructuring literature (for example, Birchall and Wild 1973; Blackler and Brown 1975; and Walters and Associates 1975) have noted this obvious imbalance in the reporting and have urged greater scientific rigor in the design of projects and the interpretation of outcomes. Such rigor has not been a characteristic of experimental design of projects, as Birchall and Wild (1973, p. 42) noted after examining over 80 job-restructuring studies:

> Although a considerable number of experiments are reported, few show evidence of thorough experimental investigation. Little use was made of control groups for comparison. Only slight attention has been paid to the evaluation of benefits. Unsuccessful applications seem to have been forgotten. Only two such reported experiments having been found.

The purpose of this chapter is to summarize the claims regarding the efficacy of job restructuring in 28 projects and, secondly, to evaluate thoroughly the scientific status of those claims. There is also a discussion of contingencies and the process of implementation.

ACTION LEVERS AND THEIR EFFECTS

The term action levers refers to the dimensions or aspects of the organization changed in the course of the various projects. Table

3 reveals the extent to which different action levers were manipulated and the outcomes reported in each case. There is also information about the target group, the numbers involved, and other contextual factors.

The most commonly manipulated action levers in this set of studies were, in order of decreasing frequency, autonomy/discretion, task variety, information/feedback, and training. This group of dimensions corresponds very closely to Herzberg's (1966) motivators and the core dimensions of Hackman and his associates (1975). In contrast, the levers least often changed were interpersonal/group process, pay/reward systems, organizational structure, support, and technical/physical. These levers correspond closely to the hygiene factors of Herzberg. A number of commentators have noted that it is advisable to ensure that the hygiene needs are adequately met before the benefits of improving the motivators can be attained. In general, then, it can be seen that the emphasis in these experiments is consistent with the main theoretical bases of job restructuring.

The number of action levers manipulated in the various projects ranges from one to six. Ten studies (36 percent) reported change involving one or two action levers, and the outcomes for these relatively simple interventions seem no more or less successful than the results obtained by changing a greater number of dimensions. Significant improvements can apparently result from even a few simple changes in the design of jobs.

The effects of the changes made in the 28 cases reviewed are shown in Table 3. In all of the studies but one (Lawler, Hackman, and Kaufman 1973), some degree of success was reported; in a total of six cases (29 percent), a deterioration on one of the outcome dimensions was recorded. The general pattern of results suggests that the changes had a predominantly positve effect. It is impossible with the information provided by these studies to separate out the relative efficacy of each of the action levers in producing specific outcomes. A great deal more research is required to establish the relationships between separate changes and outcome variables.

A more detailed examination of the pattern of outcomes reveals that the most common effect of job restructuring was an improvement of attitudes—in 64 percent of cases. Improvements on the other outcome variables occurred in the following proportions of cases: quality (61 percent), productivity (54 percent), costs (32 percent), and withdrawal (21 percent). The few negative results that were reported do not fall into any discernible pattern that might suggest the reasons for deterioration on the dimensions in question.

The overall picture that emerges from this mosaic of findings is that job restructuring is typically successful. The question arises, however, as to the validity of these claims: Did the manipulation of

TABLE 3

Job Restructuring: Contextual Variables and Action Levers and Their Effects

	Authors								
	Alderfer, C., 1969	Conant, E., Kilbridge, M., 1965	Cox, D., Sharp, K., 1951	Davis, L., Valfer, E., 1965	Davis, L., Werling, R., (a), 1960	Davis, L., Werling, R., (b), 1960	Ford, R., (a), 1969	Ford, R., (b), 1969	Ford, R., Sheaffer, H., 1969
Contextual variables									
Type of work	Production process	Manufacturing assembly line	Assembly line	Manufacturing supervisors	Distribution in chemical plant	Maintenance in chemical plant	Clerical in telephone company	Summary of 19 experiments in telephone company	Telephone circuit installation
Sex	?	?	Male/female	?	?	?	Female	Male/female	Male
Occupational status	Blue	Blue	Blue	White	Blue	Blue	White	Blue/white	Blue
Number treated	?	61	?	?	?	?	36	1,000	38
Unionized	?	Yes	Yes	?	Yes	Yes	?	Yes	Yes
Participation in change	?	?	Yes	?	No	No	No	No	No
Country	United States	United States	Great Britain	United States	United States	United States	United States	United States	United States
Treatment took effect	?	Yes	?	Yes	No	Yes	Yes	Yes	?
Action levers									
Pay/reward systems		x							
Autonomy/discretion		x		x	x	x	x	x	x
Support					x	x			
Training	x			x	x	x			
Organizational structure									
Technical/physical	x	x	x						
Task variety	x	x	x		x	x	x	x	x
Information/feedback							x	x	x
Interpersonal/group process									
Effects									
Costs		−		+	−	−	+		−
Productivity		+	+	0	+	+	+	+	0
Quality		+	+	+	−		−	+	+
Withdrawal							−		−
Attitudes	+−	+	+	+		+	+	+	

86

	Authors								
	Foulkes, F., 1969	Gorman, L., Molloy, E. S. (a), 1972	(b), 1972	King-Taylor, L. (a), 1972	(b), 1972	Lawler, E. et al., 1973	Maher, J. et al., 1969	Marks, A., 1954	Marr, D., 1970
Contextual variables									
Type of work	Assembly line	Clerical	Key punching	Assembly line	Clerical	Telephone operator	Inspection	Assembly line	Service-ticket agent
Sex	Female	Male/female	Female	Male	Female	Female	?	Female	Male/female
Occupational status	Blue	White	White	Blue	White	White	White	Blue	White
Number treated	?	16	42	?	?	39	?	29	16
Unionized	?	?	?	Yes	?	Yes	?	Yes	?
Participation in change	Yes	Yes	?	No	?	No	?	Yes	Yes
Country	United States	Ireland	Ireland	Great Britain	Great Britain	United States	United States	United States	United States
Treatment took effect	?	?	?	?	?	Partial	Yes	Yes	Partial
Action levers									
Pay/reward systems	x	x	x	x	x		x		x
Autonomy/discretion			x	x	x	x	x	x	x
Support									x
Training			x	x	x		x		
Organizational structure			x				x		
Technical/physical	x		x				x	x	
Task variety		x	x	x	x	x	x	x	x
Information/feedback		x		x	x	x	x	x	
Interpersonal/group process		x	x						
Effects									
Costs							0		
Productivity	+	+	+	+			+	0	0
Quality	+			+			+	+	
Withdrawal	−		−	−	−				
Attitudes	+	+	+	+		0 −	+	+	+ −

(continued)

TABLE 3 (continued)

| | Authors | | | | | | | | | | |
| | Paul, W., et al. | | | | | Pauling, T., 1968 | Randall, R., 1973 | Sorcher, M., 1969 | Van Beek, H., 1964 | Walker, C., 1950 |
	(a), 1969	(b), 1969	(c), 1969	(d), 1969	(e), 1969					
Contextual variables										
Type of work	Engineering supervisor	Fabricating supervisor	Sales	Design engineering	Laboratory technician	Assembly line	Key punching	Assembly line	Assembly line	Machinists
Sex	?	?	?	?	Male	Female	Female	Female	?	?
Occupational status	White	White	White	White	White	Blue	White	Blue	Blue	Blue
Number treated	?	?	15	?	40	?	?	131	104	?
Unionized	?	?	?	?	?	?	?	?	?	?
Participation in change	No	No	No	No	No	?	?	Yes	?	?
Country	Great Britain	Great Britain	Great Britain	Great Britain	Great Britain	Australia	United States	United States	Netherlands	United States
Treatment took effect	Yes	?	Yes	Yes	?	?	Yes	?	?	Yes
Action levers										
Pay/reward systems										x
Autonomy/discretion	x	x	x	x	x	x	x	x		x
Support	x	x	x	x	x				x	
Training								x		
Organization structure										x
Technical/physical										x
Task variety	x	x		x	x	x			x	
Information/feedback	x	x					x		x	x
Interpersonal/group process										x
Effects										
Costs	-	-	-			-		-		
Productivity	0	+	+			+	+	+	+	+
Quality	+				+	+			+	+
Withdrawal								0		
Attitudes	+	0	+	+		+-	+		+	+

Code: blank = not relevant; x = variable manipulated; ? = insufficient data; + = variable increased; - = variable decreased; 0 = variable static.

Source: Srivastva et al. 1975, pp. 104-06.

these action levers actually produce the outcomes reported? Or was there another cause, like an upturn in the economy, a new boss, or some other factor not accounted for in the reports? To answer these questions, that is, to assess the internal validity of the studies, each experiment was examined to ascertain whether factors, other than the action levers, could have accounted for the results. Whenever a rival explanation seemed plausible, this was taken to constitute a threat to the validity of the findings. Each experiment was evaluated, and an inspection was made of the pattern of threats to validity in the total set of 28 studies. The assumption was made that if a particular threat was found to impinge on most studies in the set, then the internal validity of the positive trend in the results would be questionable. If, on the other hand, a particular threat was present in only a few of the studies, such a pattern was unlikely to account for the findings. The internal validity of performance and attitudinal findings are now discussed.

Validity of the Performance Findings

Twenty-four of the projects reviewed took account of some aspect of performance—either costs, productivity, or quality. No single study controlled for all threats to the internal validity of the performance findings. Threats from history were controlled in almost half of the studies by the use of comparison groups. A threat was posed by instability in 87 percent of cases where it was relevant. Testing was always controlled or else was not relevant. This particular threat was eliminated by the fact that the data were commonly obtained from nonreactive measures of performance; that is, the measurement was usually unobtrusive. Instrumentation was a source of threat in 50 percent of the studies where it could be considered relevant. The most common reason why instrumentation posed a threat to internal validity was that the performance improvements could plausibly have been attributed to changes in the organization's assessment procedures. In less than half of the cases where they were relevant, there were plausible threats from statistical regression (38 percent), selection (21 percent), and selection interaction (45 percent). The possibility of threats due to mortality, that is, differential loss of subjects from the comparison groups, occurred in nearly every case.

Briefly, then, the designs of the separate experiments were generally quite weak, but when the set of studies was taken as a whole, it was found that the converging positive outcomes could not reasonably be attributed to factors other than the manipulation of action levers. The greatest threats came from instability and mortality. With regard to the former, it should be noted that even though this threat could have been eliminated by simple statistical testing of differences, the improvements in performance were so great in several studies that such testing was apparently considered unnecessary. We are left, finally, with the greatest threat coming from mortality, and it is felt that the performance findings could not reasonably be discounted on this basis alone.

Validity of Quality of Work Life Results

Twenty-one studies reported some kind of attitudinal finding. The causal inferences made on this set of results are open to more alternative explanations than were the performance findings. Approx mately one-third or fewer of the studies controlled for instability, statistical regression, mortality, and selection interaction. The threat from history was avoided in 61 percent of the studies; instrumentation threats were controlled in 76 percent of the experiments where it was a relevant threat; and testing was ruled out in 67 percen of cases. Despite these three relatively strong features of the research designs, the weaknesses are such as to call the quality of work life findings into question.

The failure to make use of time series data, nonreactive measures of attitude, and other such devices weakened seriously these 21 designs for investigating quality of work life dimensions. Althougl several of the studies included additional anecdotal data, such as managers' or consultants' favorable judgments of the outcome, it must nevertheless be concluded that neither a causal connection between the action levers and attitude improvements has been proven by this group of studies nor, of course, has such a connection been confirmed between extraneous factors and the outcomes reported.

CONTINGENCIES

There are two sources of information regarding the factors upo which the reported results might be contingent: the design of the research project and certain contextual details contained in the reports and summarized in Table 3. The following discussion of contingencie does not distinguish between performance and attitudinal findings, except in preference to the study's research designs.

Table 3 provides information about the subjects and contexts of the experiments. Unfortunately, the unsystematic reporting of these data means that there are many question marks in the table, which make it difficult to identify trends or clear differences. It can be ascertained, however, that the sex of subjects is unlikely to be a contingency, since successes were reported for both males and females. Nor does the type of occupation or task seem to be a moderating factor, although there are no reports of job restructuring among executives or senior technical or professional personnel. Insofar as the numbers of subjects treated in any one project were specified in the reports, it seems that the strategy has been confined to numbers of less than 100. It remains to be proven, therefore, whether a job-restructuring project would be able to embrace much larger groups. Approximately one-third of the experiments specified that the subjects were unionized, so unionization clearly does not operate as a general constraint, and may even be a facilitator. Finally, Table 3 shows that job restructuring is applicable in Western industrialized societies. It remains to be seen whether type of society or stage in a nation's "development" might constitute contingency variables.

The experiments' research designs were examined for three threats to external validity: testing/treatment, selection/treatment, and experimental arrangements. The first of these occurs when pretesting has the effect of sensitizing the subjects to the treatment. Since the performance data were gathered from company records, which are largely nonreactive, this particular threat did not arise. The attitudinal findings were, however, subject to this threat to external validity in the majority of studies. The second threat, selection/treatment, puts a constraint on generalizing both sets of findings beyond the population from which the subjects were drawn because of the interaction of selection biases and experimental treatment. Several studies reported that experimental groups were chosen for reasons of cooperativeness and accessibility rather than randomly. Also, some of the studies reported that volunteer subjects were given the experimental treatment. Given such biases in the choice of subjects, the findings are unlikely to be typical of the universe of populations to which one might want to generalize. Hence, selection/treatment is a threat to external validity in all cases. The third threat, experimental arrangements, occurs in all studies, because almost any kind of field experiment involves the creation of some kind of unusual situation—for example, extra attention paid to workers and consultants coming and going.

While the examination of the research designs limits the automatic generalization of the findings to other groups and situations, this does not necessarily mean that the same job-restructuring technique would not produce similar results elsewhere. As indicated above, Table 3 suggests that this technique for improving productivity and quality of work life is quite robust in that it seems to work in a wide variety of situations and with a wide range of subjects.

Given the design of the 28 studies and the background information that was reported, the success of job restructuring may be contingent on the process of selecting people for such projects, on sensitization by some form of pretesting, and on special experimental arrangements. It may also be contingent upon the organizational level of subjects and unionization—among other possible contingencies. Only further research can confirm to what extent and in what way these contingencies do in fact operate to mediate the effects of job restructuring on productivity and quality of work life.

IMPLEMENTATION OF JOB RESTRUCTURING

Unlike the strategy for forming autonomous work groups, which was well formulated from the early stages of its use, a comprehensiv approach to job restructuring has emerged only recently, after scores of projects that depended, perhaps, more on the ingenuity of the instigators than on any firm set of guidelines. Not surprisingly, therefore there are few common threads running through the implementation strategies of the 28 studies reviewed here—that is, insofar as aspects of implementation have been reported. Only rarely was there any indication that a formal diagnosis of the organization took place, though this kind of analysis probably was carried out informally in many cases. In a small proportion of projects, typically European, considerable attention was paid to building commitment by setting up formal committees to supervise the project. Educational sessions were also common. Some kind of detailed diagnosis appeared to be part of the strategy adopted in most cases, though the methods of data collection varied from consultation with supervisors, through systematic interviewing, to both tailor-made and standardized questionnaires.

The technique of brainstorming, or greenlighting, to generate suggestions for change was reported in less than half of the studies. In Table 3, it can be seen that in five projects, the subjects themselve participated in formulating the changes, and in 12 cases, there was apparently no such consultation with subjects. The proportion of studies that simply did not report this kind of information makes it im possible to generalize on the relative wisdom of participation in the change process. Finally, the evaluation of studies was far from rigorous, especially with regard to attitudinal data. The fact that pretreatment measures of performance could be extracted from company records after a project had been completed probably explains the relatively stronger research designs for performance better than any suggestion of careful planning to evaluate from the outset. In other words, evaluation often seemed to be an afterthought for purpose of demonstrating some improvements.

Clearly, there is no single implementation formula to suit every situation. Even if one were to follow the steps outlined in the previou

chapter, considerable flexibility and ingenuity still seem to be required. The very instigation of some of the projects stemmed from
the opportunism of managers, who spotted the opportunity to append
job restructuring to other organizational changes already contemplated
or under way. With regard to the impetus for job restructuring, it is
also worth noting that the motive was, in several cases, simply to
improve an already satisfactory situation and not necessarily to solve
a morale or productivity problem. A striking feature of these projects is the involvement of line managers and internal consultants in
implementation and follow-up. The need for help from external consultants does not appear to be so great as, for instance, in projects
involving autonomous group redesigns. Another feature of this strategy, from the practicing manager's point of view, is that job restructuring can be introduced to a wide variety of situations with minimal
disruption of the work. In the Gorman and Molloy (1972) chapter
that follows this one, for instance, the actual time required to complete the various steps was six hours, that is, three two-hour periods.
In this same chapter, there are indications of the type of flexibility
mentioned above; although the members of the target group were not
involved in formulating the changes, they were consulted and given
the option to accept or reject their supervisor's proposals. In this
case, they accepted all but one recommended change.

In summary, success in job restructuring requires a systematic
approach, allied to considerable sensitivity to possible constraints
and the creativity to adapt to these constraints. The studies reviewed
here have been characterized more by the ingenuity of the pioneers
in this field than by the orderliness and rigor of their approach. If,
however, job restructuring is to outlive its pioneers and become a
reliable management tool, a more systematic strategy needs to be
adopted.

SUMMARY

Job-restructuring projects have been conducted in several countries and among subjects in an exceptionally wide variety of occupations. In general, a review of 28 projects reveals that job restructuring produces improvements in performance and quality of work life.
Careful scrutiny of the experimental designs and of the inferences
made from the data points out the need for caution in interpreting the
claims made, especially regarding attitude improvements. Since
reports of the implementation strategies varied greatly, a more systematic approach is urged if jobs are to be restructured effectively.

7

THE PROCESS OF "JOB ENRICHMENT"

Liam Gorman
Edmond S. Molloy

INTRODUCTION

In this chapter, a description is given of one approach to the "enrichment" of jobs. The purpose of job-enrichment programs is to redesign jobs so that they include those characteristics that research findings have shown to lead to the greater involvement of people in their work, to increased levels of job satisfaction, and, often, to higher levels of performance.

There are two main reasons for presenting this chapter:

To give a practical example of the steps involved in a job-enrichment project in order to demonstrate to managers and others, who might wish to use this approach, how to set about redesigning jobs in their own organizations.

To illustrate some of the benefits, such as productivity increases and increased levels of job satisfaction, that can result from modifying the nature of people's work.

The term job enrichment is derived from the work of Herzberg and his associates (Herzberg, Mausner, and Snyderman 1959; Herzberg 1966; and Paul, Robertson, and Herzberg 1969). A brief outline of Herzberg's ideas on work motivation will first be given. Herzberg research work led him to postulate that aspects of an individual's wor situation that lead to job satisfaction differ from those that lead to dis

===========

This chapter first appeared in People, Jobs and Organizations by Liam Gorman and Edmond S. Molloy (1972), and is reprinted here by kind permission of the publishers, Irish Productivity Centre, Dublin.

satisfaction. He holds that the actual work a person carries out is critically important in determining the satisfaction he derives from his job. More specifically, Herzberg's view is that a person needs opportunities for achievement at work, opportunities to take responsibility, recognition for achievements, and opportunities to advance and develop in his job if he is to be involved in his work. The factors that, according to Herzberg, are important in causing dissatisfaction are relationships with superiors, peers, and subordinates; the company policy and the way the company is administered; working conditions; the degree of job security offered; the status the job has; and the salary offered. The process of job enrichment involves putting more of the _motivators_ (Herzberg's term for the factors that give rise to satisfaction) into jobs.

The writers do not necessarily accept that the empirical validity of Herzberg's so-called two-factor theory has been established. However, many of the job characteristics categorized as motivators by Herzberg are referred to by other authorities on job design as qualities that are necessary in jobs if people are to become involved in their work. Other writers list additional factors not specifically referred to in Herzberg's work, such as task integration, that is, that the different operations one carries out should have some meaningful relationship to each other (Emery and Thorsrud 1969); feedback— a more extensive term than Herzberg's concept of recognition (Lawler 1969); opportunities for using higher-level abilities, such as one's judgment or capacities for decision making (Argyris 1964); and an optimal degree of variety in one's work. It is the authors' view that the job characteristics mentioned by these writers, as well as those derived from Herzberg's work, are relevant in job redesign programs.

A DESCRIPTION OF THE REDESIGNED JOB

The job that was redesigned was in the "long-haul" section of an airline telephone reservation office. The section dealt with long distance travel to and from continental Europe and America and travel on other airlines throughout the world. A separate "short-haul" section dealt with Ireland-United Kingdom bookings.

The work involved answering questions concerning particular travel arrangements from prospective passengers; offering appropriate services; quoting fares (complicated or unusual fares not immediately available in a manual were referred to a separate desk manned by a fares specialist); and checking and putting in reservations through a device linked to a real-time computer system. It also involved making special arrangements for some passengers, such as vegetarians, disabled passengers, unaccompanied children, and so on. The com-

puter with which the clerk dealt might not be able to give information
on the definite availability of particular accommodation, especially
if accommodation on certain other airlines was being requested.
In such cases, the computer automatically initiated a teleprinter message to the other airline requesting the accommodation. The reply,
when received, was relayed by the computer to the requesting section,
and a clerk would then telephone the passenger back to give him the
reply. In all, 16 people carried out the type of work described here.

STAGES IN A JOB-ENRICHMENT PROJECT

The following stages are useful to distinguish when undertaking
a job-enrichment project:

1. Introduction of the relevant concepts to those who will carry out the
   change program.
2. A brainstorming session, in two parts. In the first part, all ideas
   that might suggest possible ways in which the relevant jobs could
   be enriched are produced but not evaluated. In the second part,
   each idea that has been put forward is carefully evaluated in order
   to examine the problems involved in its implementation, and a
   list is drawn up of those ideas that can be put into action.
3. Implementation of the changes.
4. Evaluation of the effects of the changes.

Stage 1: Introducing the Relevant Concepts

It is the authors' experience that job-enrichment projects are
usually initiated by the training or staff development departments of
organizations through their contacts with line management. A well-
informed training or staff development department can generally identify sections or departments of the company where redesign of work
would be practicable and useful. In addition, training programs conducted by staff development personnel provide a good opportunity to
communicate to those in charge of line departments the possibilities,
benefits, and problems of redesigning jobs. It was during a training
program that the person with overall responsibility for the telephone
reservation office was introduced to job redesign ideas and saw their
relevance to his section. While he did not have serious morale problems among his staff, he felt, however, that the approach might help
people to become more involved in their work and take more initiative.
At the invitation of the section head, the staff development department
of the company and one of the authors became involved in the project.

The first step taken was to acquaint the immediate supervisors of the telephone reservation staff with ideas concerning job design. To achieve this purpose, a procedure similar to that used by Herzberg in his original study of motivation at work was adopted. Thus, members of the supervisory group were asked to recall a period when they felt highly involved in, and satisfied with, their work and to describe it and, likewise, to recall and describe a period when they were dissatisfied and uninvolved in their work. They were then given a list of factors that had been identified (by Herzberg) as sources of satisfaction and dissatisfaction at work, for example, the supervision one experiences, the pay one gets, the recognition one is given, and so on. By referring to this list, they were able to determine the main job factors alluded to in the incidents they had described. In this way it became clear that for them, aspects of work such as the degree of responsibility they experienced, the recognition they got, and the opportunities for self-direction they had were relevant to their satisfaction at work. Since the relevance of these factors to job involvement had been demonstrated from within their own experience, they were much more convinced of their importance and committed to attempts to implement action based on these ideas than if they had been told directly of their relevance.

This exercise was followed by the showing of a film about Herzberg's work, and afterwards, discussion took place on the subject matter of the film. The ideas brought out in the writing of their own themes were thus reinforced and elaborated on. At this stage, the members of the group were sufficiently convinced of the usefulness of the notion of job redesign to undertake to explore its potential contribution to their own work situation and to the work of the people they supervised. The session (which lasted two hours) ended with the group being given two articles describing job-enrichment projects in an office situation. These showed that an exercise like that which was being undertaken had been carried out successfully elsewhere and had yielded worthwhile results.

It is worth noting that in this particular project, the main planners of the project were the supervisory personnel. The authors usually tend to have the people whose jobs are being enriched more directly involved in the process, but here, this was not regarded as the best approach. The people whose jobs were to be redesigned, that is, the clerks in the telephone reservations office, were of course consulted before the changes were made, and any changes they did not agree with were not implemented.

Stage 2: Brainstorming Session

In this session, the supervisors again got together with a member of the staff development department and the consultant. The supervisory personnel were now familiar with job-enrichment concepts, and through their reading of the articles they had been given, they had met some examples of the implementation of these ideas in a situation somewhat similar to their own. They had been asked to consider, in the interval since the last meeting, how job-redesign ideas could be used in their own area. The session was taken up with a brainstorming exercise in which supervisors suggested ways in which the relevant jobs could be enriched. There were two distinguishable phases in this exercise. In the first phase (which lasted for approximately 30 minutes) ideas were produced freely, participants did not evaluate the ideas of other group members, and every idea that was produced was recorded by the staff development department representative. This phase of a brainstorming exercise is sometimes called, for obvious reasons, an idea-getting session. A large number of ideas, about 50 in all, was produced at this session.

The second part of the exercise is known as the "idea evaluation" phase. In this phase, all the ideas produced are systematically evaluated. Ideas are evaluated on the basis of two criteria:

1. The desirability of implementing the idea, for example: Would it be welcomed by the people directly affected?
2. The feasibility of implementing the idea, for example: Would implementation give rise to serious problems in other parts of the organization, such as encroachments on other sections' work? Would it have wider policy implications, such as implications for the overall grading and salary structures in the organization? Or how much time would be needed in order to implement the idea?

Ideas were eventually categorized into four groups, according to the ease with which, and speed at which, they could be implemented. The session ended with a list being compiled of the most readily implementable ideas. All participants in the meeting undertook to investigate problems surrounding the implementation of the ideas, such as the cost, if any, involved in their implementation, how they would affect other departments, whether industrial relations problems might arise because of the jobs involved being changed in such a way that others would feel threatened, and so on. In all, this session lasted just under two hours.

Stage 3: Implementation of the Proposed Changes

At the third meeting, definite proposals were formulated, which the supervisor who had overall responsibility for the area subsequently put to the personnel whose jobs it was proposed to redesign. The main changes proposed were the following:

1. The staff would themselves deal with requests for special handling from passengers booked in by them. Requests for special handling, such as for stretcher treatment or kosher food, were formerly passed to a supervisor for action.
2. The group would, in the future, arrange their own roster, provided that manning requirements were met.
3. The staff would be encouraged to compute and quote complex fares to passengers. Previously, these had been automatically passed to a special section.
4. The staff would play a more active market research and selling role. For example, they would pass on information on potential cargo sales arising from passenger bookings; also, they were given authority to initiate canvassing calls to major business accounts.
5. On a group basis, they would monitor the performance of the section against the agreed telephone-answering standards.
6. Personal contact would be established between telephone reservation staff and the secretaries to senior executives of the airline so that the reservation staff themselves would handle bookings directly rather than having these processed through their supervisors.
7. The staff would be consulted on the periodic modifications to the computerized reservations system.
8. Feedback on individual performance would be provided by having each person keep a record of the number of calls he dealt with.
9. Staff would participate in the training of juniors and new entrants.
10. Each staff member would be responsible for maintaining tariff manuals and a personal file of travel information.

The proposals put forward were accepted by the staff, except the one that dealt with increasing feedback by having people keep a record of the number of calls they dealt with. One or two people objected to this change, so it was not implemented. The other changes were implemented.

Stage 4: Evaluation of the Changes

These were the results found four months after the changes described here had been implemented:

1. There was an increase of almost 50 percent in the number of bookings that were transferred to the airline in question here from

the airlines with which the bookings had originally been made. These transfers occurred as a result of passengers' contacts with the telephone reservations staff.

2. The staff whose jobs were enriched were considered by their managers and supervisors to be showing far more initiative generally in seeking out new business through telephone contacts with, for instance, business firms and various types of associations.

3. Morale was generally considered to be very high by the supervisors in the area. To quote one supervisor: "People take a more active rather than a passive approach to their work. Such procedures as are required to be followed are followed voluntarily."

REFERENCES

Argyris, C. Integrating the Individual and the Organization. New York: Wiley, 1964.

Emery, F. E., and E. Thorsrud. Form and Content in Industrial Democracy. London: Tavistock Publications, 1969.

Herzberg, F. Work and the Nature of Man. Cleveland: World Publishing Company, 1966.

Herzberg, F., B. Mausner, and B. Snyderman. The Motivation to Work. New York: Wiley, 1959.

Lawler, E. E., III. "Job Design and Employer Motivation." Personnel Psychology 22 (Winter 1969): 426–35.

Paul, W., Jr., K. B. Robertson, and F. Herzberg. "Job Enrichment Pays Off." Harvard Business Review 47 (March/April 1969): 61–78.

8

PARTICIPATIVE MANAGEMENT:
THEORY AND CHANGE STRATEGY

Participative management is an approach for increasing the amount of participation by workers in those decisions directly affecting their work lives. The focus of this work-improvement strategy is work groups and their involvement in work-related decisions. Such democratic procedures constitute a shift in the hierarchical allocation of decision making from higher to lower levels in the organization. The distinct features of this approach are a democratic style of leadership and worker involvement in wider aspects of the workplace. Although the primary aim is increased decision making, improvements in organizational structure, work methods, and group process frequently result from greater worker participation. The effects of participative management are twofold: workers increase their satisfaction as a result of making different and more need-satisfying decisions, and motivation to produce rises as workers are more committed to carrying out their own decisions.

Participative management grows directly from a series of studies concerning the effects of democratic methods. Starting with the pioneering study by Lewin, Lippitt, and White about the results of different leadership styles (as reported by White and Lippitt 1960), the theory and practice of this strategy have undergone considerable refinement. Much of this development has been under the direction of researchers from the Survey Research Center at the University of Michigan (Coch and French 1948; Morse and Reimer 1956; and French, Israel, and As 1960). Their research represents a systematic attempt to understand the conditions necessary for effective involvement in decision making in organizations. This chapter presents the theoretical basis of participative management and a change strategy for implementing it in organizations.

THEORETICAL FOUNDATION

Participative management can be traced to a set of seemingly unrelated studies concerning the effects of leadership style on children's play groups (Lippitt 1940; Lippitt and White 1943). This research, a part of the University of Iowa Studies in Child Welfare, wa a powerful impetus for the study of democratic procedures in a varie of organized settings. Its major objective was a comparison of the effects on children and their play groups of three distinct styles of adult leadership: authoritarian, democratic, and laissez faire. Brid five-member groups of ten-year-old boys who were engaged in after-school hobby activities were subject to each style of leadership. Authoritarian leaders tended to remain aloof from active group participation, while determining group policy, dictating work tasks, and specifying techniques and activity patterns. Their praise and criticism of team members was personal rather than objective. Democratic leaders tended to encourage group discussion and decision on such matters as policy, activity patterns, and division of tasks; feedback to group members was objective or fact-minded. Finally, laissez faire leaders were relatively uninvolved with the hobby group they gave children complete freedom of decision making, while supplying materials, information, and feedback only when requested.

The major results of the groups' exposure to the three styles of leadership were quite revealing. First, laissez faire leadership was not the same as democracy: it was less efficient, less organizec and less satisfying. Second, democracy resulted in both high work e fectiveness and member satisfaction, while autocracy achieved only work goals and laissez faire met only social objectives. Third, autocracy tended to create hostility, aggression, and scapegoat behavic it also produced submissive dependence and a lack of individuality. Last, there was more group-mindedness and friendliness in democra than under the other styles of management. When taken together, these findings demonstrated the significant impact of leadership style on important dimensions of group behavior. Furthermore, they provided clear evidence of the performance and satisfaction benefits to be gained from democratic forms of decision making.

Starting from the solid base of the Iowa leadership studies, research into the effects of democratic procedures spread to a variety of organized settings. These studies tended to focus on two related issues: the impact of group decisions on social change and the conditions by which participative management leads to improved productiv and human satisfaction. The former line of inquiry uncovered much about the process of social change itself, while experimenting with changes in such diverse areas as food habits, work production, crim nality, alcoholism, and prejudices (Lewin and Grabbe 1945). The lat ter research led to an increased understanding of employee participation in decision making by experimenting with democracy in on-going work groups (Coch and French 1948; Morse and Reimer 1956; French, Israel, and As 1960). Both areas of research refined the concept of participative management and demonstrated that individuals can participate responsibly in wider aspects of their work lives. Such knowledge challenged traditional notions of managerial authority, while demonstrating empirically the impact of democratic decisions on employee's behavior and attitudes. Two major findings emanated from this research: group methods of decision making facilitate social change, and increased rank-and-file decision making increases both productivity and worker satisfaction.

Group Decision and Social Change

, Lewin's (1947) conceptualization of social change provides a useful framework for understanding how group decision making affects change. His theory rests on a number of assumptions about the process of change itself. First, the object of social change, such as the level of productivity of a worker, is considered a process rather than a thing. A certain standard of productivity, for instance, means that certain actions, such as planning how much to produce, occur with a certain frequency within a given time period. Changing the amount of productivity means changing the level at which these actions proceed. Second, study of the conditions for change starts with an analysis of the conditions for no change or the current state of equilibrium. A state of no change is not stationary but represents a "quasi-stationary equilibrium, the equivalent to a river that flows with a certain velocity in a given direction. The conditions for remaining in equilibrium represent two forces of equal strength operating in opposite directions: forces that tend to lower the level of behavior and forces that tend to raise its level. Both types of forces set up a gradient about the current level of behavior such that forces against raising the level increase with the amount of raising, while forces against lowering the level increase with the amount of lowering. Thus, it is possible to change the strength of the opposing forces without changing the level of behavior. Third, changes in the current equilibrium level may be instituted in two ways: by adding forces in the desired direction or by diminishing opposing forces. Although both strategies may lead to a different level of behavior, their secondary effects are quite different. Adding forces in the desired direction is likely to produce more tension, since opposing forces increase in conflict. On the other hand, reducing opposing forces is likely to lead to less tension, because positive forces operate without opposition. Therefore, methods of social change that lower opposing forces seem preferable to those that pressure for change. The application of Lewin's theory of change to group decision making concerns the power of group standards as forces against change. Specifically, individuals tend to behave fairly close to the standards of the groups to which they belong. Deviations from these standards are met with ridicule and eventual expulsion from the grou. Thus, group standards serve as opposing forces against change. Attempts to change levels of activity will be resisted as long as group standards opposing the change remain unchanged. If the group standard itself is changed, the resistance to change is removed, and individuals will probably operate at the new level. This is the main reason for the effectiveness of group decisions, especially those involving group participation in the planning of change. When group members participate in setting new levels of behavior, existing standards for resisting change are removed. This leads to a new level of activity, with a relatively low level of tension.

The power of group decisions for changing levels of behavior raises an interesting issue: how to assure that the new level of activity remains permanent. Frequently, a change to a higher level of group performance is short lived, as the group soon returns to its previous standard. This suggests that in addition to setting new stan. dards through group decisions, one must also plan for the permanenc of the change. Lewin (1947) proposes that a successful change involv three stages: unfreezing the present level, moving to the new level, and freezing group life at the new level. Since any level is determine by two sets of opposing forces, permanency depends on the new sets of forces being made relatively secure against change. This demand careful attention to the specific forces operating in a particular situa tion, as any attempt to change group behavior without such diagnosis is likely to fail.

Participation's Effects on Productivity and Satisfaction

Worker participation in decision making has been shown to increase both productivity and human satisfaction (Morse and Reimer 1956; French, Israel, and As 1960). One explanation for this finding concerns individuals' needs and their motivation to perform to satisf these needs. Management's willingness to allow workers to participate in important work-related decisions implies that workers are competent and valued partners. This satisfies workers' needs for recognition, independence, and appreciation by others. Furthermor the process of decision making itself appears to be satisfying to a large number of employees. Thus, participative management is satisfying to the extent that it meets workers' valued needs.

Participation's impact on productivity is more indirect than its effects on satisfaction. Greater rank-and-file decision making increases workers' motivation to produce and, hence, productivity. The link between participation and motivation is employees' expectations that productivity is a path to greater need satisfaction. Specifically, when workers plan and put into effect their own decisions, satisfaction of the needs and values inherent in those decisions is dependent on the decisions' execution. Therefore, performance is a path to meeting workers' own needs and values rather than those of external sources, such as management. Also, to the extent that participation leads to better plans and decisions, productivity may benefit from the new methods and procedures.

The positive effects of participative management may also be explained in terms of the social-control processes operating in complex organizations. The need for rationality in organizations requires a system for regulating and controlling human behavior. Hierarchy, the allocation of control to different levels in the organization, serves this function in two ways. First, it binds people into the organization by motivating them to enter and fill the necessary roles. This binding-in function is typically accomplished through the use of monetary inducements, though all forms of motivation serve this purpose. Second, hierarchy controls human behavior by means of a binding-between process, which integrates workers' role behavior around a common goal. Work charts and job assignments are examples of how organizations meet this integrative need. Any means for controlling behavior in complex organizations needs to serve these two functions. The traditional approach of allocating decision making to higher levels in the organization results in a greater emphasis on the binding-between process, while the binding-in function is left primarily to an external reward system. This results in greater productivity (an indication of binding between) but with few motivational sources for satisfaction (an indication of binding in). Participative management, on the other hand, emphasizes both the binding-in and the binding-between functions. Employees are motivated to enter and remain in the organization because their decisions embody their own values and needs; this motivation, in turn, makes workers want to implement decisions that are rational for goal achievement. Hence, the integration of both functions, through greater involvement in the organization's decision-making processes, leads to greater productivity and worker satisfaction.

The above explanations for participation's effects have been stated in general terms. There is evidence to suggest that at least four variables may moderate the impact of participative management:

legitimacy of participation, manner of introducing the change, the in portance of the area of participation, and the relevance of participation (French, Israel, and As 1960).

Legitimacy of participation refers to the extent to which workers consider it right and proper to engage in decision-making processes. In all organizations, there is a set of social roles defining the relations among the employees and prescribing how much these individuals should participate in different areas of decision making. Since the role structure specifies the pattern of legitimate participation in decision making, individuals will be motivated and satisfied only to the extent to which their participation is considered legitimat Therefore, the amount of decision making given to workers must be consistent with the organization's norms and values if it is to be effective.

The manner of introducing participative management may also condition its results. Frequently, individuals are resistant to chang such as increased decision making. Such resistance results from in duced forces opposing the change. One kind of opposing force is the manner in which management introduces increased decision making. If workers resent the participation procedures used, they are likely to resist the change and, hence, reduce their motivation to perform.

Participative management is likely to produce its greatest effects when it concerns decisions that are important to the participant The significance of the area of decision making is especially critical because it relates to the satisfaction of employees' needs. If the decision is of little or no importance to the worker, his participation will not provide a means to satisfying valued needs.

Finally, the relevance of participation moderates the outcomes of increased rank-and-file decision making. The specific content of the decision determines, to a large extent, the kind of effect produce A decision about working hours, for example, will affect behavior and attitudes toward this dimension of employment more than it will impact behavior and attitudes with respect to production or fringe benefits. In general, the more the content or process of the decisior is related to performance and specific areas of need satisfaction, the more participation should affect these variables.

Summary

Participative management is a means of increasing workers' involvement in the decision-making processes directly affecting thei work lives. Such participation usually takes place at the group level because groups have a significant impact on individuals' behavior an attitudes. Group decisions are an effective means of changing emplo ees' behavior. When members participate in setting new levels of behavior, existing standards opposing change are removed, and the group is able to move to a new plateau of performance. Similarly, group decisions may also lead to increased productivity and worker satisfaction. Participation in decision making leads to these results by providing workers with a path to greater need satisfaction. In terms of organizational control processes, participation is an integrative means for motivating workers to join and remain in the organization and for coordinating individuals' behavior around a common goal. The positive effects of participative management are moderated by at least four factors: legitimacy of participation, manner of introducing change, the importance of the area of participation, and the relevance of participation.

CHANGE STRATEGY

Participative management, like most approaches to work improvement, does not require a specific method for implementation. Rather, there are innumerable ways to increase workers' involvement in decision making. Examination of several studies in this area, however, reveals a noteworthy characteristic distinguishing participative management programs from other strategies of workplace change. This quality concerns the methodological rigor associated with implementation and evaluation. Those who have experimented with increased employee decision making tend to start from an explicit theoretical base from which one or more researchable problems are identified. Then, conditions for testing these propositions are carefully formulated. Finally, an organizational experiment is conducted under relatively controlled circumstances, so that results may be evaluated properly. The outcome of this experimental strategy has usually been improved organizational behavior, as well as development of the existing knowledge base. In short, theory is put to the practical test of improving the organization.

Given the methodological rigor of most participative management experiments, it is not surprising that knowledge in this area has tended to be cumulative, each study refining the results of previous research. Although this method of change may seem more appropriate for academic researchers than for managers and workers, there are at least four steps that appear to increase the probability of obtaining positive results: gaining commitment and planning the change, training supervisors, introducing the change to employees, and evaluating results.

Gaining Commitment and Planning the Change

A necessary condition for implementing a participative-management program is organizational commitment to experimenting with increased employee decision making. Although this step may seem rudimentary, it is important to note that participative management is not a packaged program instituted overnight. Rather, it involves a major commitment to democratic ideals and leadership styles. Management must not only understand and accept this approach but must actually treat workers as valuable partners. In most instances, this requires considerable preparatory work to ensure a supportive organizational climate. Like experimentation with autonomous work groups, participative management is best suited to an organization whose members are high in openness, trust, and risk-taking behavior. Indeed, the classic experiment in worker decision making, conducted by Lester Coch and John French (1948) at the Harwood Manufacturing Corporation, underscores the significance of a supportive organizational climate. In this case, the company's labor relations were liberal and progressive; a high value was placed on fair and open dealings with employees; and managers were encouraged to resolve their problems using human relations approaches. Furthermore, the president of Harwood, Alfred J. Marrow, was actively committed to a democratic, managerial philosophy. Given these positive conditions, Harwood provided workers with considerable involvement in important areas of decision making. This resulted in less resistance to technological changes and less conflict with management. The major point to be gained from this and similar studies is the need to address commitment and organizational-climate issues prior to the change program. This provides for extensive reality testing as to the present state of the organization, and it gives both management and workers an opportunity to assess the relevance of participative management and their commitment to this form of change.

Once sufficient commitment is attained, a plan for instituting rank-and-file decision making is formulated. In most cases, a small part of the total organization is chosen for experimentation. Existing work groups and department-level units are prime targets for change. These provide relevant task boundaries within which group standards impeding change are likely to be strongest. This is a pertinent point since failure to identify and change group standards may thwart attempts to improve important work-related behavior. The actual content of the change program varies according to the situation. Typically, specific areas for increased decision making, such as product goals, work methods, and quality standards, are identified. A timetable for implementing the change is devised, as well as explicit plans for evaluating outcomes. Specific training needs and related organizational changes are also identified, so that important contingencies for implementing participative management can be integrated into the change program. In those instances where researchers are involved in strategy formulation, an explicit statement of the research problem and conditions for testing it are included. Since the research design is related directly to existing organizational problems, the dual goals of organizational improvement and development of knowledge are incorporated in the change strategy.

Training Supervisors

The explicit goal of participative management is to delegate decision making from higher to lower levels in the organization. Since this often involves changes in the hierarchical distribution of control in the organization, management is the prime agent of change. Specifically, managerial delegation of decision making is the mechanism for increased employee involvement. To facilitate this handing-over process, supervisors are trained in the theory and methods of participative management. This ensures that formal changes in decision making result in actual changes in relations between people. Depending upon the existing knowledge and skills of management, training ranges from informal discussions about what changes are relevant and feasible to formal classes in human relations and democratic procedures. A major aim of the training program is to legitimize hierarchically new roles before they are actually instituted. By training supervisors to formally delegate authority to subordinates, employees' utilization of this authority is legitimized in the organization.

Introducing the Change to Employees

The specific method of introducing participative management to workers varies with the situation. In most instances, however, the program is implemented in small group meetings involving relevant employees and first-level supervision. Though the size of these groups varies, they tend to be rather small—6 to 12 individuals—so that a more open and intimate atmosphere can be established. Once management explains the need for increased rank-and-file decision making, workers are encouraged to air their views and to discuss relevant areas for involvement. This may include a number of successive meetings, as employees gain confidence in their decision-making ability and learn to trust management's willingness to delegate authority. This testing-out process seems to be a necessary prelude to establishing a working partnership between supervisors and workers.

Its success depends, in part, on employees' perceptions that increase decision making is a legitimate part of their role behavior and that areas for decision making are important to their work lives. The ability of supervision to introduce the changes in a democratic manner also appears to affect workers' responses to the program. Indeed, a critical variable for implementing this strategy is management—its willingness to formally delegate authority to subordinates and to behave democratically in the day-to-day operations of the firm.

Evaluating Results

Those who have experimented with participative management have tended to use rigorous research designs to assess the efficacy of their programs. Typically, a quasi-experimental design employing pre- and posttest measures for both experimental and control groups is employed. While not as strong as randomized experiments, such quasi-experiments permit tests of whether participative management leads to increased productivity and worker fulfillment. In addition to assessing the outcomes of increased rank-and-file decision making experimenters also examine the extent to which workers actually experience increased decision-making opportunities. This allows researchers to test the success of their experimental changes. Such information is especially relevant for assessing the results of a work improvement program, since it provides evidence of whether the program was, indeed, implemented.

Summary

The change strategy for implementing participative management in organizations starts from a sound theoretical base and a commitment to democratic procedures. Once management has decided to increase rank-and-file decision making, it must legitimize the authority of subordinates' new roles. Training supervisors in human relations skills provides the expertise needed to accomplish this task and to introduce this approach to workers. Careful evaluation of both the change process and its outcomes completes this cycle of experimental events.

9

PARTICIPATIVE MANAGEMENT:
A REVIEW OF SEVEN
SELECTED EXPERIMENTS

Participative management is a significant approach for improving work. Although many experiments to increase rank-and-file decision making are not identified formally under this name, the basic tenets and methods of participative management are practiced widely in modern organizations. The purpose of this chapter is to review seven selected studies employing the participative-management approach. These experiments represent some of the more rigorous attempts to document and test this change strategy. Because of their methodological refinement, these studies offer a particularly valuable insight into the effects of increased worker decision making. The chapter is divided into three sections: action levers and the validity of their effects, contingencies for producing successful outcomes, and the implementation of participative-management strategies.

ACTION LEVERS AND THEIR EFFECTS

Unlike most change strategies reported in this book, the seven participative-management studies manipulated only one action lever—autonomy/discretion (the only exception being Bartlett's [1967] study, which also changed the action levers of training and organizational structure). Table 4 identifies these studies by author and lists contextual variables and action levers and their effects. In all cases, the experimenters reported that the participative-management program was implemented successfully. Though it is not possible to determine how much autonomy was actually given to workers, these data substantiate the organizations' ability to change this action lever in the desired direction. The specific form of autonomy/discretion given to employees concerned greater involvement in the decision-making

TABLE 4

Participative Management: Contextual Variables and Action Levers and Their Effects

	Authors						
	Bartlett, A., 1967	Bragg, J., Andrews, I., 1973	Coch, L., French, J., 1948	French, J., Israel, J., As, D., 1960	Lawler, E. E., III, Hackman, J. R., 1969	Morse, N., Reimer, E., 1956	Powell, R., Schlacter, J., 1971
Contextual variables							
Type of work	Manufacturing supervisor	Laundry in a hospital	Garment making	Footwear assembly	Janitorial	Clerical	Maintenance
Sex	?	?	Male/female	Male/female	?	Female	Male
Occupational status	White	Blue	Blue	Blue	Blue	White	Blue
Number treated	100	32	41	20	46	206	?
Unionized	?	Yes	?	Yes	?	No	?
Participation in change	Yes	Yes	Yes	Yes	Yes	?	Yes
Country	United States	United States	United States	Norway	United States	United States	United States
Treatment took effect	Yes	Yes	Yes	Yes	Yes	Yes	Yes
Action levers							
Pay/reward systems							
Autonomy/discretion	x	x	x	x	x	x	x
Support							
Training	x						
Organizational structure	x						
Technical/physical							
Task variety							
Information/feedback							
Interpersonal/group process							
Effects							
Costs	−						
Productivity	+	+	+	0	+	0	0
Quality	+						
Withdrawal	−	−	−			−	+
Attitudes	+	+	+	+		+	+ +

Code: blank = not relevant; x = variable manipulated; ? = insufficient data; + = variable increased; − = variable decreased; 0 = variable static.

Source: Srivastva et al. 1975, p. 119.

114

processes of the organization. Depending upon the situation, workers were able to decide on such matters as productivity, methods of work, technological changes, and job designs.

Table 4 reveals that increased rank-and-file decision making produces positive results. Costs and quality were measured in only one study (Bartlett 1967), and both of these outcomes were positive. All of the experiments measured productivity, but positive findings appear in only four of the seven studies. Of the five experiments concerned with withdrawal, four showed positive results. Finally, attitudes were totally positive in four of the five experiments measuring this variable. It is interesting to note that in the one study changing action levers in addition to autonomy/discretion (Bartlett 1967), additional benefits were gained in terms of reduced costs and higher-quality production. This suggests that related organizational changes —training and organizational structure in this case—may interact with increased decision making to produce more pervasive outcomes.

To assess whether participative management produced the positive results listed above, the exerpiments' research designs were examined for both the productivity and attitudinal data. Because of the limited number of studies measuring these variables—seven and four, respectively—only those threats to validity present in more than one-half of these experiments are reported.

Validity of Performance Findings

All of the participative-management studies measured some aspect of performance—costs, productivity, or quality. Of the seven experiments, only four showed an improvement on this variable. Examination of the research designs for this set of studies shows that only one threat to validity was relatively uncontrolled—mortality. Mortality was judged a questionable threat to validity because of the failure to report pretest withdrawal data. Without such information, it is difficult to assess whether there was differential loss of subjects from the comparison groups. Furthermore, three of these studies showed reduced incidences of withdrawal as the result of the experiment, thus making the likelihood of a mortality threat plausible. Since it is possible that there was some selective dropout of experimental subjects from these studies, the effects of increased worker decision making on performance must be interpreted with some caution.

Validity of Quality of Work Life Results

Five experiments measured some dimension of quality of work life—for example, job satisfaction, morale, and attitudes toward man-

agement. Inspection of the research designs for the four studies
showing totally positive results reveals that three uncontrolled factors threaten the validity of the attitudinal findings—selection, mortality, and selection interaction. Selection was a possible threat to
validity either because comparison groups were not used to equate
subjects on the pretests or because repeated measures were not obtained from experimental subjects. Like the performance results,
mortality was a plausible threat because of lack of sufficient withdrawal data. Finally, selection interaction was a confounding factor
because of the failure to employ time series measures. Although
each of these uncontrolled variables is a plausible, rival explanation
for improvements in quality of work life, anecdotal data about employ
ees attitudes toward increased decision making suggest that the quality of work life outcomes may have some justification. Careful reading of the research reports for these studies shows that employees
were generally receptive to the participative–management programs
and responsive to management's democratic style of leadership.
Given this additional information, the effects of participative management on quality of work life remain questionable but not altogether im
plausible.

     In summary, the efficacy of the participative–management out-
comes appears to be justifiable. The validity of the performance find
ings was stronger than that of the quality of work life outcomes. This
is not surprising in light of the stronger research designs associated
with performance types of data. Generally, performance measures
are easier to obtain for longer periods of time than attitudinal data.
This permits expedient use of control groups and time series data,
two factors strengthening the internal validity of research findings.

CONTINGENCIES

     Given the relative validity of the participative–management re-
sults, the question of contingencies arises—those factors that limit
the general applicability of the findings. Three sources of informatic
were used to assess the external validity of the experiments' outcome
First, the contextual variables in Table 4 include organizational and
research population data that suggest possible limiting conditions.
Second, examination of the studies' research designs reveals the presence or absence of certain threats to external validity. Finally, one
of the participative–management studies tested explicitly certain contingent factors (French, Israel, and As 1960). Since direct examination of contingencies is rare in work-improvement experiments, the
results of this analysis are presented in detail.
     Four studies reported totally positive improvements in perfor-
mance (Bartlett 1967; Bragg and Andrews 1973; Coch and French 194

and Lawler and Hackman 1969). The contextual variables in Table 4
suggest that these findings are applicable to both service-oriented
and manufacturing kinds of work, as well as supervisory tasks. Information about the characteristics of workers involved in these
studies is quite limited, especially for sex and union status. Data
on occupational status, however, shows that both white and blue collar
workers were involved in the experiments. This implies that occupational status is not a contingent factor. The number of individuals
involved in these projects ranged from 32 to 100, with a median of
43.5. Since most of the participative-management experiments concerned small groups of workers, these figures represent gross numbers of experimental subjects rather than the size of the work groups.
If anything, these data suggest a wide latitude in the total number of
workers who can be included successfully in this kind of experimentation. All studies reporting improvements in performance revealed
that workers were involved in the change process. This appears to
be a limiting condition; indeed, it is difficult to imagine how organizations could implement participative management without direct employee involvement in the change program. Finally, the performance
findings seem to be limited to only one country—the United States.
This seems to be more a function of the studies chosen for review
than an actual threat to the general applicability of results. Given
these data, the major limiting factor in achieving positive performance
outcomes seems to be worker involvement in the change process.

Like the performance findings, only four experiments reported
totally positive increase in quality of work life (Bragg and Andrews
1973; Coch and French 1948; French, Israel, and As 1960; and Morse
and Reimer 1956). Examination of Table 4 reveals data similar to
those reported for performance improvements, the major exception
being the inclusion of another industrialized country—Norway. In
sum, the quality of work life outcomes also appear to be contingent
upon employee involvement in the change program.

Inspection of the research designs of the participative-management experiments shows two threats to the external validity of both
the performance and quality of work life findings. The first contingency concerns special experimental arrangements, the inability to
apply the outcomes to nonexperimental settings. The collaborative
nature of the participative-management projects, their presentation
as out-of-the-ordinary events, and the extra attention paid to workers
by managers and researchers probably created a special setting for
the experiments. These reactive arrangements make generalization
to ordinary organizational settings questionable. The second threat
to external validity involves selection/treatment interaction, the inability to generalize the results to other groups of workers. Since
many of the participative-management studies took place in organiza-

tions where both managers and workers were receptive to behavioral science techniques and experimentation, it is doubtful whether such studies would be as successful with less responsive subjects. Although both of these contingencies appear to limit the general applicability of the participative-management outcomes, considerably more research is needed to determine to what extent the findings are actually constrained by these factors.

In addition to the contextual variables and assessment of research designs, knowledge of contingencies is provided by one of the experiments (French, Israel, and As 1960). Here, researchers tested whether the effects of participative management are moderated by four factors: legitimacy of participation, resistance to methods of introducing the change, importance of areas of decision making to workers, and relevance of areas of decision making to intended outcomes. A major finding of the study was that experimental workers showed greater job satisfaction and more favorable attitudes toward management. These quality of work life effects became significant the more workers perceived that their influence was legitimate (that is, that they have as much influence as they should have) and the less they were resistant to the methods of introducing the change. Further, the researchers were able to explain a lack of significant performance improvements in terms of relevance of areas of decision making. Specifically, the areas of increased decision making were not related directly to production, hence the experimental treatment did not affect this outcome. The findings of this important piece of research suggest that the above-mentioned factors may condition the effects of participative management. Further research along the lines reported here would greatly expand knowledge of contingencies in the work-improvement area.

In summary, several contingencies appear to limit the general applicability of participative-management effects. Worker involvement in the change process seems to facilitate both performance and quality of work life. Perhaps involvement in the change program allows employees to determine directly the amount of influence they should have, thus legitimizing their participation. It may also reduce workers' resistance to change, since they have some say in the change program. Although the number of individuals who may be involved successfully in participative-management programs appears to be large—upward to 100 employees—the small group and collaborative nature of this change strategy appears to favor small groups of workers. Special experimental arrangements, such as collaboration between workers and managers and similar out-of-the-ordinary events, may facilitate positive outcomes. Similarly, workers and managers who are supportive of behavioral science techniques and experimentation may be especially responsive to this strategy. Finally, legitimac of participation, acceptance of methods of implementing change, relevance of areas of decision making, and importance of areas of decision making to workers may increase the performance and quality of work life effects of participative management.

IMPLEMENTATION OF PARTICIPATIVE MANAGEMENT

The participative-management experiments contain useful advice for implementing this strategy. Though such suggestions must be tailored to the specific circumstances of each work setting, they provide a valuable checklist for those contemplating this approach. Similar to most strategies of work improvement is the need for top-level sanction and support. This is especially relevant for participative management experiments, which require good management/labor relations, as well as an organizational climate responsive to democratic ideals. Since increased rank-and-file decision making is contingent upon managers giving employees greater authority, management must feel secure enough to allow individuals such freedom and responsibility. Supervisors who are already successful and who support a democratic style of leadership seem to have this security. Choice of experimental unit can also facilitate the acceptance of this approach. Work systems that have previously established trust between workers and supervision and which already have high levels of performance appear to be ideal. They have both an appropriate work climate and the freedom to experiment without fear of having to improve their performance. Similarly, work systems that are relatively isolated from other oganizational units are prime change targets. Their isolation allows for greater acceptance of suggestions about such things as working hours, choice of holidays, and control over work breaks. Finally, the process of implementing participative management frequently involves a change in existing group norms and behavior. If change is to be successful, previous group standards must be unfrozen before new standards can be instituted. This unfreezing process requires direct involvement in the change program. Group members must be advised of the need for change and given the opportunity to participate in setting new norms of behavior. Small group meetings where individuals can communicate freely seem to provide the atmosphere required for change. Also, supervisory involvement in such meetings appears to be mandatory for legitimizing workers' participation in important organizational decisions.

SUMMARY

Participative management is an effective strategy for improving productivity and the quality of work life. A review of seven experiments shows that increased rank-and-file decision making—as represented by the action lever of autonomy/discretion—has positive effect in work systems. The efficacy of these outcomes appears to hold for a variety of organizational settings and different types of workers Possible contingencies exist, however, in such areas as worker involvement in the change process, legitimacy of participation, relevance of participation, and special experimental arrangements. Consideration of these moderating factors, as well as certain practical suggestions, provide experimenters with a powerful strategy for improving work.

PARTICIPATIVE DECISION MAKING:
AN EXPERIMENTAL STUDY IN
A HOSPITAL
J. E. Bragg
I. R. Andrews

Since several excellent summaries of previous work on participative decision making (PDM) are already available (for example,
Bucklow 1966; Campbell, Dunnette, Lawler, and Weick 1970; Lowin
1968), this chapter will not include the usual literature survey. In
general, the experimental design and analyses in this chapter were
most influenced by Lowin's (1968) theoretical model, which defines
PDM as "a mode of organizational operation in which decisions as to
activities are arrived at by the very persons who are to execute those
decisions," and by his prescriptions for PDM research. Stated quite
simply, our hypotheses predicted that the introduction of participative
decision making into a particular hospital laundry would improve employee attitudes, reduce absenteeism, and increase productivity.

METHOD

In the section "Experimental Studies in Organizations," Lowin
specified six standards that such an experiment must meet. In addition, his theoretical definition of participative decision making implies
a seventh standard. Each of these standards will be considered in
turn as they apply to this chapter.

Reprinted by special permission from The Journal of Applied
Behavioral Science 9, no. 6 (1973): 727-35, copyright © 1973 NTL
Institute.

Standards

1. "A determined effort must be made to unfreeze the system in
preparation for the PDM program." In the present study, the attitudes and values of the chief nonmedical administrator were
modified by three behavioral science courses in an executive
M.B.A. program. According to the administrator, his experienc
in the courses sharpened and intensified an already favorable
feeling about a participative-management style.

Another key figure, the foreman in charge of the laundry, had
already established himself as a highly effective supervisor, with a
driving, authoritarian style of management. When first approached
by the chief administrator about the possibility of trying a participativ
management style, the foreman was dubious and negative. It was
not until six months after the first discussion that the foreman electec
to accept the challenge of trying a new management style. A key factor in his acceptance of the challenge was his own very positive respo
to the high degree of decision-making autonomy that he had been giver
by the chief administrator. Another important factor was his participation in a weekend sensitivity-training workshop with nonmedical
management personnel.

In anticipation of PDM, the foreman prepared a list of 18 problems that might be encountered during the changeover. He also re-
stated the goals of his department to make them consistent with the
PDM philosophy.

When PDM was introduced to the 32 laundry workers, the foreman was able to state in all honesty that the basic purpose of the program was to make jobs more interesting. The workers were told
that PDM sometimes does result in higher productivity but that this
was unimportant to top management because their current level of
productivity was already excellent. They were also told that they
would have the right to discontinue PDM if they found it unsatisfactory

One other important factor in the total system was the union
leadership. Because of previously established trust and respect
(without love, it might be added) for top management, it was fairly
easy to obtain union approval for the tentative introduction of PDM.
Active support for the program, however, was not offered.

Finally, the unfreezing process was greatly expedited by the
results of the first two PDM meetings. One of the key employee suggestions in these early meetings was the revision of work hours to
begin and end two hours earlier. Because the laundry unit was com-
pletely isolated from other subsystems in the hospital, there was no
reason for not acting immediately upon that suggestion. In the follow
ing week, the work hours were changed, and PDM was off to a good
start.

2. "Attitudinal data should be collected to document the adaptation to PDM or its rejection." At the end of every two-month period in our study, a seven-item questionnaire was completed by all 32 laundry workers. Included were such questions as, "Should we continue with PDM?" and "Do suggestions get a fair trial?" The data from these questionnaire responses are reported in the "Results" section.

3. "Similar changes in organization behavior should be recorded." Most closely related to the attitudinal data would be the data on absenteeism, which are reported in the "Results" section. Less closely related to the attitudinal data are changes in rate of productivity, also reported in the "Results" section.

4. "Appropriate control groups must be utilized." Two other hospital laundries in the same city were used as comparison groups for evaluating changes in productivity. Strictly speaking, these were not "control groups," since the workers in the comparison laundries were not aware that their performance data were of interest to persons outside their own organization. It is also true, however, that postexperimental interviews with PDM employees showed that they were not aware that they were subjects in an experiment. They knew only that for the first three months of PDM, the chief administrator seemed to be interested in what they were doing.

During the period studied there was only one technical innovation to confound the productivity data. Fortunately, it was possible to correct the data for this one factor (the introduction of some polyester fabrics into the linen supply).

Since the comparison hospitals were not able to provide suitable data on absenteeism, results for the PDM group were compared with absence data for other nonmedical staff in the PDM hospital. Neither the PDM nor the comparison groups were aware that their absence records were being monitored in other than routine ways.

In the first three or four months of the study, any differences between the experimental and comparison groups could have been confounded by a strong Hawthorne effect (in the usual sense of "increased attention, novelty"). However, it is highly unlikely that such an effect could have lasted over the 18 months of the study. Active interest and participation by the chief nonmedical administrator ceased after the first three months. As stated above, the PDM workers were not aware at any time that they were subjects in an experiment.

5. "Long-term research is essential." The 18-month time period of the study provided ample time for worker adjustment to PDM and reduced the likelihood that any observed differences were due

either to random fluctuations or to a Hawthorne effect. Moreover, both attitudinal and behavioral data showed gradual improvement throughout the study period. It is unlikely that some extraneous factor stabilized behavior at an improved level and continued to do so throughout the study.

6. "The validity of organization records should be checked." The basic record-keeping procedures for absenteeism and productivity were constant throughout the study period and throughout the period preceding. The absentee record-keeping procedures were identical for the PDM group and the comparison group (other non-medical employees who worked in the same hospital). With regard to productivity data, the inclusion of pre- and postmeasures for the PDM group and the comparison hospital laundries reduced the likelihood that any differences would be an artifact of record-keeping procedures.

7. In defining PDM (as quoted above), Lowin continues: "The PDM process shifts the locus of some decisions downward—from superior to subordinate." In the present study, decision-making power was transferred from the laundry foreman to a committee composed of all the laundry employees. Any and all aspects of managing the laundry could be considered by the committee. It was agreed, however, that union matters and personal gripes would not be discussed in the meetings.

Role of the Foreman

In the initial PDM meeting, the laundry foreman was elected to serve as a discussion moderator. By the fifth meeting, the role of discussion moderator was taken over by several of the laundry employees, with the foreman's main tasks reduced to agenda setting and the scheduling of meetings. During the meetings, the foreman refused to be active as a task expert, even in cases where the group's decision was, in his opinion, incorrect. Once the group reached a decision, the foreman did what he could to assist the particular employees charged with the responsibility of implementing the changes agreed upon. Because the foreman himself was operating with a very high degree of autonomy, there was seldom need to obtain approval from higher management before taking action. This made it possible to implement most of the proposed changes within one or two weeks of the date of the committee's decision.

It was agreed that meetings should be restricted in length to 30 or 40 minutes and that they should be called only when there were specific proposals to discuss. From this, it is clear that most of the PDM work was accomplished outside of the formal meetings.

Throughout each working day, the foreman tried to make himself easily available to individual employees (or groups of employees) who wanted to discuss new ideas or problems. In these informal meetings, the foreman concentrated on being a good listener—on acting as a sounding board, so employees could develop their own ideas with a minimal amount of help from him. Also, whenever it seemed appropriate, the foreman attempted to transfer his task expertise to the employees, thereby reducing their dependence on him. Lastly, because the overall climate in the laundry became supportive and cooperative, even shy employees were able to develop, present, and gain acceptance for their ideas.

RESULTS

PDM Group Meetings

The laundry foreman kept a record of the 28 meetings that occurred during the first 15 months of PDM. An analysis of his minutes revealed that 147 employee suggestions were discussed. Of these, 11 involved hours of work and working conditions, 90 had to do with the work flow (process and methods), 44 involved minor equipment modifications, and 2 were concerned with safety. No record was kept of the innumerable additional ideas discussed on the shop floor between meetings.

Attitudes Toward PDM

It was anticipated that some of the older workers would react negatively to PDM, while younger workers would be more receptive. As it turned out, however, the only strong negative reactions came from three younger workers, who objected to the transfer of decision-making power from the foreman to the laundry committee. Fortunately, their attempts to sabotage participative decision making were overcome by the enthusiastic supporters of it; eventually, their resistance changed to active support.

For each of the seven items on the employee attitude questionnaire, an employee could write in "yes," "no," or "?." For scoring purposes, the "?" responses were added to the "no" responses, and this total was compared with the number of "yes" responses. The following percentages of "yes" responses are reported by two-month intervals for the first 14 months of the study: 62 percent, 64 percent, 75 percent, 71 percent, 79 percent, 84 percent, and 90 percent. As is apparent from these data, the employees' initial uncertainty about PDM gave way to a positive attitude by the end of the first two months. From that point, there was almost a steady climb to a highly favorable attitude toward PDM.

Absenteeism

In the 38 reporting periods that immediately preceded the introduction of PDM, the absence rate for the laundry group was less than the overall hospital absence rate, 23 out of 38 times. In the 38 reporting periods after the introduction of PDM, the absence rate for the laundry group was less than the overall hospital absence rate, 32 out of 38 times. This shift in proportions from .61 to .80 was highly significant ($Z = 1.9$, $p < .03$). Thus, an already superior absence record became substantially better after the introduction of PDM. It is of possible interest that immediately after PDM began, the absence rate for the laundry group was worse than the overall hospital rate in 5 out of 8 reporting periods. After that unimpressive beginning, the absence rate for the laundry group was lower than the overall hospital rate in 29 out of 30 reporting periods. Expressing that remarkable record in different terms, the absence rate for the laundry group averaged 2.95 percent before PDM versus 1.77 percent with PDM. For other nonmedical staff, the rates were 2.80 percent before the study began versus 3.07 percent during the study. Expressed in yet another way, the 1,791 hours of sick time in the laundry group in the year before PDM fell to 1,194 hours in the first year of PDM. There were no long- or short-term trends in the hospital at large to account for this drop in absenteeism.

Productivity

In the year prior to the introduction of PDM, productivity in the experimental group averaged approximately 50 pounds of laundry processed per paid employee hour. In the first six months of PDM, production rose gradually to an average of approximately 61 pounds. In the second six-month period, production surged to 78 pounds, but this was followed by a slight drop in the third six-month period to 73 pounds per paid employee hour. As shown in Table 5, the productivity rate in the two comparison hospitals remained constant, or perhaps even declined slightly, during the year-and-a-half study period.

Since the rate of productivity in the experimental group was already higher than the rates for the two comparison hospitals, these initial differences in favor of the experimental group had to be discounted before testing for the significance of mean differences during the study period. After this adjustment, the mean difference between the experimental group and each of the comparison groups was 23 pounds per paid employee hour. For each of the two comparisons, this difference in mean productivity was significant ($t = 8.43$ for comparisons A and B, respectively, $df = 34$, $p < .01$, two-tailed). Though cost savings through increased productivity was not an important objective of the PDM program, significant economic benefits to the hospital were realized, equal to approximately $1,000 per employee per year.

DISCUSSION

In this chapter, which attempted to adhere closely to Lowin's (1968) recommendations for PDM experiments in ongoing organizations, it was found that attitudes improved, absence declined, and productivity increased. No such changes were observed in the comparison groups. The differences between the experimental and comparison groups were statistically significant and in the direction hypothesized. Because of the long duration of the study and because the more substantial performance improvements were not realized in the early months of the PDM program, it seems highly improbable that the reported results can be explained in terms of a Hawthorne effect.

There are several factors in the subsystem studied that favored a successful PDM effort: the program was initiatied and actively encouraged for three months by the hospital's chief nonmedical adminis-

TABLE 5

Productivity Rates for the PDM Laundry and for Two
Comparison Laundries[a]

Time Period	PDM Laundry[b]	Comparison A	Comparison B
12 months before study	50	47	39
18 months during study	71	45	37

[a]Pounds of laundry processed per paid employee hour rounded to the nearest whole number.

[b]Figures corrected to allow for the introduction of some polyester fabrics into the linen supply.

Source: Compiled by the authors.

trator; an already successful laundry foreman existed who felt secur
enough in his position to experiment with a radical change in his man
agement style and was able to effect PDM; the foreman had been give
a high degree of decision-making autonomy well in advance of the
PDM program; previously established trust and an already high leve
of productivity made it easier for the union leaders to believe management when they said that the primary objective of the PDM program was job improvement for the workers; the isolation of the
laundry subsystem made it easier for management to comply with
some of the initial employee suggestions about such things as hours
of work, choice of holidays, and self-control over work breaks; and
lastly, the middle class work values of several foreign-born immigrants in the work group might have facilitated the establishment of
group norm in favor of PDM.

At the time of this somewhat belated report (1972), PDM has
been in effect in the hospital laundry for over three years. Neither
the foreman nor the workers have expressed any desire to return to
the old style of management. The foreman has said that it would be
easy for him to revert to his old style of autocratic management, bu
he would "miss the satisfactions he derives from PDM." He has als
mentioned that he has not had to reprimand a worker since PDM began.

The success of PDM in the laundry has encouraged other subsystems in the hospital to follow suit. In a medical records section
where there was an adequate unfreezing of the system and strong sup
port (but no involvement) by the chief nonmedical administrator, a
serious turnover problem has been eliminated through PDM, and a
high level of union grievances has been reduced to zero. With the
nursing staff, on the other hand, a deficiency of unfreezing activitie
and substantial resistance by the head nurse caused PDM to flounder
badly for the first six months. In fact, PDM was a dismal failure
until the introduction of a new head nurse with a favorable attitude
toward PDM, and until the chief nonmedical administrator found tim
for some involvement in the program. With these changes, the tide
was turned, and after a year and a half, the PDM program for nurse
is still alive. However, continued resistance by some of the admini
trative medical personnel has kept PDM from flourishing in the nurs
ing group.

In closing, it might be of value to ask why production increase
when top management's main concern was job improvement for the
laundry workers. Looking back at the foreman's record of PDM me
ings, it can be seen that 90 percent of all employee suggestions involved technological modifications in the laundry subsystem. This
suggests quite convincingly that the creation of a genuine PDM atmo
phere led employees to adopt organizational goals as their own. Mo

over, since there was no economic gain for employees' contribution of ideas for technological improvements, it is safe to assume that the underlying motivational force was higher-order need fulfillment. We thus believe that releasing this rich vein of heretofore untapped energy led to technological and attitudinal changes that substantially increased productivity. The relative impact of these two sources of productivity improvement should be tested in future research. For example, one group might experience PDM, and the technological changes they develop might be introduced into other groups by conventional managerial methods. This would enable distinguishing the productivity-raising effects of methods improvement as such from the attitudinal changes occurring in PDM.

REFERENCES

Bucklow, M. "A New Role for the Work Group." Administrative Science Quarterly 11 (March 1966): 59-78.

Campbell, J. P., M. D. Dunnette, E. E. Lawler, III, and K. E. Weick. Managerial Behavior, Performance, and Effectiveness. New York: McGraw-Hill, 1970.

Lowin, A. "Participative Decision Making: A Model, Literature Critique, and Prescriptions for Research." Organizational Behavior and Human Performance 3 (February 1968): 68-106.

11

ORGANIZATION-WIDE CHANGE:
THEORY AND CHANGE STRATEGY

Organization-wide change is a work-improvement program where the focus of change is on the total organization rather than the individual job or work group. In contrast to the other strategies reviewed in this book, organization-wide change does not have a common theoretical base or a standard method of change. These experiments possess, however, a number of similar characteristics that justify treating them as a separate work-improvement strategy. Probably their most distinguishing feature is a concern for the whole organization as comprised of interrelated parts functioning toward a common goal. This systems approach suggests that change in one part of the firm—in the number of hierarchical levels, for example—frequently requires corresponding modifications in related parts, such as company policy, supervisory practices, and communication channels. To affect systemic change, organization-wide change focuses on both the managerial and operating structures of the firm. In most cases, the change program is aimed at reducing ambiguity in reporting relationships and increasing the rational flow of work and information through the organization. This may necessitate such diverse changes as new configurations of work groups, a more formal managerial structure, clearer company policy, and a more equitable reward system. Regardless of the specific modifications in organizational structure, the goal is to design a more rational organization, with clear bounds to the use of judgment and discretion. In fact, many of the organization-wide studies reviewed were attempts to bring order to an organization that had recently undergone a dramatic increase in growth or size.

A second characteristic of organization-wide change is a focus on structural modifications as a means to improved organizational functioning. By structural change, we mean improvements in the formal organization as it would appear in a typical organization chart, including the grouping of job occupants from top management to the shop floor. A concern for organizational structure emanates from the need to bring rationality to the organization. Structure provides such order through the specification of organizational roles and the grouping of these roles into discrete yet interrelated units. Since structure sets the parameters for many of the more dynamic proces of the organization, such as communication, control, and task integr tion, its design is a prerequisite to significant improvements on the related dimensions. Without appropriate structure, members of the organization are left frequently to their own wits in communicating task-relevant information; managers are often thwarted in their attempts to control behavior; and related organizational units are face repeatedly with conflict as they integrate around a common task. Given the predominance of structure as a major organizational varia ble, it is not surprising that it is among the first concerns of organi zation-wide change.

A third feature distinguishing organization-wide change from other approaches to work improvement is the diversity of theories appropriate to this form of change. For example, one study describ ing change in a printing firm (Sadler and Barry 1970) used sociotech nical theory as a base. Here, both the social and technical and the systemic and environmental relationships were analyzed and rede-signed. Another experiment concerned with a packaging materials firm (Bowers and Seashore 1963) employed Likert's (1961) modified theory of management to direct the change program. Using the group as the basic organizational unit, the primary goals were to build high amounts of influence, support, and responsibility among group members and to link the various groups in the organization through a pattern of overlapping membership. The diversity of theories represented in these experiments points to the complexity of organization-wide change. Given the variety and interrelatedness of variables affecting total organizational performance, no single theory of organization seems capable of affecting change in all situa-tions.

Based on the above-mentioned characteristics of organization-wide change, there appear to be at least three consequences for the process of change itself. First, the time scale of change is longer for total system change than for other methods limited to jobs or work groups. This follows from the simple fact that structural changes affecting several parts of the organization take longer to af-fect than changes in selected units of the organization. Presumably, analyzing the organization, gaining commitment to change, and im-plementing the program require considerable time and effort. Secoi the amount of disruption in organization functioning seems greater for organization-wide change than for other approaches to work improvement. This is particularly evident in those instances where modifications affect different parts of the organization simultaneously. A reduction in the number of hierarchical levels, for example, may disrupt existing communication channels, task allocations, and control procedures. Until these related variables are integrated with the change, significant organizational functioning may suffer. Finally, related changes affecting the whole organization are likely to interact in unpredictable ways. The causal networks present in complex organizations are often richly interconnected and fused with a change gradient. This makes it difficult to predict how single changes may affect diverse parts of the organization or how multiple changes may interact to produce specific results. Thus, the unintended consequences arising from organization-wide change may amplify greatly, either tempering the intended effects of the program or causing additional problems in the organization.

Although the organization-wide change studies do not follow a common implementation strategy, they offer a number of useful suggestions intended to deal with the consequences of change at this more complex level. Starting with the time scale of change, the longer the time from the start to the end of the implementation process, the greater is the need to monitor the change program to see if it is progressing as intended. Structural changes frequently take from several months to more than a year to implement. During this time, many factors, such as the organization's environment, technology, and workers' attitudes, may impact the change in unintended ways. Unless the change program is monitored, the changes may either proceed in abnormal ways or they may produce undesirable effects. Information about the change process and its effects can provide organizational members with a useful barometer of what is transpiring. Such knowledge may be used to modify the change program to meet emergent circumstances or to institute additional changes needed to produce positive results.

The disruption in organizational functioning that is likely to occur from organization-wide change may be mitigated if careful attention is given to planning the change program and to obtaining sufficient organizational support. A first task of the experimenter is to formulate the purposes of change in language appropriate to the organization. If organizational members understand the change program and see its utility to the organization, they are less likely to resist the change or sabotage its implementation. Similarly, a planned-change program provides a strategy for integrating separate yet related changes and for timing them to minimize organizational disturbance. Although several of the organization-wide change studies were responses to unusual situations—for example, the start-up of a new plant, an economic crisis, a change in leadership—their change programs were planned to give the organization sufficient stability during the implementation process. Thus, stability in organizational functioning seems to be a prerequisite to engaging in successful change.

In addition to planning the change strategy, organizations must also obtain commitment and support from relevant members if they are to modify their structures successfully. This is especially relevant for change at the organizational level. For it is here that commitment to change takes on its greatest complexity, as members from top management to the shop floor are either involved directly in the change program or are affected by its consequences. Organizational commitment to change provides the climate needed to work through the myriad of difficulties encountered in the change process. Rather than ignoring these disruptions, members confront their problems in a supportive milieu. This minimizes unnecessary disturbances and provides the organization with a realistic basis for implementing change.

It is almost an inescapable fact that organization-wide changes are likely to interact in unpredictable ways. The interrelatedness of the parts of an organization and the presence of a change gradient make it particularly difficult to judge how one change may interact with another to produce specific outcomes. Rather than ignore these possible interaction affects, it seems more appropriate to study the change process itself to detect if subtle yet powerful relations among the separate changes are producing unintended results. Thus, for instance, a new configuration of production units may combine with a modification in pay structure to produce an inequitable distribution of rewards in the organization. This, in turn, may result in less motivation to perform and poorer attitudes toward the company. Knowledge of these effects would warn the experimenter that his change program is not producing expected results. A careful analysis of the situation would reveal that separate changes are interacting to produce negative outcomes.

Beyond studying the change process for possible interaction effects, experimenters may also time the implementation of separate changes to minimize potential interaction problems. This requires considerable planning as to the order and time scale of each structural modification. By instituting each change sequentially, organizations can reduce the likelihood that simultaneous changes interact inappropriately. Further, this allows experimenters to ascertain how each change is progressing before implementing additional changes. A realignment of organizational units, for example, may reveal that an intended change in communication channels is unwarranted. This knowledge would not only save the organization time and resources in implementing an unnecessary change but it would also avoid potential interaction problems between the two modifications.

In summary, organization-wide change is a work-improvement strategy concentrating on the total organization as the unit of change. These experiments employ structural modifications as a means to greater productivity and worker satisfaction. The diversity of theories guiding these studies points to the complexity of system-wide change, where no single theory is appropriate to all situations. The consequences of an organization-wide change strategy are threefold: the time scale of change is longer, the amount of disruption in organizational functioning is greater, and the likelihood that separate changes interact unpredictably is greater. To deal with these difficulties, experimenters can monitor the change program to discover if it is progressing as intended and to detect possible interaction effects among the separate changes. They can also plan the change program to integrate separate yet related changes and to gain members' understanding of the purposes of change. Finally, organizations can obtain member commitment and support for the change so that difficulties encountered during implementation may be worked through in a supportive milieu.

12

ORGANIZATION-WIDE CHANGE: A REVIEW OF SEVEN SELECTED EXPERIMENTS

Organization-wide change represents a systems approach to improving the organization's managerial and operating structures. The seven studies reviewed here implemented an assortment of structural changes to increase both productivity and the quality of work life. The different technologies, workers, and cultural settings included in the experiments provide a diversified introduction to this change-strategy. Like the other experimental reviews reported in the book, this chapter is divided into three parts: action levers and the validity of their effects, contingencies upon which successful outcomes are dependent, and guides to implementing this strategy in organizations.

ACTION LEVERS AND THEIR EFFECTS

The seven organization-wide change experiments modified a number of structural variables, or action levers, to produce positive effects. Table 6 lists these studies by author and presents information about contextual variables, action levers, and their effects. Since the contextual variables provide considerable data about the organizational settings of the studies, they are discussed in the next section of this chapter as contingencies, those factors affecting the general applicability of the findings. Turning to action levers and their effects, Table 6 shows that each study made from two to six separate changes to implement this approach. The most prevalent modification was organizational structure, with all of the experiments reporting some change in this action lever. This was followed closely by change in information feedback (five of the seven studies). The remaining action levers were modified in less than one-half of the seven experiments.

Organization-Wide Change: Contextual Variables and Action Levers and Their Effects

			Authors			
	Blain, I., Keohane, J., 1969	Bowers, D., Seashore, S., 1963	Cumming, E., Clancey, I. L. W., Cumming, J., 1956	King-Taylor, L. (c), 1972	Mann, C., Hoffman, L., 1960	O'Connell, J., 1968	Sadler, P., Barry, B., 1970

	Blain, Keohane 1969	Bowers, Seashore 1963	Cumming 1956	King-Taylor 1972	Mann, Hoffman 1960	O'Connell 1968	Sadler, Barry 1970
Contextual variables							
Type of work	Manufacturing supervisor	Manufacturing assembly line	Nursing	Purchasing	Power plant workers	Insurance sales supervisor	Printing company
Sex	?	Male/female	Male/female	Male	Male	?	Male
Occupational status	White	Blue	White	White	Blue	White	Blue
Number treated	131	215	?	20	140	22	?
Unionized	No	Yes	Yes	No/yes	No	No	Yes
Participation in change	?	Yes	Yes	?	?	No	Yes
Country	Great Britain	United States	United States	Sweden	United States	United States	Great Britain
Treatment took effect	No	Yes	Yes	Yes	Yes	Yes	Yes
Action levers							
Pay/reward systems					x		
Autonomy/discretion	x	x			x	x	
Support		x	x		x		
Training		x	x	x			
Organizational structure	x	x	x	x	x	x	x
Technical/physical					x	x	
Task variety					x		
Information/feedback	x	x		x		x	x
Interpersonal/group process	x	x	x	x			
Effects							
Costs				−		0	
Productivity		+		+		+	+
Quality		+	+				+
Withdrawal		−	0		−+−		
Attitudes	+	+		+			−

Code: blank = not relevant; x = variable manipulated; ? = insufficient data; + = variable increased; − = variable decreased; 0 = variable static.

Source: Srivastva et al. 1975, p. 126.

autonomy/discretion (three), support (three), training (three), inter-personal/group process (three), pay/reward systems (two), and vari (one).

Examination of the studies in terms of the two predominate action levers—organizational structure and information/feedback—reveals that structural changes, such as decreases in the number of hierarchical levels or new departmental redesigns, were frequently accompanied by modifications in communication channels and information systems. This suggests that both types of action levers may be highly interdependent, with changes in one requiring modifications in the other. Theoretically, this interdependence may be explained in terms of the differentiated parts of an organization and the information needed to integrate them into a functional whole. Information integrates the separate parts around the firm's task or mission. Therefore, changes in the structure of the organization's parts often demand requisite modifications in the information exchanges relating the units to each other.

The results of the organization-wide experiments were generally favorable. Table 6 reveals that all of the studies measuring productivity (four) and quality (two) showed positive outcomes. Of the two experiments presenting cost data, one showed an improvement and the other revealed no change. Workers' withdrawal from work declined in two of the three studies measuring this variable. Finally six studies reported attitudinal data: three showed totally positive improvements, two revealed mixed results (positive on some attitude and negative on others), and one showed a decline. Since all but one experiment reported that the change program was implemented successfully, the positive outcomes appear to be the result of the organizational changes.

Assessment of whether the experiments actually produced positive improvements followed the method used throughout this book. Each study's research design was examined for possible threats to the validity of the findings. The results of this analysis are summar below for both the performance and quality of work life findings.

Validity of Performance Results

Five of the organization-wide change studies measured some aspect of performance—costs, productivity, or quality. Since each study showed some improvement on this outcome, the entire set of studies was assessed for internal validity. Four out of the five studies used one-group pretest/posttest experimental designs, which are subject to several serious threats to internal validity—history, instrumentation, statistical regression, and selection interaction.

Failure to control for history is particularly damaging, since a multitude of external influences, such as the state of the economy, changes in the amount of available work, and fluctuations in the costs of raw materials, could have conceivably caused the performance improvements. While not as serious as the history threat, the other uncontrolled factors reduce considerably the efficacy of the performance findings. In the absence of a control group, it is difficult to discern whether changes in the way performance was measured (instrumentation) caused the positive results. Similarly, a lack of time series data raises the question of whether the experimental systems may have been selected because of their extreme scores on this outcome variable (statistical regression) or whether selection interacted with one of the other threats, such as history, to produce the improvements (selection/interaction). Given the predominance of plausible threats to internal validity, the positive performance findings seem highly questionable.

Validity of Quality of Work Life Findings

The quality of work life results—for example, job satisfaction, morale, and involvement—are, if anything, weaker than the performance findings. Five studies reported some improvement in attitudes. Only one of these experiments (Bowers and Seashore 1963) used a research design that controlled for most threats to internal validity—a nonequivalent control group design with pre- and posttests. The remainder of the studies employed research designs with many inherent threats to internal validity. When taken as a whole, the experiments showing increases in the quality of work life are subject to such uncontrolled factors as history, testing, instrumentation, statistical regression, selection, mortality, and selection interaction. While it is difficult to believe that all improvements in attitudes are merly artifacts rather than experimental effects, the validity assessment makes these findings extremely doubtful.

The efficacy of both the performance and quality of work life results does not appear to be justifiable. Serious threats to validity reduce considerably our confidence in the findings. This raises two pertinent questions about the organization-wide change experiments. The first issue concerns the conduct of inquiry in this area: Why do experimenters use such weak research designs to test the effectiveness of their change programs? One explanation is that the complexity and size of the experimental units—organizations in this case—reduce researchers' ability to use tightly controlled research designs. For example, locating a comparable control group is more difficult at the organizational level than at the job or work group levels. A second interpretation concerns the relative unpredictableness of organization-wide change processes. It is difficult to control data measurement when the initial change program encounters unexpected problems requiring continual modification of the proposed changes. In one study, for instance, the control groups demanded to be included in the change program; accommodation to their request reduced considerably the strength of the research design. Given these problems inherent in the conduct of organization-wide research, it is not surprising that the experimental designs were generally weak.

The second question arising from the assessment of the validity of the organization-wide experiments involves generalization of the findings: If the results are so questionable, why bother with a discussion of contingencies? It may be argued that whenever a set of experiments displays low internal validity, then the issue of external validity, or contingencies (the term used in this book), does not arise From a strictly scientific perspective, this argument has much meri On the other hand, a review of the contingencies associated with the seven organization-wide experiments would provide readers with a more comprehensive view of this change strategy. Assuming that this approach to change has some validity—that is, that the findings are not totally antifactual—discussion of contingencies may provide potential experimenters with knowledge of those factors limiting the general applicability of results. Before turning to contingencies, however, the reader should be reminded that the efficacy of the organization-wide change results is extremely questionable. Until further studies are reviewed along the lines used in this book, cautio must be exercised in accepting the claims of this work-improvement strategy.

CONTINGENCIES

Contingencies are those factors, such as technology, character istics of workers, organizational settings, and cultures, which limit the general applicability of experimental findings. Two sources of data were used to evaluate the studies' external validity: the contextual valuables in Table 6 and the experiments' research designs. Both sources of information provide knowledge about which variables modify the effects of organization-wide change.

Five experiments reported positive improvements in performance (Bowers and Seashore 1963; Cumming et al. 1956; King-Taylo [c] 1972; O'Connell 1968; and Sadler and Barry 1970). Examination of the contextual variables in Table 6 shows that these outcomes are applicable to service-oriented, manufacturing, and supervisory kinds of work. Information about characteristics of workers suggests that sex, occupational status, and union membership are not limiting factors, as both female and male, white and blue collar, and union and nonunionized workers were included in the experiments. The number of persons involved in the studies ranges from 20 to 215, with a median of 81. Since the median number of workers is considerably higher for this set of experiments than for most others reviewed in this book, the size of the work force does not appear to be a severe constraint, at least for the numbers reported in these studies. Workers' involvement in the change process may be a contingency, as four out of five experiments reported such inclusion. Perhaps worker participation is required the more structural changes demand new forms of behavior. Direct involvement in the change program would reduce workers' resistance to such changes by giving them some say over the implementation strategy. Finally, the performance effects appear to be limited to industrialized countries likely to support a positive work ethic—Great Britain, Sweden, and the United States. Based on the contextual variables in Table 6, the performance findings of the organization-wide change studies seem to apply to a wide range of settings and workers. The primary factors limiting the general applicability of these results are workers' involvement in the change process and industrialized countries supporting a positive work ethic.

Similar to the performance outcomes, five experiments showed some improvement in quality of work life (Blain and Keohane 1969; Bowers and Seashore 1963; Cumming, Clancey, and Cumming 1956; King-Taylor [c] 1972; and Mann and Hoffman 1960). The contextual variables in Table 6 reveal information similar to that reported for the performance findings. This suggests that the quality of work life results are also applicable to a variety of settings and workers, with the possible contingencies being worker involvement in the change process and industrialized countries.

Examination of the research designs of the organization-wide experiments reveals that none of the studies reporting increases in performance or quality of work life controlled for any of the threats to external validity. Testing/treatment is not a problem for the performance findings because they constitute unobtrusive measures, such as company records. Unfortunately, this contingency limits the general applicability of the attitudinal outcomes, as three out of the five studies reviewed used attitudinal surveys as pretests. These more obtrusive measures are likely to sensitize workers to the subsequent change program, thus making applications to unpretested populations questionable. Selection/treatment and special experimental arrangements appear to constrain the generalizability of both sets of outcomes. Several studies reported that experimentation was feasible only because organizational members were receptive to be-

havioral science methods. This selection/treatment bias makes generalizations to less receptive audiences doubtful. Like most experiments reviewed in this book, the organization-wide studies included
a number of special experimental arrangements, such as external
consultants, participation in the change program, and extra attention
paid to workers. Indeed, the very fact that organizational members
referred to these change efforts as projects or experiments sets
them apart as something out-of-the-ordinary. These reactive arrangements appear to facilitate the change process by giving workers
the feeling that they are special or important to the organization.
Application of the organization-wide change findings to more ordinary
situations may not produce the positive outcomes reported here.

In summary, the organization-wide change projects' performan
and quality of work life effects appear to be applicable to a diversity
of organizations and workers. Several contingencies seem to modify
these positive outcomes, however. Worker involvement in the chang
process and application to industrialized countries may limit the
findings. Similarly, testing/treatment seems to condition the quality
of work life effects, while selection/treatment and special experimen
tal arrangements may limit both the performance and attitudinal results to groups of workers who are receptive to behavioral science
techniques or to organizations presenting the experiments as nonordinary or special events.

IMPLEMENTATION OF ORGANIZATION-WIDE CHANGE

Organization-wide change is one of the most complex and power
ful work-improvement strategies reviewed in this book. Its complexity derives from the very nature of modern organizations, where diverse parts function together toward a common objective. Similarly,
its power to improve the organization emerges from the structural
modifications aimed at the total organization rather than at limited
units, such as jobs or work groups. Because of its complexity and
power, organization-wide change requires a comprehensive strategy
to plan and implement structural change. The seven experiments included a myriad of suggestions about facilitating such change processes. Although much of this advice was situation specific, applying primarily to the organizations under study, three conditions seem
to facilitate change across a variety of settings. The first factor
concerns the support of top-level executives. In most of the studies,
a key figure, such as the plant manager, was personally committed
to the change program. The power of his position and of his personal
influence gave added weight to advancing the goals of the program.
While the support of top management is important for other strategies

of change, such as autonomous work groups and participative management, it is especially significant when the focus of change is the total
organization. Here, the change program affects both managerial
and operating levels of the organization. Management's commitment
to change legitimizes the new organizational structure and provides it
with meaning for the rest of the firm.

A second condition that seems to enhance organization-wide
change is an underlying atmosphere of trust and mutual confidence
among members of the organization. A supportive organizational climate gives members the freedom to experiment, without fear of negative reprisals and evaluations. Workers have confidence that whenever problems arise, they can be worked through in a positive manner. Thus, for example, a departmental reorganization may require
a new set of intergroup relationships. Interpersonal trust among
workers and managers can facilitate the establishment of such link-
ages.

The final factor facilitating organization-wide change is the establishment of strong union-management relationships. Contrary to
popular belief, a strong union with able representatives is a benefit
for change programs. Such unions are frequently accustomed to working with management on various problems, including some out-of-
the-ordinary bargaining relationships. Since organization-wide change
often affects such contractual issues as work classifications and payment systems, active union involvement is almost mandatory if such
changes are to be implemented. Furthermore, a good union-management relationship provides the trust and cooperation needed to undertake a work-improvement program of uncertain scope and duration.

SUMMARY

Organization-wide change is a powerful strategy for improving
performance and the quality of work life. A review of seven studies
shows a predominance of positive outcomes. The validity of these
findings, however, is extremely questionable in light of the weak
experimental designs employed to evaluate these projects. Assuming
that not all of the improvements are artifactual, positive results may
be enhanced by worker collaboration in the change process, application to industrialized countries, special experimental arrangements,
and the selection of organizations responsive to behavioral science
methods. Attention to these moderating factors, in addition to sound
advice for implementation, furnishes organizations with a structural
approach to improving work.

13

IMPROVING PATIENT CARE THROUGH
ORGANIZATIONAL CHANGES IN
THE MENTAL HOSPITAL

Elaine Cumming
I. L. W. Clancey
John Cumming

The authors of this chapter, working as a team, undertook,
with the support of the hospital superintendent, Dr. Humphry Osmond
the general task of designing and carrying out changes that would lead
to improved patient care. One member of the team was a sociologist
whose role included research and consultation. Another was clinical
director of the hospital and, thus, had an executive role, and the thir
was a senior psychiatrist, who had administrative, clinical, and research duties and whose role on the team was a linking one.

At the beginning of our study, the hospital described in this
chapter, like many other large, state-supported mental hospitals,
constituted a reasonably permanent social system. Its location in a
geographically remote place, far from cities, gave it a striking "tota
community" quality. The social structure of its staff was granulated
that is, crosscut horizontally by caste lines and vertically by the func
tional autonomy of its parts. The medical staff turnover was high, a
few patients were treated with insulin and electric shock, and the patients on the "back wards" were "deteriorated."

On paper, the formal structure of the hospital staff was that of
a modern bureaucracy; promotion was based upon specified standards
of qualification and performance, jobs were described in terms of
specific functions, and authority lines were clear-cut. But much of

---

Reprinted by special permission of the William Alanson White
Psychiatric Foundation, Inc., from E. Cumming, I. Clancey, and
J. Cumming, "Improving Patient Care Through Organizational Chang
in the Mental Hospital," Psychiatry 19 (August 1956): 249-61. Copy-
right ©1956 by the William Alanson White Psychiatric Foundation,
Inc.

this was on paper only; informally, the hospital had many of the features of a paternalistic, traditional society rather than a democratic, rational one. There were cliques of elite who exercised power that went far beyond their legitimate authority; this they could do because some members abrogated their authority through ignorance, error, or a desire to be relieved of it. As traditional ways of doing things were emphasized, once such authority was abrogated, it was difficult to return it to its legitimate holders. Since one group of legitimate authority holders, the doctors, were often not the people with the longest tenure in the hospital, tradition tended to support ways of doing things that resulted in the withholding of power from them. In consequence, informal groupings were very important, a fact expressed in phrases such as, "So-and-so really runs the place." No one knew how this had come to be; it was vaguely attributed to "political influence" or nepotism.

With this pattern of traditional ways of doing things, there was a devaluation of new ways, and a compensating ideology that "this is the best hospital in this part of the country." Obviously, innovations were not needed in a society that was already so satisfactory! In the higher reaches of the hierarchy, few regulations were committed to paper; rules, guiding principles, and even the personal records of the nurses[1] and attendants were filed in the memories of the senior staff members. This lore was passed from role-holder to role-holder by word of mouth. Rumors were the lifeblood of the institution because they were often the only way of receiving vital information.

In this hospital, like most insitutions of its kind, there was seldom more than one doctor for every 200 patients. This meant that although the doctor might influence the condition of the patients, he must do it through the nurses. But the doctor was often much less acquainted with the hospital and its lore than were the nurses. Furthermore, there was little interaction across the caste lines.[2] Because of this, and because of traditionalism, it became important to "know the ropes," seniority was valuable, and having "been through the mill" was a virtue. Young doctors attempting to make changes were discouraged by the repeated, "When you've been here as long as I have, Doctor . . . ," which they heard from senior ward staff. Traditional and static, such a mental hospital is hard to change, and especially hard for the doctor to change because he is always outnumbered and usually outmaneuvered.

These were not the only reasons why this mental hospital was hard to change; just as important was the low level of integration at which it operated. There was, in other words, a high level of functional autonomy in the various hospital departments regarding both goals and methods of reaching them. For example, the farm had its traditional patterns of using patient labor in order to reach its goal of food production, while the wards had different goals and patterns of reaching them. The members of these two systems seldom interacted, except in the ritualistic handing over of patients in the morning and evening. Thus, the policies and procedures throughout the hospital were not closely integrated, and there was little chance of effecting change by reorganizing one part of the greater social system and waiting for the other parts to fall in line through a necessary adaptive process. If, for example, the occupational therapy department changed its daily routine, all that would happen would be that a few patients affected by the change would stop attending occupational therapy sessions, and slowly a few would replace them. There would be no corresponding shift in the routines of other departments, no planned adaptive process.

Autonomy was strikingly evident between the "male side" and the "female side." For instance, during the early part of our reorganization, when some 50 female patients from a chronic ward were allowed to go out unaccompanied for the first time, the resulting incidents caused rather dramatic reactions on the part of the townfolk; but the staff on the male side did not know until these incidents had been reported in the press that the female side had even contemplated such a program.

The level of communication between departments was low, because there was little need of much communication as long as the hospital functioned mainly custodially. The resulting type of integration was the "mechanical solidarity" of Durkheim,[3] that is, the hospital organization hung together because all were concerned ultimately in the custody of the patients; it was a common task, undertaken for a common goal to earn a living. There was, on the other hand, a low level of the interdependence, or "organic solidarity," which arises from a greater division of labor. Because each person or unit did a more or less complete task—either ran a ward or administered a portion of the hospital—people were not forced to communicate and to integrate their activities. This hospital lacked that specialization that, as Durkheim says, "creates among men an entire system of rights and duties which link them together in a durable way . . . and gives rise to rules which assure pacific and regular concourse of divided functions."[4] Such integration as existed in the hospital was brought about high in the hierarchy; at the ward level, no decisions were made that might affect general policy; thus, a minimum was done, for nothing could be done without decisions.[5] Therefore, changing the hospital entailed raising the level of integration of the system.

In general, this hospital was neither better nor worse than most. Many such hospitals have wrestled with the problem of improving the condition of their chronic wards, lifting the level of their

treatment programs, and changing staff attitudes. We propose here
to describe some of the techniques employed, we believe successfully,
in our attempt.

The goal was to integrate the system so that a new "therapeutic"
policy could be introduced to displace the older "custodial" one. The
meaning assigned to these terms was a little different from that used
by other workers. Briefly, those attitudes designated as custodial
centered in the conviction that most mental illness, particularly
schizophrenia, is incurable. We called those attitudes therapeutic
that centered in the assumption that most mental illness, and particularly schizophrenia, are, like rheumatoid arthritis, chronic, recur-
rent disorders for which there is no known cure but which can be so
treated as to allow the patients long periods of remission. Two secondary assumptions we felt necessary for a therapeutic attitude were,
first, that mentally ill patients require a high level of interaction
with other patients and with staff members in order to improve; and,
second, that in almost every case, life in the community is preferable
to life in a state mental hospital. The small number of doctors made
a goal of personality transformation untenable; the last assumption
implied that in this hospital, a "social recovery" would be the goal
choice for most patients.

TWO EARLIER ATTEMPTS AT CHANGE

As with most "reforms," the authors stood upon the shoulders
of others. The first step was to examine past attempts at change in
the hospital under study. Of these, two were outstanding, although
neither had been entirely successful.

The Nurses' Training Program

The first of these attempts at change had been a new nursing
training program, which had been introduced seven years before our
study. This program was designed to introduce more modern and
humane attitudes and to raise the prestige of the psychiatric nurse.
It has been fully described by McKerracher,[6] and, as is evident from
his description, it was an excellent program. However, by the time
of our study, the new training staff had in fact failed to gain access
to the wards for teaching purposes, and the most frequent complaint
heard from the training staff was, "We train the new nurses, but after a while the ward culture gets them; the old-line staff ridicule them
if they use our ideas, and they are gradually broken down." Thus,
the training program was, in effect, encapsulated and academic, and

did not seem to have much impact upon the custodial quality of the
hospital. It was said, on the other hand, to have raised the standard
of physical nursing care, and through its affiliation with the provin-
cial university, it did raise the prestige of the nursing group.

We tried to find the answer to the vital questions, Why did the
program fail to change the ward culture? Why did not the old-line
staff learn at least as much from the new trainees as they taught them
We found three main answers. First, the failure to change the ward
culture could be attributed to the failure to introduce structural
changes in the social system so as to raise the level of integration
of the hospital. We know from many sources that values, beliefs,
and attitudes—that is, norms—are changed, as they are made, in
interaction.[7] This is as true for the work group as for the friendship group or the family group. As Brown says, "The primary group
is the instrument of society through which in large measure the individual acquires his attitudes, opinions, goals, and ideals; it is also
one of the fundamental sources of discipline and social controls."[8]

If this is true, in a granulated system where the rate of interaction is low, one must either raise the level of integration and,
hence, of interaction of the total system or else arrange for persisten
interaction between members at all parts of the system, thus changing each semiautonomous part separately. Clearly, the latter approach would require a tremendous number of training staff members.
The training staff, in fact, interacted only with student nurses, who
not only were at the bottom of the nursing herarchy but were also
unable to support one another on the wards because they were spread
out over the hospital. This failure to integrate the granulated social
structure acted against the new training course.

The second reason for the failure of the program lay with the
failure of its designers to recognize the importance of seniority in
the static hospital society.[9] They had bypassed numerous senior ward
supervisors by promoting two capable but junior staff members to
high-ranking training positions on the basis of their attitudes and
orientation. At the same time, they made the training staff independent of the nursing hierarchy and responsible, under a director traine
in pedagogy rather than nursing, directly to the medical superintendent.

As said before, little is written down in a large mental hospital;
what is actually expected of a ward supervisor, beyond a minimal
list of duties, is never recorded. If the principle of seniority is
violated in making promotions, it throws great doubt into the minds
of the old-line staff as to their own status. They have no way of know-
ing whether or not they are performing well enough to be promoted.

Moreover, just as the designers of the training program had not
reckoned with the meaning of seniority, so they had overlooked the

earlier and somewhat less adequate training program, unrecognized by the university, in which the old-line staff had been trained. There was a tendency to refer to "before the training course," and to think of the old-line staff as "untrained." In fact, most employees who had been in the hospital only two or three years were unaware that there had been an old training course. While the old-line employees were given honorary membership in the new nursing organization, their traditional training was not incorporated into the new program. It was to be new, and it failed by being too new.

A third error lay in the violation of the principle that the most highly chosen people are most likely to be the norm-bearers.[10] The two men chosen from the nursing ranks to join the training staff were both deviant by definition, for they were selected as being the least custodial people in a custodial institution. The old-line supervisors had reason to be adamant in the face of this innovation; one of the problems that faces all mental hospitals is the performance of the function of "protection of the public" without slipping into custodialism.[11] Medical men do not like being charged with the duty of "protecting the public," for it runs counter to their perception of themselves as therapists. Yet this function must be performed, and the doctor must, by giving certain orders about the patients' daily routines, take his part in performing it. But he is in conflict, and one of his resolutions of this conflict is to exaggerate the "custodialism" of the nursing hierarchy. Many times we have heard a physician complain of "nursing office" attitudes and how they cripple his attempts to give the patients maximum freedom. We believe that the senior nursing staff members had been assigned the mantle of custodialism and that they had no way of refusing it. Furthermore, the old-line nurse had certain compensations. In effect he had made an even trade with the doctors; he had tacitly agreed to wear the mantle of custodialism in return for the power to run the costodial wards himself, in his own way, and with a minimum of interference. In spite of this, when we interviewed senior ward supervisors, we found that their reference point for advice and guidance in the care of patients tended to be the medical staff and not the custodially oriented head nursing offices, as had been generally supposed. They had, in short, latent therapeutic attitudes never called into play.

When all of the foregoing factors are considered, it is not surprising that the efforts of the recently promoted training staff members to teach on the wards were blocked by the old-line people over whose heads they had been promoted. On the other hand, the training program undoubtedly did a good deal of useful work, both in teaching nursing techniques, especially of the concrete, physical sort, and in constantly reminding the students of a more ideal sort of psychiatric nursing care than they were seeing on the wards.

The "Total-Push" Ward

A second and quite different attempt at change had been undertaken four years before by an enterprising and energetic team of two
doctors.[12] They had demonstrated on a treatment ward that deteriorated and incontinent schizophrenic patients would show social improvement if they were placed in an improved social environment,
no matter whether they had physical treatment or not. This demonstration, though strikingly successful, was not followed by any sustained attempt to improve the status of deteriorated patients in the
hospital; and, indeed, it had been intended only as a demonstration.
Our assumption is that one cannot create permanent changes in attitudes, values, and behavior by such an example, no matter how good,
because there seems little doubt that values and beliefs are changed
in interaction, and only a small proportion of the staff members had
a chance to interact in the improved situation. Further, the structure
of the organization that had been serving the purposes of the old values
was literally unchanged. As soon as the tremendous energy of the
two doctors was removed, the old situation reappeared. Thus, some
of the staff said cynically, "What is the use of improving the patients'
condition if it is inevitable that they revert to a deteriorated state?"
Yet there was an important residue of change in the personal outlook
of a few staff members, who hoped that this sort of improvement
could some day be made permanent throughout the hospital. This
small group of nurses represented a strain in the nursing ranks, for
they had a constant latent role conflict. They knew that as nurses they
could be doing better, but they did not know how, and their membership in the staff group kept them from voicing this belief very often.
But had it not been for them, our task would have been much more
difficult. Our predecessors had demonstrated that change was possible
and although they were unable to interact with sufficient people to
change the culture of the total group, they had overcome an immense
hurdle by convincing a certain number of the old-line staff that something could be done.

Recapitulating, we found that we had before us the task of raising the level of integration of the formal structure and of providing
a high level of interaction with staff members so as to succeed in
motivating them to adopt more therapeutic attitudes.

THE STRUCTURAL CHANGE

So far, while we have tried to describe the general characteristics of the hospital, we have touched only peripherally on its structure.
At this point, a brief but more specific description of the old structure

will help evaluate the new one. The hospital, like many others, had two separate nursing hierarchies, one for the male side and one for the female side, each headed by a chief nursing officer.[13] One of the main characteristics of the nursing structure was a lack of coordination between these two services. In theory, both were responsible to a superintendent of nursing, but, in practice, this post was often empty. Even when it was filled—always by a woman, since the post required general hospital training as well as psychiatric nursing training—there was never an effective coordination of the two nursing services; in actual fact, the role–holder tended to do the job of the chief nursing officer on the female side, while the holder of this role did the job of her deputy.

The two chief nursing officers were responsible directly to the medical superintendent, and a system of daily reporting kept a routine communication going between them. Actually, the nursing services had been run by their chief offices almost without interference through the years. Since promotion to positions in these offices was based almost exclusively on seniority, the role–holders, on the male side of the hospital especially, were people who had been trained in those custodial principles of mental hospital care that existed when they had first joined the hospital staff.

While the two chief nursing offices were the fulcrum of the medical side of the hospital, beyond this, very little was laid down regarding proper lines of communication. Therefore, entrenched informal groupings tended to control the flow of information. These offices often received information directly when it should have come through ward supervisors, and they often withheld information that should have been distributed to the ward staffs. This, of course, greatly enhanced the power of the chief nursing offices, as the control over communication must always do.[14]

Another major characteristic of the old structure was the limited authority of the doctors. The doctors on both sides were responsible to the clinical director and, hence, to the medical superintendent, but no one was responsible directly to the doctors. Ward staff had, of course, to obey medical orders from the doctors, but in all other matters, their final authority was their chief nursing office. Differences of opinion between doctors and one or the other of these chief nursing offices were resolved by the medical superintendent usually in favor of the nursing hierarchy, for doctors were, by and large, expendable, but the good will of the nursing hierarchy was not. The doctors, themselves, furthermore, did not wish the responsibility for running the wards that authority over the staff would entail.

One of the outstanding aspects of the structure of the nursing service was the small size of the executive echelon, which consisted of the two chief nursing officers, a deputy for each, and three administrative assistants on the male side and two on the female side. Considering that there were nearly 2,000 patients and a nursing staff of about 350, the nursing executive echelon was large enough for only the most routine daily administrative duties. This, together with an almost total absence of meetings with staff and the lack of formal job specifications, practically guaranteed that the minimum would be done and that integration would be low.[15]

All sociostructural changes in this hospital were timed to take place on one day. Just prior to this, meetings were held with various staff groups, and formal announcements were made of the new social structure within which they had to work. We did this not because we felt that they would absorb the information particularly well, but to put the formal intention of the highest hospital authorities before the total staff. This move had a latent purpose—preventing rumors about the change. In a sense, it was a rite of passage: the formal announcement of a new status for the hospital.

The New Executive Echelon

Our first move was to expand the executive echelon by creating ten new "coordinating" roles in the nursing hierarchy. Two of these were at the deputy nursing officer level, and the remainder at the assistant nursing officer level. The general purpose was a double one—to increase the efficiency and improve the quality of the nursing service, and to integrate ward activities. The number selected was small enough for intensive interaction with the medical doctors in discussions and meetings, yet large enough to meet with the ward staffs sufficiently often to have an appreciable effect upon their attitudes and beliefs—that is, to change their norms. In this way, the new therapeutic approach could be spread out fan-wise through the hospital.

Among their specific duties, these new officers were charged with the job of total hospital planning for the ancillary services, such as recreational and occupational therapies, and of securing the cooperation of the people engaged in these services. Since the development of the special therapeutic departments had been slight, there were no entrenched positions to consider in placing the new nursing officers in a coordinating role with respect to them.

Furthermore, the simple matter of getting things and getting things done fell within the scope of these new roles—the kinds of activity necessary in a large bureaucracy for procuring needed equipment and material. Hitherto, the nursing hierarchy had been too weakly staffed at the executive level to spend any time on such matters, especially if anything the least bit out of the ordinary was required. For instance, the doctors who had run the total-push ward had experienced great difficulty in getting wood for carpentry activities; since carpentry had not been done on the ward before, obtaining the materials was a major operation.

The new roles, then, in their acting out, were to provide a more efficient, integrated, and therapeutic nursing service, and the medical staff could use the nursing structure to introduce their own attitudes right down to the ward level.

The New Formal Lines of Authority
Communication

As a second step, we laid down firm lines of communication and announced that, for the time being, protocol would in all cases be observed. We did not want people to fall back into their old patterns of informal communication, which would be bound to short-circuit some of the new role-holders, especially as most of these people had only recently been subordinate to the chief nursing offices. Furthermore, although we were prepared to allow some informal channels to develop, we were determined that this should not happen until the proper channels were institutionalized enough so that every time any person used an informal channel, he would be perfectly well aware he was doing it. If vital information was withheld or misdirected, formal sanctions could be employed against the act. Sanctions had, in fact, to be used in this regard on several occasions.

The Training Office

A drastic change was made in the authority position of the training office. It had stood outside the nursing hierarchy, and the old-line nurses in the chief nursing offices had had no power to discipline the training staff, who, in turn, had no power to force their program upon the nursing hierarchy. The result was an almost inevitable stalemate, and encapsulation. Nursing training was restored to the nursing service under a well-qualified nursing officer. The creation of a personnel department to perform a previous function of the training staff informally allowed some members of the training staff to remain outside the nursing hierarchy, but the training staff—itself long insulated from the nursing service—once again became an integral part of it.

This step not only greatly facilitated the use of ward staff for practical training purposes but also was designed to break up the granulation of the structure and to bring the training staff, with its

therapeutic orientation, into close contact with the ward staffs. At
the time of writing (1955), the process of institutionalization is in-
complete, and the training staff and personnel staff informally appear
to consider themselves unitary.

Authority of the Medical Staff

A final change in lines of authority gave the doctors authority
over the new nursing officers in charge of coordinating therapeutic
activities. In administrative matters, these nursing officers were
still responsible to the superintendent of nursing, and, therefore,
formal regulations regarding communication with the nursing office
were introduced. It was important not to have overlapping areas in
the divided authority;[16] moreover, until the responsibilities of the
new officers to the nursing office were institutionalized, we felt that
they might be tempted to communicate solely with the medical staff,
who were, after all, in charge of the more interesting of the activitie
required by their roles.

Integration of the Two Sides

Getting the hospital to operate as one institution was the bigges
single undertaking. After all, it had run along fairly comfortably for
years without much contact between the two sides. It is true that
some female nurses had been nursing on the male side, but only because of the inability of the hospital to recruit male staff in sufficient
numbers and not because anyone had planned it as a desirable thing.
The first step we took in this direction was to place the two
chief nursing officers together with all the new appointees and the
training office staff in new common quarters.[17] Previously, they had
been separately housed on their own sides, but now they were in the
administration wing of the building together, on neutral ground.
Since the choice of people to fill the new coordinating positions
was very important to hospital integration, we will digress here to
discuss the selection process. The new appointees had to be able to
work with both male and female patients if necessary—not an easy
task for some; they had to be amenable to the therapeutic approach,
although we did not feel that they had to be already enthusiastic about
it; and finally, they had to be acceptable to the nurses with whom they
would have to work.
With these considerations in mind, we took advantage of the
waiting period, while the new posts were being formally approved
through bureaucratic channels, to conduct a campaign of anticipation.

The following examples of the preliminary work are taken from the male side, because, while that term is fast becoming less meaningful in this hospital, two of us were working closely with the male staff at the time of the reorganization.

A meeting of all the ward supervisors was called; the new jobs, of which 6 were to be filled by men, were described to them, and they were asked to fill out sociometric ballots indicating which male staff members they thought should be promoted to these new positions, as well as to 2 administrative nursing posts that happened to be vacant. Although the voting did not follow rigid seniority lines, all of the 8 men who received almost all of the votes were among the 15 most senior male staff members in the hospital. (Five of the remaining 7 men were within a year or two of retirmenet and had expressed their disinclination for promotion to the new jobs.) Thus, only 2 of the most senior old-line men were considered inappropriate for the new therapeutic positions by their peers.

When we examined this list of highly chosen men, we found it to coincide exactly with our own list of the senior men most able to do a good job. Although we knew that there were some exceptionally good young men of less seniority, we had decided that the following three principles were too important to violate:

1. Norm-bearers—those who most clearly express the attitudes and beliefs of a group—are highly chosen. New programs, to be accepted, should be introduced by norm-bearers rather than by deviants.
2. In a stable system, when all else is equal, seniority is the fairest criterion for promotion.
3. Very few roles in any society should be structured so that only exceptional people can hold them, since most people are unexceptional. [18]

The next step in anticipatory socialization was to assign special tasks to these highly chosen men in order to orient them to the type of problem with which they would be dealing when they were formally appointed. From among the chosen men, several small committees were set up to study ward procedures, such as the condemning of old clothing and the requisitioning of new, in order to recommend how these procedures could be changed so as to maximize patient welfare. A committee drafted a plan for the reorganization of a geriatrics ward, and a key man was assigned the task of preparing a weekly bulletin to keep all branches of the hospital informed of any news that might otherwise circulate only by rumor.

These activities proceeded while the men still held their old roles. Although they were never asked to work overtime, they put in many evening hours. [19] Although we asked our staff to work hard at

specific jobs for specific purposes during this period, and although
we expected them to orient themselves to the welfare of the patient,
it was through activity, not through formal teaching of any special attitude, that we hoped that a common sentiment of involvement in ther
peutic goals would emerge. These planning committees reported to
us, and in these reports, we were able to discern a good deal of the
"ward culture." In this way, we knew which of our planned changes
would be immediately acceptable, which might be acceptable eventual
and which would be intolerable to this group of men.

During this anticipatory period, we made a great many informa
contacts among the staff. A lot of our effort was spent in persuading
the "old guard" that things could be done. A great deal of their skept
cism about improving the hospital was founded upon their own experience in attempting minor enterprises of their own. The low level of
integration of the structure had convinced them, for example, that it
was impossible to get the cooperation of the tinsmith to repair the
lockers. Unless they could be fixed, how could the men be expected
to care for their clothes? There was a tendency to some defeatist
grumbling about past frustrations, even among the new appointees.
A certain amount of "charisma" was needed at this stage, as well as
demonstrations that the reorganizing team meant business.

All of the above-mentioned activity took place before the new
appointments were made. By the time we made them, we had a fairl
good idea of the kind of people we were dealing with and the kind of
job we could expect them to do. The restructuring of the nursing hie
archy followed.

Besides the establishment of the new executive positions, two
main changes were made in the interests of a closer integration of th
two sides. The three top nursing roles, the superintendent of nursin
—long unfilled at this time—and the two chief nursing officers were
consolidated into two posts, the superintendent of nursing and her
deputy. It was stipulated that if the superintendent were a woman, th
deputy would be a man, and vice versa, and that one of them must ha
a general nursing training. These two role-holders were made jointl
responsible for nursing services, and charged with the duty of unifyi
these services across the two sides of the hospital.

At the same time, it was announced that applicants for the war
supervisors' posts, made vacant by promotion to the new positions,
would be received from both male and female nurses for both sides
of the hospital. This broke cleanly with tradition. Men went for the
first time into supervisors' posts on the female side of the hospital,
because many male staff members had a great deal more seniority
than any female members.[20]

Neither the sick rate nor the resignation rate among the womer
changed in the months following the introduction of this practice. Th

were undoubtedly certain advantages to the women nurses in working on teams that also included men, for certain work on the wards is more easily done by men because they are stronger, and certain work is more appropriately done by men because of the difference in male and female roles in this society. We predicted that the women would appreciate a division of labor along these male and female role lines, and we have informal evidence that they did; for instance, nurses have commented that they are less exhausted, are less afraid on certain wards, and so on. These compensations appear to offset the dissatisfaction resulting from the women's reduced chances of promotion.

Division of Labor by Function

As said before, the lack of integration in the hospital was partly a result of the low level of functional specialization. As an example of the increased division of labor at the executive level, we consolidated the booking procedures—that is, the assignment of nurses to wards and shifts—into the hands of one staff member. Previously, each side had done its own booking, and each had operated on the basis of a different set of principles. Now one person, in consultation with the deputy nursing officer in charge of training and the superintendent of nursing, was assigned this task for the whole hospital.

On the same principle, two large male wards were consolidated for the purpose of administration. One supervisor was put in charge of administration, and two shared the responsibility for the therapeutic program. This division of labor forced communication and coordination across these two wards, with a rise in efficiency. Such administrative roles seemed an important safety valve for certain senior staff members, whose old, militarylike indoctrination into mental hospital procedures made them uncomfortable in the new "therapeutic" situation.

THE CHANGES IN ATTITUDES

Interaction and Communication

The importance of changing norms and values through interaction, and of appointing norm-bearers to key positions, which we have mentioned in describing the structural changes, cannot be emphasized too strongly. The impossibility of changing norms in a didactic fashion is aptly illustrated by an unsolicited comment from a training office

staff member, now attached to the personnel office: "All my stero-
types of the old, custodial ward supervisors have gone down the
drain." He went on to say, "I see people going around doing all sort
of things that we've been trying to talk them into for years."

An important element in our program was the committee work
we have described, which is now being continued in other committees
all over the hospital. When a change was considered, we tried to as
a committee to find the most therapeutic way of doing it. We did not
ask the staff to have good attitudes toward the patients; we assigned
them the job of finding out which of several alternatives would most
favorably influence the patients. A by-product of this technique was
the delegation of the decision-making function to the executive nursin
echelon. These people had never in the past had to assume the responsibility for making decisions about changes, and a feeling of increased status and involvement resulted. They became identified
through this program of action with the goals of the medical staff,
and with the remembered goals of the two doctors who had engineere
the total-push ward.

A second by-product of our technique was a high level of communication of vital information where it was needed. Not only did
the nursing executive echelon meet together and establish therapeutic
norms in interaction, but they also started meeting with groups of
ward nurses. Their discussions were focused on the relationship of
the new jobs to the starting of therapeutic activities. Thus, for the
first time, the problems generated on the ward were discussed on
the ward, and passed on for discussion, coordination, and action at
the top of the nursing hierarchy.

To coordinate these nursing activities with medical and clinica
activities, policy-making committees were formed, composed of the
clinical director, two senior psychiatrists, the superintendent of
nursing, her deputy, and, when applicable, the deputy nursing office
in charge of training.

The Didactic Program

Since many of our older nurses were unfamiliar with the conte
of modern psychological theory, a series of evening lectures was offered, and morning meetings were held to review papers, discuss
problems, and evaluate changes. Didactic material included principles of psychodynamic psychiatry, but the emphasis was on social
dynamics and interaction patterns. The social process on the wards
was the focus.

In the meantime, one of us started a group therapy training
seminar with the new nursing officers, and each of these, in turn,

started one group therapy program among the admission ward patients and one among chronic ward patients. Thus, through the manipulation of the interaction pattern in this hospital, we were able to make the new nursing program very shortly reach the patients.

The Effects of the Changes

The success of the techniques described must be measured by the results, as indicated by better staff morale and improved patient care. For both of these, there are accepted indexes, but since the change is very recent, these cannot yet be reported on.[21] Some immediate signs of success are discernible, however. We had expected that there might be a temporary recession in morale as a result of the dislocation of old patterns, but sickness and absenteeism rates, staff resignations, and the frequency of secluding and restraining patients have remained stable. This encourages us to believe that not only have we avoided arousing the antagonism of the old-line staff but have perhaps aroused in them latent therapeutic attitudes that have, in turn, provided them sufficient satisfaction to compensate for the dislocation of their accepted ways of doing things.

This impression is strengthened by spontaneous revolt among the male nursing staff against the entrenched practice of using them to relieve shortages in the cleaning and servicing departments. They actively demanded relief from the nonnursing chores that they had always done, such as carting mattresses to and from the upholsterer. They complained that they were being hampered in their rehabilitative and nursing efforts by routine jobs of cleaning, sanitation, and maintenance, which could in no way be considered therapeutic.

Evidence of increased integration of goals has appeared in increased cooperation between departments. For example, the maintenance department, through a spokesman, has suggested that some of their patient-laborers should be placed under the supervision of the nursing staff in order that these patients might have planned therapeutic occupations.

Increased patient activity, both in occupations and in recreation, is evident. We estimate an increase to date of 25 percent in the number of chronic patients who are occupied rather than idle. All admission ward patients, and many chronic ward patients, are in group therapy. The significant point is that this raised level of activity comes from the initiative, planning, and action of the nursing staff. We believe that we have succeeded in some measure in creating a hospital less dependent for its therapeutic activities upon the initiative of the doctors, who are so few and so much less permanent in tenure than the nurses.

There have been some unexpected and negative consequences of the change, which are being worked out. On the female wards, three of the four new male supervisors were well accepted, but the fourth man was rejected in a curious way. He was cut off from ward activities by the female staff and forced into an inactive role—making out charts in the office. After complaining for some time about it, he "went off sick" and remained so for a long period.

Another problem arose when a small group of men from the old chief nursing office suffered serious loss of status relative to the new members of the executive echelon. Their complaints were of "increased work," although there was no objective reason for this complaint. They had, however, inadvertently been put in the position of working more evening and night shifts than they had done before the reorganization; and not having to do shift work is an important sign of status in any organization that works around the clock.

In many ways, our task is far from completed; for instance, the training staff are only formally attached to the nursing program, and their functional attachment awaits the restatement of training goals and the changes in function that this will imply. There are, moreover, general signs of a tendency to slip back into old patterns; perhaps the most outstanding of these is the occasional automatic response of a nurse to a doctor: "I agree, Doctor, but the ward staff don't have time for that." This is the phrase that for years was used to maintain the status quo in the face of the attacks of interfering newcomers; it usually has little to do with time and expresses mainly desire to resist. On the other hand, we have much evidence that most nurses are more involved in their work than they ever were before, and we have confidence that the hospital can never quite return, under the worst of circumstances, to where it was before.

In general, we worked with the nursing group as we would have with any other staff of workers, assuming that they would do a better job in the interests of our new therapeutic approach if they felt a sense of involvement in our goals and if their statuses were not called into question by the reorganization. Changing the attitudes and values of the staff was accomplished, as such changes are always accomplished, by interacting with norm-bearers in primary groups. We believe that our efforts have resulted in higher morale, in much improved patient care, and in a fundamental change in the basically pessimistic "custodialism" of the nursing staff.

NOTES

1. The word <u>nurse</u> in this chapter refers to psychiatric nurses trained in mental hospitals, not to registered nurses.

2. See in this connection Edwin M. Lemert, Social Pathology (New York: McGraw-Hill, 1951), p. 417; and Howard Roland, "Friendship Patterns in the State Mental Hospital," Psychiatry 2 (August 1939): 363-73.

3. Emile Durkheim, The Division of Labor in Society (Glencoe, Ill.: The Free Press, 1947); see, especially, pp. 396-409.

4. Ibid.

5. See, in this connection, C. I. Barnard, The Functions of the Executive (Cambridge, Mass.: Harvard University Press, 1938).

6. D. G. McKerracher, "A New Program in the Training and Employment of Ward Personnel," American Journal of Psychiatry 106 (October 1949): 259-64.

7. See J. A. C. Brown, The Social Psychology of Industry (Harmondsworth, Middlesex: Penguin Books, 1954). See, also, Kurt Lewin, "Group Decision and Social Change," in Readings in Social Psychology, ed. Guy E. Swanson, Theodore M. Newcomb, and Eugene L. Hartley (New York: Henry Holt, 1952); and George Homans, The Human Group (New York: Harcourt, Brace, 1948).

8. Brown, The Social Psychology of Industry.

9. Questioning revealed that no old-line supervisor could remember a doctor or training staff member ever asking his opinion on the grounds that the long tenure alone made his a valuable opinion.

10. For a discussion of this point, see, for instance, William Foote Whyte, "Corner Boys: A Study of Clique Behavior," American Journal of Sociology 46 (March 1941): 647-64.

11. This problem is discussed by Alfred H. Stanton and Morris S. Schwartz in The Mental Hospital (New York: Basic Books, 1954).

12. This program has been described by Derek H. Miller and John Clancey in "An Approach to the Social Rehabilitation of Chronic Psychotic Patients," Psychiatry 15 (November 1952): 435-43.

13. The chief nursing officer on the male side was called the "Chief Attendant," and on the female side the "Head Nurse," titles that were dispensed with in our reorganization.

14. Stanton and Schwartz, The Mental Hospital.

15. We should like to mention here that the tradesmen who attended to the maintenance of the hospital were on strained terms with the ward staffs. Without going into detail, we can say that this was another evidence of the low level of integration of the hospital structure. The tradesmen thought the nursing staff irrationally demanding; the latter considered the tradesmen to be arbitrary and withholding in their approach to ward needs.

16. This problem has been discussed by Jules Henry in "The Formal Social Structure of a Psychiatric Hospital," Psychiatry 17 (May 1954): 139-51.

17. This move was suggested to us by Dr. Robert Hyde, Assistant Superintendent, Boston Psychopathic Hospital.

18. This point is discussed by Ralph Linton in The Study of Man (New York: Appleton-Century, 1936); see chap. 8, "Status and Role," pp. 113-31.

19. We tried to avoid the pitfall of assuming that nursing is an avocation and that we were justified in asking more than a day's work for a day's pay.

20. This had resulted from the higher turnover among the female staff; approximately 3 years' seniority had been needed before promotion to the supervisor post on the female side, and 15 years on the male. However, the trend is toward a greater proportion of women, and while the supervisors' posts will be overweighted with men in the near future, almost all senior posts will eventually belong to women, if this trend continues.

21. More specific information is now available. Against a steadily rising admissions rate, there has been a slow but steady decline in hospital population. For 1954, the total admissions were 533, while the hospital population on December 31 of that year was 1,880. For 1955, total admissions were 683, while the hospital population on December 31 was 1,809. By June 19, 1956, the population had further decreased to 1,790.

While there have also been dramatic decreases in the use of isolation, restraint, and electroconvulsive therapy to control behavior clear-cut conclusions are complicated by the fact that the tranquilizing drugs have come into use during the period under study. The use of these drugs does not, however, appear to be a factor in the decrease of hospital population; the initial drop occurred well before the use of any of these drugs, and, so far as we are able to determine, the later discharges of patients have not been attributable to these drugs.

V

ORGANIZATIONAL BEHAVIOR MODIFICATION

14

ORGANIZATIONAL BEHAVIOR MODIFICATION: THEORY AND CHANGE STRATEGY

A number of different terms—positive reinforcement, operant conditioning, and organizational behavior modification—have been used to denote the theory and change strategy discussed in this chapter. The last term, coined by Luthans and Kreitner (1975), is adopted here. Organizational behavior modification, or OB Mod for short, is a recent development, with the first notable applications occurring in the early 1970s. Despite the novelty of this approach, however, the theory and techniques of OB Mod have been articulated more thoroughly than most others discussed in this book. The main reason for the relatively advanced state of OB Mod is that it represents a direct application of the theory and methods of B. F. Skinner, the noted psychologist, whose techniques have been adopted successfully to change people's behavior in countless situations—prisons, schools, stores, mental hospitals, and nursing homes, to name a few. (See, for instance, Goodall 1972; Gray, Graubard, and Rosenberg 1974; and Hall 1972.) It was inevitable that industrial and commercial organizations would come to see the potential of this approach for improving productivity. Indeed, Skinner himself (1973) has recently expressed the view that operant conditioning is applicable to business and commercial organizations. In keeping with the spirit of Skinner, proponents of OB Mod claim that it is more scientific than other approaches, principally because they confine their attention to observable behavior and avoid all reference to internal, unobservable states, such as needs or expectancies. Also, they generally make no bones about the purpose of OB Mod, namely to control and predict behavior. Articles and books about this approach are notable for their relatively scant reference to human relations, self-actualization, fulfillment, or other such notions. Rather, they see the principal value of OB Mod in its potential for increasing management's control of the "human factor."

The central idea of OB Mod is that behavior is determined or shaped by its consequences. Thus, for example, if you make a bona fide mistake at your work, you are more or less likely to do so again according to how your boss reacts. If he complains bitterly, this wi have one effect on your future behavior; if he ignores the mistake, th will have a different effect; or if he praises your efforts and says "try again," this will have a still different effect on your behavior. OB Mod seeks to systematically define the contingencies (or connec- tions) between behavior and its consequences and to show how specifi changes in the consequences—say a switch from punishment to prais —can change the original behavior.

In every field in which it has been applied, Skinnerian behavior ism has generated much heated debate about questions such as free- dom of the individual, manipulation, and the ethics of controlling an- other person. These same questions have already arisen with regar to OB Mod, but they will not be treated here. The view is taken that OB Mod merits managers' attention as a useful approach to improvin performance and one whose potential is probably far greater than is currently realized. The ethical questions raised so readily in rela- tion to this particular approach should properly be raised regarding all approaches, and indeed regarding all management controls, if these questions are to be treated adequately. It is not within the scope of this book to deal with this issue.

This chapter is divided into two main sections. The first is de voted to an exposition of Skinner's analytical framework, the fundam tals of the science of behavior, and change techniques. The second section shows how these basic tools can be applied to the modificatio of organizational behavior.

THE ANALYSIS AND MODIFICATION OF BEHAVIOR: BASIC PRINCIPLES

The Analytical Framework: Behavior, Consequences, and Cues

Skinner's success can be attributed, in part, to the simplicity of his theory of behavior. In fact, he did not try to formulate a prop theory but stuck to a very simple analytical framework, which has three terms—behavior, consequences, and stimuli (or cues). (See Skinner 1953, 1969, and 1971.)

There are two basic kinds of human behavior, respondent be- havior and operant behavior. Respondent behavior is something we do automatically in response to a specific stimulus; for instance, a hungry infant will automatically suck if given a bottle. Respondent behavior is made up of stimulus-response connections, called reflexes. We are born with a number of reflexes, and we acquire others through the process of conditioning. Operant behavior is quite distinct, and its main characteristic is that it operates on the environment. What the individual does has consequences in the situation around him. These consequences, in turn, affect the individual's subsequent behavior—that is, he learns that certain consequences follow certain behavior, and he will change his behavior according to whether he likes or dislikes the consequences.

The fact that a person learns to do X rather than Y is critical to an understanding of OB Mod. The implications for managers are very great. It means that if John Smith is frequently absent or unproductive, this is not because he is innately lazy or unmotivated but because he has learned by his experience in the company (or other places he has been) that to be absent or unproductive brings more reward and less punishment than coming to work and being productive. Put differently, the consequences of being absent and unproductive have taught John Smith that it is worth his while to behave like that frequently.

Behavior is strengthened, maintained, or weakened by its consequences, and OB Mod attempts to systematically map out the impact of consequences on the behavior of people in organizations. Apart from the connection between behavior and its consequences, there is a third piece to Skinner's explanation of behavior—the initial stimuli, or the cues, which are present when a person does X. Just as people learn that certain consequences follow certain behavior, they also learn which is the best time and place to behave in a given way. Skinner says that people learn to discriminate between stimuli in the presence of which their behavior is likely to be reinforced and stimuli in which the behavior will be ignored or punished. Hence, certain stimuli become the occasion for reinforcement, that is, signs that the reinforcement will take place.

Fundamentals of the Science of Behavior

The essential features of a science of behavior are those of any science, namely, a unit of analysis, a method of measurement, and a set of relationships. The unit of analysis for behaviorists is the behavioral event or response. Strictly speaking, there is no such thing as a discrete or separate piece of behavior, but behaviorists have been very successful in breaking down complex or gross behavior and observing it in detail. For example, they would be unlikely to speak of the unfriendly behavior of a store clerk but rather refer to her frowning, her talking to a colleague while handling your purchase, or her avoidance

of your attempts to catch her attention. Behaviorists use the term be
havior chains to refer to such complex sequences of behavior.

The method of measurement consists mainly of counting the frequencies of behavioral events or responses. The strength of a response refers to the frequency of its occurrence during a given period

The relationships that concern the behaviorists are the continge
cies that exist between stimuli, behavior, and consequences. Two si
ple sets of contingencies would be the following: if the telephone ring
(stimulus) then the secretary handles the call quickly (behavior), and
then the caller expresses appreciation (consequence). If the average
credit period has slipped from 30 days to 60 days (stimulus), then the
financial controller will issue a stern directive to salesmen to stop
selling for a few days and concentrate on collecting debts (behavior),
and then the salesmen ignore the directive (consequence). The consequence in each case is contingent upon the behavior.

The more frequently a certain behavior occurs in the presence
of a particular stimulus, and is reinforced, the more the behavior ca
be said to be under stimulus control. A person learns to associate
certain consequences with certain stimuli. In the example given,
therefore, if most callers express appreciation of prompt handling of
the call, the latter behavior is likely to come under the control of the
ringing telephone. In the second example, however, the issuance of
a stern directive by the accountant is unlikely to come under the stim
lus control of the poor credit position, since the accountant's behavio
is not reinforced by the salesmen. The secretary's behavior is
strengthened by its consequences, while the accountant's behavior is
weakened by its consequences.

Luthans and Kreitner (1975), who have written one of the few
comprehensive books on the application of behavioral modification
to organizations, propose a simple formulation of contingencies that
is easy to understand and remember:

> Since cues [stimuli] represent antecedent events or events
> occurring prior to a response being emitted, an ANTECE-
> DENT-BEHAVIOR-CONSEQUENCE, or simply, A-B-C
> model, can be used to identify each term and its relation-
> ship to the other terms in the three-term contingency.
> Functional analysis reduces complex learned or operant
> behavior to A-B-C terms. Once reduced, behavioral
> events become manageable through the systematic and
> consistent control of consequences and consequence/ante-
> cedent pairings (pp. 43-44).

The Behaviorist Change Technology

Skinner and other behaviorists have developed a technology of
behavioral change. The basic components of this method are reinforcement and punishment, shaping, and reinforcement schedules.

Reinforcement and Punishment

Reinforcement is the basic principle of learning. It refers to the fact that behavior will occur more often if it is followed by a positive or rewarding consequence. A rewarding consequence could be one of two things: It could be something desirable or good in itself, such as money, praise, or promotion. This kind of reinforcement is called positive reinforcement. Or it could simply be the removal or nonoccurrence of something unpleasant or noxious. This type of consequence is called negative reinforcement. Examples of negative reinforcement would be the following: disciplinary action is not taken because the individual comes to work on time; correspondence does not have to be retyped because the letters were initially typed with care. Note that negative reinforcement is very different from punishment. Negative reinforcement strengthens behavior. Punishment does not. Negative reinforcement strengthens behavior because, by behaving in a certain way, the person escapes an unpleasant consequence. Thus, in the above examples, the individual is likely to come to work on time and the typist is likely to type with care if these behavior obviate unpleasant consequences.

Strictly speaking, punishment can occur in two forms that parallel the two forms of reinforcement. First, punishment occurs if an act is followed by something unpleasant; for example, if a mother spanks her child for misbehaving. Second, punishment occurs if an act is followed by the removal of a pleasant consequence; for example, if the mother prevented the child from watching his favorite television show because he misbehaved. A particular form of punishment, often called extinction, is to ignore the behavior, thus producing no consequence. Whereas reinforcement strengthens behavior, punishment weakens it.

Positive reinforcement, negative reinforcement, and the two forms of punishment may be used either as separate techniques or in various combinations. Combinations are used where incompatible behaviors occur—for instance, where the salesman with the highest sales may also be allowing the most credit over the desired limit. In this case, his boss might reprimand his high credit (punishment) and give the salesman a bonus for his high sales (positive reinforcement). Several different combinations of the basic techniques are possible.

Shaping

Skinner pointed out that behavior can be shaped, that is, gradually changed, by rewarding successive approximations to the desired behavior. Each small improvement is reinforced, and no re-

ward is given for behavior that is not a step in the right direction.
Shaping is one of the cornerstones of behavior modification. It is important because the change in behavior that is desired is often too
great to attempt in a single step—for instance, where it is desired to
change a machine operator's reject rate from 15 percent to 2 percent.
In addition to such cases as this, the behavior that is desired may
rarely if ever occur, as, for instance, where constructive suggestions
rarely arise from a work group. In both cases, reinforcement of
even slight movement in the right direction would constitute shaping.
Shaping requires patience, but it is likely to bring the desired results
more quickly in the end.

The basic idea of Skinnerian behaviorism is that behavior is
shaped, strengthened, or extinguished by its consequences, and these
consequences consist of occurrences in the environment or situation
of the individual. This does not mean that the individual will be entirely passive. Actually, Skinner acknowledges that the person has
the capacity to manipulate certain environmental factors, which, in
turn, control his behavior. For example, a person who plans to build
a boat and buys the materials is controlled by the consequences of
planning and buying the materials—in the sense that he is more likely
to build the boat than waste the materials. Self-control, as understood by behaviorists, highlights the important fact that people have
to manage the consequences of their own behavior. In nonbehaviorist
terminology, if people decide, or plan, or choose, or do something,
then they have to hold themselves accountable for what they have
done and follow through on their choices and plans.

The gradual process of shaping, by reinforcement or punishment, accounts for a great deal of the behavior we observe. Some
behavior, however, cannot easily be explained in terms of shaping—
for example, behavior that appears relatively suddenly (and so was
not acquired by a long process of shaping). The main explanation
offered by behaviorists for the appearance of such behavior is that it
is learned by imitation of others. Imitation, or modeling, accounts
for much of the behavior observed in organizations. Not surprisingly
therefore, one of the strategies for changing behavior involves the
systematic use of models or examples of the desired behavior. (See,
for instance, Johnson and Sorcher [1976].)

Schedules of Reinforcement

The purpose of reinforcement is to strengthen and maintain behavior. One of the discoveries of Skinner and his followers is that
behavior is not necessarily strengthened and maintained by continuous
reinforcement. Considerable attention must be given to the schedules
of reinforcement, that is, the particular pattern according to which
reinforcers (or punishment) follow behavior.

Six distinct schedules of reinforcement have been distinguished, and considerable research has been carried out to establish the various effects of each kind of schedule on behavior. The simplest schedule is continuous reinforcement, in which reinforcement is always given for a particular behavior. Intermittent reinforcement involves reinforcing only some occurrences of the behavior. Intermittent reinforcement can be randomly given, or else given according to a certain ratio or at a certain interval—that is, reinforcement after a certain time. Ratios and intervals may be fixed or variable. Examples of the six types of schedule are as follows: continuous reinforcement—newlywed husband praises all of his wife's cooking; intermittent reinforcement (random)—catching a fish; intermittent reinforcement (fixed ratio)—piece rate payments; intermittent reinforcement (variable ratio)—winning on a slot machine or lottery; intermittent reinforcement (fixed interval)—11:00 a.m. coffee break or 5:00 p.m. finish to work; and intermittent reinforcement (variable interval)— the start of the warm summer weather.

ORGANIZATIONAL BEHAVIOR MODIFICATION: INTERVENTION STRATEGY

Organizational behavior modification is the term used to distinguish the adaptation of Skinner's techniques to solving organizational problems, such as low productivity or absenteeism. It is not usually possible to maintain the same scientific rigor in changing organizational behavior as when carrying out a laboratory experiment. There are a number of steps that can be followed, however, to ensure as much rigor as possible, given the constraints of time, money, and other organizational pressures. Nine steps in the overall strategy can be identified: (1) initial scanning of behavior, (2) identification of key behavior, (3) measurement of the frequencies of focal behaviors, (4) analysis of contingencies, (5) setting of behavioral targets, (6) formulation of the modification program, (7) piloting of the program, (8) implementation, and (9) evaluation of the project.

Initial Scanning of Behavior

Assuming that the target group (or individual) has been chosen, either because there is a problem to be solved or an opportunity to be exploited, the first step is to analyze the behavior of the group. What do they actually do all day? The answer to this question can be obtained by asking people involved, as well as others who may be familiar with them, and by observing what they do. A diary method may be used to compile a general picture of what subjects do. This diary may be filled in by the subjects themselves or by the observer. A diary of a day's activities of a hypothetical salesman might contain such entries as greetings and small talk with colleagues (18 minutes), answered two phone calls from customers (3 minutes), looked at mail while having coffee (10 minutes), answered two letters (15 minutes), drove to visit customer (30 minutes), meeting with customer (60 minutes), had lunch with salesman of another company and exchanged idea (90 minutes). When a diary at this level of generality has been kept for a representative number of working days, it will be possible to estimate the average amount of time spent at each kind of activity. Frequencies may be entered if they are considered useful. Once estimates have been made of the activities of the target individual or group, it is possible to move to the next step of the change strategy.

Identify Key Behaviors

Obviously, the activities revealed by the initial scanning do not have equal importance for the organization, so priorities need to be established. Priorities will be related ultimately to the goals or targets of the organization and, at a lower level, to the performance standards set for the individual or group. For example, the targets of the organization might be to increase profit after interest and tax by 15 percent and to increase the proportion of the market by 5 percent. The first of these targets would be related closely to the success of salesmen in keeping credit to a minimum. Furthermore, the degree of success of the salesmen in controlling credit would presumably be related to the frequency of calls made on customers when payment is overdue. Behaviors that have a direct relationship to company goals and to employee performance take priority over other behavior.

The process of sorting activities may involve using a set of categories that take account of the fact that among performance-related activities, some are more central than others. Also, the sorting should acknowledge that there exist productive, counterproductive, and unproductive activities. For example, reading the newspaper would be unproductive and peripheral, whereas open exchanges with competitors could be counterproductive and central. Similarly, face-to-face meetings with customers would be productive and central, while phone calls might be considered productive but peripheral. This sorting of activities of the hypothetical salesman assists in the establishment of priorities for further investigation. In this case, there is clearly a greater need to focus on the open exchanges with the competitor's salesman and on visits to collect money and sell goods than on the other activities listed.

The purpose of the first two steps of the OB Mod strategy, just described, is to ensure the proper focus. In other words, it is a process that directs attention to more critical behaviors. These are not always as obvious, even to the experienced manager. In the case of the salesman described here, for instance, it would not be at all unusual to find a boss concentrating more on eliminating the newspaper reading and small talk that goes on every morning than on improving the handling of correspondence or increasing the number of credit collector visits.

Measure the Frequency of Focal Behaviors

The frequencies of focal behaviors must now be measured. The particular method of measurement should take account of a number of factors, including the availability of frequencies on already compiled company records—for example, absenteeism figures; sensitivity of subjects to observation by another person; and the nature of the behavior, which may, for instance, be so frequent that a sample should be counted instead of all occurrences. Various kinds of hand counters and tally sheets have been used for frequency counting. The interpretation of a set of frequencies can be greatly facilitated by depicting them in graph form.

Analysis of Contingencies

Since behavior is strengthened, maintained, weakened, or extinguished by its consequences, it is necessary to establish what follows the focal behavior. Also, since certain stimuli constitute the conditions in which behavior occurs, we want to know what was happening before the behavior in question.

Considerable rigor is needed at this stage in the unfolding of OB Mod strategy. Some cues and consequences will appear to the observer to be very obvious. But other more important ones may be less obvious and will be detected only by careful observation. The presence of incompatible behavior—desirable and undesirable behavior occurring simultaneously—should be noted.

In describing these first four steps of OB Mod, relatively discrete or separate units of behavior have been used for illustration purposes, but, in reality, it may not be so simple. If the behavior under scrutiny is complex, the analysis of contingencies may involve breaking the complex behavior into a chain of more simple behaviors.

Set New Behavioral Targets

There is now wide agreement among managers that the practice of goal setting facilitates performance improvement. The process of consciously setting targets to be achieved is the cornerstone of several new developments in management practice and training, such as management by objectives, achievement motivation training, and the shift to behaviorally stated objectives in appraisal systems. (The importance of this step in the strategy has been noted in a recent review of OB Mod projects by Hammer and Hammer 1976.) The goals that are set constitute a prediction based on the data gathered in the first four steps, and also a prediction regarding the effects of the change strategy to be employed. Targets should be realistic, neither too high nor too low; they should be measurable; the time by which targets will be reached should be stated; obstacles to achievement should be anticipated as far as possible, resources that might help toward achievement should be listed; and the intermediate steps to the end target should be stated.

Formulation of the Modification Program

This sixth step is the most crucial. In line with the basic features of behavior modification discussed earlier, there are three interrelated decisions to be made: the pattern of reinforcement or punishment; the mix of shaping, self-control, and imitation; and the schedules of reinforcement. These factors are now discussed in detail as they relate to the OB Mod.

Organizational rewards do not necessarily reinforce desirable behavior. Some rewards, in fact, have no effect or a bad one (Duerr 1974). Ideally, the connection between behavior and a consequence should be observed or demonstrated. The analysis of antecedents/ behaviors/ consequences contingencies is time consuming, so practitioners have developed a number of questionnaire-type instruments for identifying potential and actual reinforcers. Blood (1973), for instance, has developed the job orientation inventory, which identifies the priorities an individual would assign to certain types of reward. Such instruments may be supplemented by interviews with subjects in order to identify reinforcers.

Various classifications of rewards have been devised, including a useful one by Meacham and Wiesen (1969), which Luthans and Kreitner (1975) have adapted to suit OB Mod. The first four categories are consumables (for example, Christmas dinner); manipulanda (for example, company car, clothing); visuals and auditories (for example, private office, piped music); and tokens (for example, vacation trips, theater tickets). These four types may be thought of as "contrived rewards," that is, rewards brought into the natural work setting. Apart from the disadvantage of costing money in most cases, people tend to become more easily satiated with contrived rewards than with "natural rewards," and they may more easily come to take the former for granted. There are two types of natural reward—social (for example, praise, smile) and Premack. According to the Premack Principle (after David Premack 1965), reinforcers already natural to the job can be made contingent on the completion of unattractive or difficult tasks. An example of Premack would be to indicate that the more interesting activities (which have to be carried out anyway) can be started once the boring work is finished. Another example would be to allow, on completion of an unattractive task by a certain deadline, an extension to a coffee break that has to occur in any case. These six categories of rewards are used to generate a comprehensive list of concrete reinforcers.

Negative reinforcement and punishment are used widely in organizations, even though there are serious problems related to both forms of negative control. The main problems are that people will engage in all sorts of escape or avoidance behavior to avoid negative consequences; the undesirable behavior may only remain weakened so long as the punishing agent is actually present. The punisher may lose the potential to reward a subject because the subject may come to fear or suspect the punisher. Punishment may extinguish behavior —for example, showing initiative—that may be required at a later date. Colleagues of the punished individual may react badly; irrational behavior may result; and the costs of administering a system of punishment may be enormous. Therefore, a combination of positive reinforcement and less-punitive forms of negative control is probably the best approach if the desired behaviors are to be strengthened. The side effects of punishment will tend to be less marked when the punishment is balanced by positive reinforcement.

The second major question to be raised in formulating the modification program concerns use of shaping, imitation, and self-directed changes. Strictly speaking, there are a number of more basic questions underlying these three methods. There is the contentious matter of the agent of control. In shaping, the other person is largely in control vis-a-vis the subject; in imitation, the subject can choose his own models or be deliberately presented with models chosen by the other; in self-directed changes, there is relatively more scope for the subject to exercise control. Another distinction is that regarding the gradation of the change targets—that is, whether they involve a single step or a series of intermediate steps. A third consideration is the speed of change. Imitation can occur quite suddenly, whereas a process of shaping could take years. Although shaping,

imitation, and self-control are treated here as separate techniques
for behavior modification, it should be noted that they are commonly
used in various combinations to constitute the core of the overall
strategy described here. Luthans and Kreitner (1975) list in detail the steps to be follow
in shaping, modeling, and self-control. The steps are essentially th
same in all cases, except that if a modeling approach is used, it is
necessary to identify suitable models and to systematically present
these to the subjects.

It is a question of judgment about the number of steps of the
overall strategy in which the subjects should be involved. With a
cooperative group, it may be possible to involve them at every stage
from scanning their own behavior, through formulating the change pr
gram, to evaluating the eventual outcome. There would seem to be
considerable scope in organizations for a form of self-control that
consists of subjects monitoring their own behavior. This process wa
a key feature of the Emery Air Freight Case (Organizational Dynami
1973), where self-feedback was available to the dock workers, who
kept notes of container utilization throughout the day. Another form
of self-control is mentioned by Luthans and Kreitner (1975, p. 156),
who adapted a behavior modification technique called contingency con
tracting. The contract essentially involves an agreement that if the
subject does X, then Y will happen as a consequence.

To summarize this step of the overall strategy, the formulatio
of the actual treatment is at the heart of OB Mod. All the other step
revolve around it. A suitable mix of positive or negative reinforcers
must be adopted, and the specific details of reward and punishment
specified; an appropriate combination of shaping, imitation, and self-
control also has to be chosen. Schedules of reinforcement are a
critical element in the intervention program. Recall, for example,
that a continuous schedule tends to be more effective with new or wea
behaviors, but an intermittent schedule is generally more effective
in maintaining behavior.

Pilot the Intervention Program

This step is optional. Provided that people responsible for the
project are satisfied that the intervention program has been sufficiently refined and that there are few, if any, risks in implementing
it, they should bypass this step. In some cases, however, it makes
a great deal of sense to conduct a pilot project before implementation
on a wider basis.

There are several factors that might commend a dry run of the
change program. First, if it has been necessary, for whatever rea-

son, to short-circuit some of the more scientific aspects of the initial steps, then it will be wise to test the intervention in order to detect and correct any faults it might contain. For example, a pilot project might reveal that certain rewards were reinforcing incompatible behaviors. A case could also be made for a pilot implementation where large number of subjects will be affected by the change program. Even small refinements could have a big payoff. Furthermore, an ideal opportunity is provided for supervisors or managers to practice their skills as reinforcing agents. The third kind of situation where it would be wise to pilot the change program is where there is risk of a bad reaction from the target group or of some other consequence that could jeopardize the whole project.

Implementation

At a certain point, the investigation and planning must stop and the change program begun. Implementation involves two things: the contingent presentation of reinforcers and punishment, and the process of measuring the target behaviors. No matter how much care has gone into preparation for the actual change program, it is unwise to adopt the attitude that plans are a blueprint to be carried through mechanically. Rather, the experimenter should be prepared to adjust the project to meet unexpected circumstances.

Evaluation of the Change Program

It is good practice to formally evaluate the change program. The most important data will already have been collected as part of the implementation itself, namely, the behavior frequencies. Ideally, behavioral changes should be related to performance criteria and company objectives. Recall that the target behavior was not chosen at random but because it related to broader individual and company performance standards or objectives.
Evaluation serves many useful purposes:

1. To demonstrate that the program objectives have been achieved,
2. To demonstrate that the behavioral change makes a real difference to performance,
3. To compare OB Mod with other change techniques, on a cost basis, for instance,
4. To improve subsequent attempts to change behavior,
5. To bring to light unexpected or unwanted results of reinforcement and punishment,

6. To provide well-documented case study material for other departments that may be interested in trying OB Mod.

SUMMARY

The theory and techniques of Skinner have been extended to the field of organizational behavior. The notion that behavior is a functi of its consequences has immense implications for managers. OB Mod practitioners advocate the use of less punishment and more pos tive reinforcement on a regular, systematic basis. A step-by-step strategy for implementing OB Mod programs was outlined here.

Writers on OB Mod tend to make the claim that their theory an technology of change are more scientific and, therefore, better than other approaches. Such a claim diverts attention from the fact that OB Mod can be seen as complementing rather than superceding othe approaches. Beatty and Schneir (1975) have proposed some ways in which OB Mod might be integrated with job enrichment, management by objectives, Scanlon plans, and other approaches.

15

ORGANIZATIONAL BEHAVIOR
MODIFICATION: A REVIEW OF
SIX STUDIES

Practitioners of organizational behavior modification claim that their theory and practice are more scientific than others discussed in this book. It is more scientific, they say, principally because its subject matter is observable behavior and because careful measurement is a feature of OB Mod. In this chapter, six OB Mod studies are evaluated to assess their degree of scientific rigor. The action levers and their effects are noted and summarized. An attempt is made to specify the contingencies that mediate the effects of the various action levers. The chapter concludes with a brief review of the implementation strategies adopted in the six experiments.

ACTION LEVERS AND THEIR EFFECTS

Two closely related action levers—feedback/information and pay/reward systems—were manipulated in all six cases, as one can see from Table 7. In only one case (Pedalino and Gamboa 1974) did the change in pay/reward systems actually involve money. Rather, a variety of other types of reward or positive reinforcement were used, including electrical appliances, verbal reinforcement, an extended coffee break, and making use of a person's suggestions. Information/feedback consisted of detailed information, commonly on a daily basis, about the performance of individuals or groups. In two cases, the changes included a modification in the amount of contact between supervisors and subordinates—for instance, in group discussions about work problems (Luthans and Kreitner 1975). The single case of an increase in autonomy/discretion consisted of subjects taking responsibility for keeping track of their own performance (Organizational Dynamics 1973); in this case, there is also reference

TABLE 7

Organizational Behavior Modification: Contextual Variables and Action Levers and Their Effects

	Authors					
	Adam, E. E., 1975	Business Week, 1972	Luthans, F., Kreitner, R., 1975	Nord, W., 1970	Organizational Dynamics, 1973	Pedalino, E., Gamboa, V. D., 1974
Contextual variables						
Type of work	Die-casting operation	Telephone operators	Production line operators	Secretaries, sales, porters	Container handling	Assembly line
Sex	Male	Male/female	Male/female	Male/female	Male	Male
Occupational status	Blue	Blue	Blue	White/blue	Blue	Blue
Number treated	12	1,000	?	?	?	215
Unionized	Yes	Yes	?	?	Yes	Yes
Participation in change	No	?	Yes	?	Yes	No
Country	United States	United States	United States	United States	United States	United States
Treatment took effect	Yes	?	Yes	Yes	Yes	?
Action levers						
Pay/reward systems	+	+	+	+	+	+
Autonomy/discretion					+	
Support						
Training						
Organizational structure						
Technical/physical						
Task variety						
Information feedback	+	+	+	+	+	+
Interpersonal group process	+		+			
Effects						
Costs	-				-	
Productivity	+		+		+	
Quality	0		+	-		
Withdrawal		-				
Attitudes	0			-		-

Code: blank = not relevant; ? = insufficient data; + = variable increased; - = variable decreased; 0 = variable static.

Source: Compiled by the authors.

182

to people setting their own performance standards. Some reports (for example, Organizational Dynamics 1973; Luthans and Kreitner 1975) mentioned that the intervention included some training. This consisted of preparing supervisors to carry out behavior modification programs with their subordinates.

The main outcomes of these changes show no definite pattern, although in all cases, some improvement and no deterioration were reported. Costs were reduced in three instances; productivity gains were reported in three studies; and withdrawal rates dropped in three cases. In one out of six studies, there was evidence of improved quality. Finally, the fact that there was reference to attitudes in only one study (Adam 1975) is probably a reflection of the explicit concern of OB Mod practitioners with performance and their disregard for the concept of attitude, which they associate with "internal," or "mental," states. In the Luthans and Kreitner (1975) study, however, one of the outcomes noted was a reduction in the frequency of "complaining behavior" of a particular subject. Such a change would very likely have been formulated in terms of an attitude change by theorists who do not adhere to the Skinnerian tradition. Nevertheless, the following discussion of validity refers only to performance results.

VALIDITY OF PERFORMANCE RESULTS

In OB Mod experiments, the treatment typically consists of repeated reinforcement and feedback, interspersed with measurement. The measurement itself is part of the treatment in some cases, as for instance where subjects keep track of their own daily performance. The research design employed in all cases but one (Nord 1970) was a variant of the "equivalent time samples design," which Campbell and Stanley (1966, p. 43) describe as "a form of the time-series experiment with the repeated introduction of the experimental variable." The same writers also note that

> for most purposes, the simple alternation of conditions and the employment of a consistent time spacing are undesirable, particularly when they may introduce confounding with a daily, weekly or monthly cycle, or when through the predictable periodicity and unwanted conditioning to the temporal interval may accentuate the difference between one presentation and another (p. 44).

The significance of these comments in the present context is that OB Mod experiments seek not to avoid conditioning of the behavior by the presence of stimuli and reinforcements other than the specified treatment but to actively strive for conditioning by antecedent stimuli and consequences that occur about the same time as the treatment. (See Luthans and Kreitner 1975, pp. 42-44, 52-54.) Consequently, it may be difficult to determine whether a particular piece of behavior is caused by the treatment (that is, usually positive reinforcment or feedback), by the situation in which the behavior is manifested (for example, Monday morning or when the boss is looking), or by something else that occurs at the same time as the positive reinforcement.

These features of OB Mod experiments make the assessment of internal validity a more difficult task than in the case of the change experiments critiqued in other chapters. None of the six studies reviewed tried to distinguish the effects of the treatment from the effects of other possible conditioning factors just mentioned. Only very detailed research will separate out these various determinants of the phenomena investigated in OB Mod experiments.

Nord's (1970) study took the form of a "one-shot case study" (see Campbell and Stanley 1966, p. 6), and Nord himself admits the weaknesses of his design. The discussion here will be confined to the other five studies.

The remaining five studies have a high degree of internal validity. There are no threats from history, unless the antecedent stimuli are considered to be historical events. Repeated measurement excludes threats from instability; variations are unlikely to be accounted for by purely random fluctuation if the repeated measurements follow a definite pattern or trend. As indicated earlier, testing is, in some respects, part of the treatment when self-measurement is involved, but in most of the studies, other unobtrusive measures were used, and these are the ones referred to in Table 6 under "Effects." The research designs employed in all five studies—except that part of Adam's (1975) study which investigated attitudes—exclude threats from testing. None of the remaining possible threats to internal validity were a source of plausible alternative explanations for the findings.

Three of the studies—Luthans and Kreitner (1975), Pedalino and Gamboa (1974), and the attitude part of Adam (1975)—used comparison groups, which further enriched their research designs and greatly strengthened their internal validity. Briefly, then, the claims made for the efficiency of OB Mod have a high degree of validity.

CONTINGENCIES

The analysis of contingencies is an essential step in OB Mod strategy, as discussed in the previous chapter. Here, the discussion of contingencies is confined to contextual, psychological, and social factors that might mediate the effects of reinforcement or influence the applicability of OB Mod in other respects. The experiments' research designs were also assessed for general applicability of the performance findings.

The amount of detail given in the six reports concerning contingencies was limited, but those that gave a good description of the experiment stressed that the focal performance problem must be at least partly due to human behavior and not just tools, materials, or some other nonbehavioral factor. It helps if the focal performance is quantifiable; indeed, one of the major contributions of OB Mod is to show how qualitative aspects of performance can be quantified. In the Emery Air Freight case (Organizational Dynamics 1973), several factors contributed to the success of the OB Mod program, including the absence of financial incentive programs; the fact that the organization was going through a period of growth, which gave rise to more than the usual number of opportunities for promotion; and the active fostering of a noncompetitive climate within the company. A noncompetitive climate was developed by encouraging people to compare their performance over a given period with their own previous performance and not with the performance of others. OB Mod may also be less effective if subjects do not have the ability or training to improve performance and if performance standards have been set too high.

From Table 7 it can be deduced that both men and women are amenable to OB Mod interventions; that the technique can be used with blue collar and lower-level white collar workers; that participation by subjects in the program, say by choosing their own reinforcements, seems neither to inhibit nor facilitate the intervention; and that fairly large numbers of people can be handled within a single project. OB Mod has been applied successfully in unionized companies in the United States, so only further studies will reveal whether or not unionization or country moderate the effects of this approach to improving productivity. Quite a wide variety of production and service jobs were included in these six studies, although it is noteworthy that no executive or other senior technical, service, or administrative jobs were treated. Its applicability to these latter categories of work has yet to be proven.

A contingency noted by Adam (1975) was the existence of a trade union embargo on the granting of additional financial payments without formal negotiations regarding additional payments for all, including those who were not subjects of the OB Mod experiment.

An analysis of the research designs of the six studies throws additional light on the matter of contingencies. The studies are weak on testing/treatment interaction because the method of pretesting used involved a detailed study of people's behavior. This process of testing would undoubtedly have sensitized people, for better or for worse to the subsequent treatment. A second aspect of external validity, experimental arrangements, is interesting in that none of the studies raise the matter, even though certain ethical questions arise when subjects are not aware that they are being shaped. Insofar as subject were aware of what was going on, experimental arrangements would pose a threat to external validity; that is, it might reasonably be argued that OB Mod would not necessarily have similar effects on a population that was aware. In the Emery Air Freight Case (Organizational Dynamics 1973), however, it is claimed that OB Mod continued to produce the same effects long after any Hawthorne effect might have been present. Selection/treatment interaction was a common source of threat to external validity, because the choice of target gro was not made on a random basis but usually on the grounds that there was a problem in the group, such as absenteeism; because most pote tial for improvement existed in the chosen group or organization (Organizational Dynamics 1973); or because the organization was willing (Adam 1975).

What this analysis suggests about contingencies is that generalization of the findings may well be limited to work populations where something akin to the pretesting process occurs—for example, wher people are accustomed to continuous, detailed measurement of their performance. This kind of prior sensitization apparently helped toward the success of the six projects. There is also insufficient infor mation to judge whether or not awareness of the methods and purpose of OB Mod would facilitate or inhibit success. The method of selecting groups or organizations for inclusion in the six projects was, in most cases, not done randomly; hence, automatic generalization to other situations is not warranted. It might well be that OB Mod will only work where there is a problem to be solved or where the potential for improvement is very great.

IMPLEMENTATION OF ORGANIZATIONAL
BEHAVIOR MODIFICATION

Insofar as the six reports gave details of implementation, they mentioned most of the nine steps described in the previous chapter. A formal initial scanning, however, did not seem to be common. Instead, OB Mod tended to be seen as a potential solution to an already defined organizational problem. Identification of key behaviors, mea surement of the frequency of target behavior, and the analysis of contingencies were all embodied in the systematic analysis that typically preceded intervention. In a number of cases, there was setting

of behavioral targets in concrete terms; for example, Pedalino and
Gamboa (1974) set a goal to reduce absenteeism from 3.01 percent
to 2.31 percent, a reduction of precisely 0.7 percent.
    It is clear from the studies that considerable thought and inge-
nuity went into the formulation of the modification program. Contingency contracting and a combination of extinction and positive reinforcement were used on different subjects in the Luthans and Kreitner
(1975) case; Adam (1975) reported the use of verbal reinforcement;
in the Nord (1970) study, a lottery method, with prizes of electrical
appliances, was adopted; and Pedalino and Gamboa (1974) used a similar method, based on the principles of a poker game, with prizes
of up to $20 for the winner. Incidentally, this was the only instance
of money being used as a reinforcer.
    Careful attention was given to the specification of schedules of
reinforcement. Experiences in the six cases generally confirmed
Skinner's views that frequent reinforcement is required at the beginning to strengthen the target behavior and that less frequent reinforcement at variable intervals or ratios maintains the desired behavior.
(See Organizational Dynamics 1973.) Various combinations of shaping
and self-control were used. Modeling apparently did not form part
of the strategy of any of the six studies.
    There was some evidence of piloting the program, as, for in-
stance, in the Business Week (1972) case. Finally, evaluation of the
change program took place in every case, although not always with
the degree of forethought and planning that would ensure a thorough
evaluation.
    In addition to following a definite implementation sequence, such
as that outlined in the preceding chapter, a number of other features
of OB Mod implementations were mentioned in the reports reviewed.
There were a number of examples of considerable effort having gone
into training the appropriate supervisors and managers to conduct
the reinforcement program. An apparently useful addition to the implementation strategy, adopted in the Emery Air Freight Case (Organizational Dynamics 1973), was the provision of detailed instruction
workbooks containing concrete examples of how supervisors might
give recognition and feedback.
    Pedalino and Gamboa (1974, p. 698) sound a note of caution in
explaining why their experimental incentive system was terminated
after 16 weeks: "The reason for doing so was that a bargaining date
for a new union contract was approaching and the company did not want
to find itself negotiating this incentive system into the contract."
This problem must surely represent one of the biggest stumbling
blocks to the long-term usefulness of positive reinforcement, especially
if it involves any form of material reward. On a more hopeful note,
the same two writers found it possible to stretch the schedule of re-

inforcement from weekly to biweekly without any loss of effect. The Emery case (Organizational Dynamics 1973) is also instructive regarding scheduling of reinforcement; there was an insistence on reinforcing specific behavior; on reinforcing as quickly as possible after the behavior; on reinforcing frequently, that is, at least twice weekly in the early stages in order to shape and strengthen the desired behavior; and on moving to less frequent and more random reinforcement once the appropriate behavior had been well established. There is insufficient evidence, as yet, to specify the minimum rates of reinforcement and feedback that will sustain a given level of performance.

SUMMARY

A review of six OB Mod studies reveals that they are probably "more scientific" than some of the other approaches discussed in this book in two ways—namely, in their use of systematic observation and measurement of the variables to be changed and the use of a research design that produces results that are subject to relatively few threats to internal validity. The principal action levers manipulated were feedback/information and pay/reward systems. Improvements in the areas of costs, withdrawal, productivity, and quality were claimed, and judging from the research designs employed, these claims can be accepted as valid. Experiments have been generally confined to lower-level white and blue collar jobs in which performance is easily measured. The skill of OB Mod practitioners for expressing qualitative aspects of performance in concrete terms suggests that the technique is potentially applicable to a much wider variety of jobs.

16

THE PRODUCTION CASE
Fred Luthans
Robert Kreitner

Because of the newness of OB Mod, only a few empirically based research studies have been conducted to date. This chapter presents one of them. It represents a viable approach to building a meaningful body of knowledge about OB Mod. The firm in this study is a medium-sized industrial plant engaged in light manufacturing. Two groups of nine first-line supervisors from the production division participated in the study. One of the groups went through a training program and served as the experimental group. The other group, which was matched with the experimental group on the basis of age, education, experience as foremen, and mental test score, did not undergo any training and served as the control group. Spans of control for the supervisors ranged from 10 to 30 employees. All had worked their way up from operative positions in the plant. For the most part, each had gained his managerial knowledge from the "school of hard knocks" rather than from formal education or supervisory training.

This chapter is reprinted with kind permission of Robert L. Otteman, Assistant Professor of Management, the University of Nebraska at Omaha, who holds the copyright, and of Fred Luthans and Robert Kreitner, authors of Organizational Behavior Modification (1975), where the chapter originally appeared. Organizational Behavior Modification is published by Scott, Foresman and Company, Glenview, Illinois, in the "Management Applications Series," editor Alan C. Filley, University of Wisconsin, Madison.

BEHAVIORAL CONTINGENCY MANAGEMENT TRAINING

OB Mod was applied by training the first-line supervisors how to use behavioral contingency management (BCM). The training sessions were held in the plant's training room for 10 90-minute sessions spread over 10 consecutive weeks. A process, rather than content-training, approach was used. This approach replaced the traditional lecture format, where the trainer has a dominant role, with a relatively free give-and-take discussion format, where the trainees themselves dominate.

In general, the content of the sessions was preplanned and sequenced but not rigidly structured during the session itself. Some of the assumptions made by the trainers included: it is easier to change the trainees' behavior first and overall style later than the reverse; appropriate trainee responses must be reinforced immediately and frequently; complex trainee behaviors must be gradually shaped; and allowances must be made for individual differences in learning speed.

The process approach resulted in an informal and relaxed learning environment. Importantly, the trainers served as models of what they were teaching by first cueing and then contingently reinforcing appropriate trainee behavior. Among the reinforced trainee behavior were attendance, contributions to discussion, and data presentation and analysis. In effect, the BCM approach was taught to the trainees through the use of BCM.

The steps of BCM as taught to the trainees were as follows:

1. Identifying target behavior: The focus was on objective behavior rather than on internal states. Initial reliance upon internal explanations, such as, "Joe has a bad attitude," was eventually replaced in the training sessions and on the job by an attention to observable behavior. Identification of performance-related behavior was stressed. The trainees in the study identified behavior such as work-assignment completions, absences, rejects, quality-control problems, complaints, excessive breaks, leaving the work area, and scrap rates.

2. Measuring the frequency of behavior: After learning the measuring techniques, the trainees charted real behavioral data on the job and discussed it during the training sessions. The resulting frequency charts provided both training session data and feedback for the trainees on their progress with implementing the BCM approach.

3. Functionally analyzing behavior: The trainees were taught to identify the three elements in the behavioral contingency (antecedent-behavior-consequence). By analyzing antecedents and, especially contingent consequences, the supervisors began to see for themselves how target behavior could be predicted and controlled. Emphasis was

placed on managing contingent consequences to change on-the-job behavior.

4. Developing intervention strategies: Strengthening desirable performance behavior and weakening undesirable behavior was the goal of the intervention. Shaping, modeling, and reinforcement were discussed in terms of strengthening behavior. Extinction, reinforcement of incompatible behavior, and, in exceptional cases, punishment were examined as strategies for reducing the frequency of unproductive or counterproductive behavior. Because of the difficulty of identifying reinforcers ahead of time, methods of selecting and establishing effective reinforcers were given a great deal of attention. Potential reinforcers that were proposed and used included attention, work scheduling, positive feedback on performance, approval, recognition, praise, responsibility, and contingent assignment to favorite tasks.

5. Evaluating results: The supervisors continually monitored their interventions through measurement to see whether the intended effects were in fact taking place. The goal of the evaluations was to determine if performance improvement was occurring.

Importantly, emphasis throughout the entire 10-week training program was on getting the supervisors to identify and solve behavioral problems on their own. As much as possible, the trainers resisted offering any direct prescriptions. Occasionally in the sessions, a problem would be brought up by trainees and solutions suggested by the trainers, but mainly the trainees became problem-solving behavior contingency managers.

Results were measured on two levels to evaluate the overall effectiveness of the BCM training program. First, individual and group performance of the trainees' workers were analyzed to determine the trainees' ability to put the BCM approach into actual practice. Second, since performance improvement is the ultimate test, a comparison was made between the experimental and control groups in terms of the overall "bottom-line" performance to determine if the training had a significant impact on improving the performance of the experimental group's respective departments. These results are discussed below.

CHANGES IN SPECIFIC ON-THE-JOB BEHAVIOR

Frequency of response was the dependent variable, and the intervention strategy was the independent variable in measuring on-the-job behavioral changes. The supervisory/trainees measured the frequency of a target behavior of an individual subordinate or a group of subordinates during a baseline period and, subsequently, during the intervention period. Thus, the data for the behavioral change analysis was contained on response frequency charts. Four representative illustrations of these behavioral change problems are discussed in the following sections. They involve both individual and group problems and different types of intervention strategies.

The Disruptive Complainer

A particularly disruptive female machine operator was selected as a target for BCM by one supervisor/trainee in the program. She often complained bitterly about the production standards to the supervisor. In addition, she seemed to adversely affect the productivity of her co-workers by talking to them about their rates and production sheets. According to her, everyone else in the plant had an easier job. Close review of her case revealed that her complaints were unfounded.

After identifying the complaining behavior, the supervisor gathered baseline data on this behavior during a 10-day period. No new contingencies were introduced during this "before" baseline measure. In conducting a functional analysis of the target response during the baseline period, the supervisor determined that he was probably serving as a reinforcing consequence by paying attention to the complaints.

Armed with the baseline data and information gathered in the functional analysis, the supervisor decided to use a combination extinction/positive reinforcement intervention strategy. Extinction took the form of his withholding attention when she complained. Satisfactory production and constructive suggestions were socially reinforced by praise in an effort to strengthen the incompatible behavior. In addition, her constructive suggestions were implemented whenever possible.

The supervisor's chart, shown in Figure 1, illustrates that the combination intervention strategy did, in fact, have the desired effect. The complaining behavior decreased in frequency. The chart shows that a time-sampling technique was used. Rather than carrying out time-consuming measures every day, the target response was charted on randomly selected days (the 1st, 5th, 7th, 10th, 13th, and so on). Implementing constructive suggestions turned out to be especially reinforcing in this case. The supervisor noted to the trainers that the rapid reduction in frequency of complaints was amazing because it had been such a long-standing problem.

FIGURE 1

Frequency of Complaints

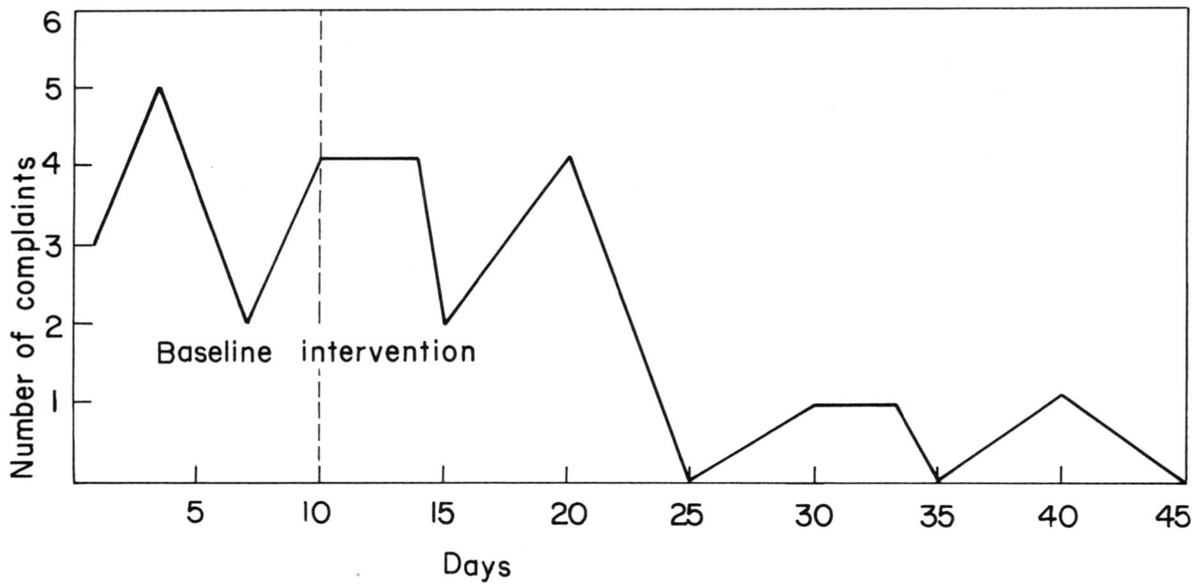

Source: Figures in this chapter have been compiled by the authors.

Group Scrap Rate

Another supervisor/trainee identified group scrap rate as a growing performance problem in his department. Attempts at reducing the scrap by posting equipment maintenance rules and giving frequent reminders to his workers had not produced any noticeable improvement. The specific target response to be strengthened was identified as stopping the stamping mill when a defective piece was sighted and sharpening and realigning the dies.

During a two-week baseline period, the supervisor kept a careful record of the group's scrap rate. Importantly, no new contingencies were introduced during this baseline period. The extent of the problem had to be determined before any intervention was attempted. After conducting a functional analysis, the supervisor decided to install a feedback system to inform the group of their scrap rate. This was accomplished by measuring, charting, and posting in the department work area the group scrap rate. The supervisor then actively solicited ideas from his workers on how to improve the scrap rate. Providing the feedback and implementing the suggestions turned out to be potent reinforcers. Figure 2 shows the results of the intervention.

In this case, group, not individual, behavior was charted. In addition to the improved scrap rate, the supervisor noted an increase in interaction between himself and his workers and among the workers themselves. A number of social reinforcers were discovered in the process.

Group Quality Control

A third supervisor/trainee identified quality control in the paint line as a major performance problem in his department. The paint line attendants' job consisted of hanging pieces on a paint line conveyor, removing the painted pieces, and inspecting them for acceptance or rejection.

"Getting on the men's backs" by the supervisor typically produced only temporary improvement in quality control. Soon after the supervisor reprimanded the men, the defective pieces would again pass unnoticed. As defined by the supervisor, a desirable target response consisted of identifying and removing defective pieces from the paint line. An undesirable response involved overlooking a defective piece.

During the two-week baseline period, the average daily number of overlooked defective pieces was recorded for the entire work group. Figures were charted weekly during both the baseline period, where

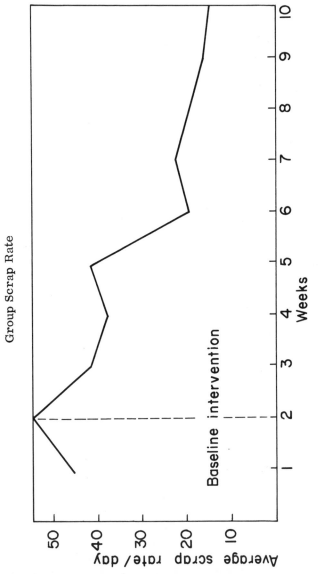

FIGURE 2

Group Scrap Rate

contingencies remained unchanged, and the intervention period. The supervisor had noted to the trainers that after conducting a functional analysis, he had concluded that he had a group of "clock watchers" on his hands, particularly around break time, lunch time, and quitting time.

The supervisor developed his intervention strategy during a discussion session with his work group. It was decided that a group rate of eight or less overlooked defective pieces a day would qualify the group for an extra five minutes for each of two coffee breaks the next day. To increase the value of the potential reinforcer, the paint line attendants were told each morning if they had qualified for the extended breaks. Figure 3 shows that the extra time off in the form of extended coffee breaks did, in fact, prove to be reinforcing.

Contingency contracting had been effectively used. With the average daily rate of defectives down to around two or three, the supervisor confided to the trainers that he could not see much more room for improvement.

Individual Performance Problem

A fourth supervisor/trainee was having a problem with the quality of assembled components in his department. Upon detailed analysis of the problem, the supervisor discovered that most of the rejects were coming from a single assembler. The assembly work entailed the precise manipulation of intricate subcomponents, and the individual in question had satisfactory scores on screening tests for dexterity and coordination. In addition, this assembler had received the standard training in assembly and checking. After initial consideration, the supervisor rejected the alternative of running the assembler through more training. In his previous experience with similar cases, more training had failed to improve poor performance. Thus, he decided to use the BCM approach on this particular employee.

The supervisor specifically identified undesirable behavior as more than 2 rejects per 100 assembled components and desirable behavior as 2 or less. Without changing the existing contingencies, the supervisor obtained a two-week baseline measure. To facilitate measuring, boxes of assembled components were randomly sampled, and the per box average recorded on a weekly basis. After a function analysis, the supervisor decided that feedback on performance and compliments and praise for desirable behavior would be an appropriate positive reinforcement intervention strategy.

Beginning a shaping process at five or less errors, the supervisor contingently praised the assembler for any improved quality. As the reject level began to drop, the reinforcement schedule was

FIGURE 3

Frequency of Overlooked Defective Pieces

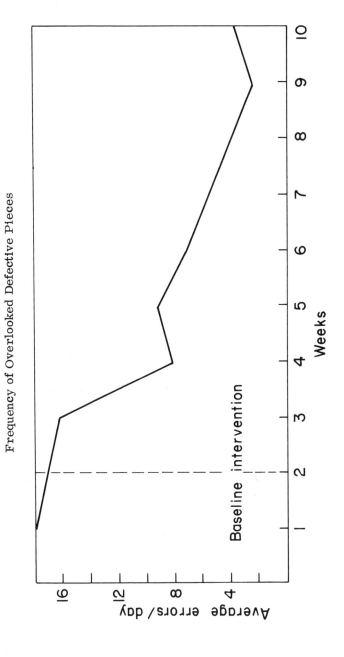

FIGURE 4

Assembly Reject Rate

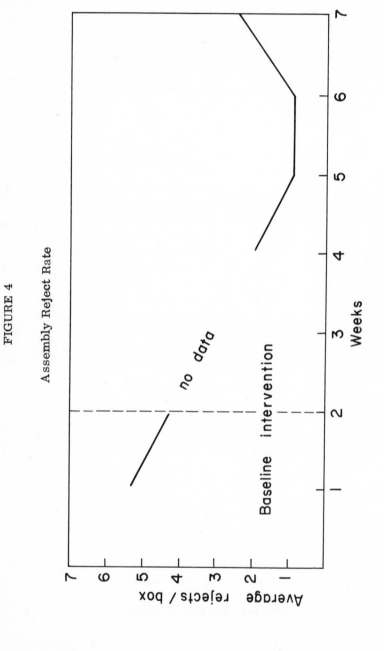

gradually stretched. In other words, the worker had to have four, then three, and eventually only two rejects before praise was given by the supervisor. Summarized reject statistics were charted and presented to the assembler as a form of feedback on performance. Discussions of this feedback data between the assembler and the supervisor provided the opportunity for the supervisor to reinforce desirable behavior and ignore undesirable behavior. Figure 4 illustrates the rapid improvement resulting from the feedback and positive reinforcement intervention strategy.

OVERALL PERFORMANCE IMPROVEMENT

The supervisors' ability to modify specific on-the-job individual and group behavior represents only one level of evaluation in BCM. Of more importance is overall performance improvement. The supervisors worked on the specific problems discussed above during the training program, but the trainers' ultimate objective was to have BCM apply to the supervisors' total method of managing their human resources. To evaluate the effectiveness of BCM as an overall method of managing, direct labor effectiveness (a ratio of actual to standard hours stated as a percent) was measured for each of the supervisors' departments both in the experimental group (those who received BCM training) and in the control group (those who received no training). Figure 5 shows the results of the overall performance evaluation.

The figure shows the experimental group's and the control group's mean direct labor effectiveness curves over a six-month period subsequent to the start of the training program at the end of September. The training program itself lasted 10 weeks (until the middle of December). The figure clearly shows that the overall performance of the control group remained relatively stable over the six-month period, but the performance of the experimental group significantly improved and seemed to be maintained even after the training period was over. This evaluation demonstrated that the BCM training had generalized and paid off in terms of overall performance improvement.

Although not all the supervisors were able to obtain as clear-cut results of behavioral change as the four reported above, the overall performance was impressive. The other cases presented in this chapter do not provide as systematic and precise an evaluation. Some of the significant features of this production case are the following:

1. Specific performance-related problems were identified by the supervisors and reduced to desirable/undesirable behavioral events.

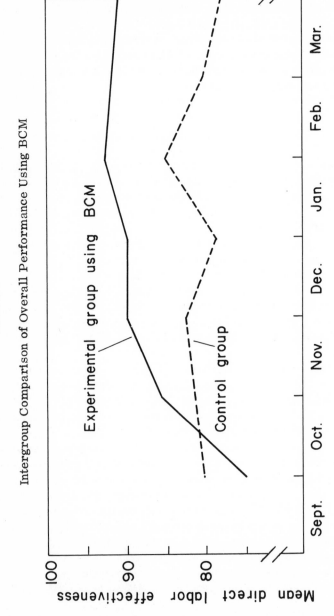

FIGURE 5

Intergroup Comparison of Overall Performance Using BCM

2. Baseline measures were obtained on target behavior. The frequency measures were accomplished with little difficulty.

3. A functional analysis was performed by the supervisors that determined actual and potential contingent consequences for positive control.

4. Making use of the functional analysis, the supervisors were able to design and generally successfully implement intervention strategies. Natural positive reinforcers were readily identified and contingently applied by the supervisors.

5. Both behavioral change and significant overall "bottom-line" results were achieved by first-line supervisors using a BCM approach.

PART

VI

**FLEXIBLE
WORKING
HOURS**

17

FLEXIBLE WORKING HOURS: THEORY AND CHANGE STRATEGY

Flexible working hours is an arrangement whereby employees have a degree of freedom in choosing the hours they will work each day. The idea of FWH was the brainchild of Christel Kammerer, a German management consultant, who first introduced the system in 1967 to the German aerospace company Messerschmitt-Bolkow-Blohm. Since then, this new way of organizing working hours has spread throughout the world, and if earlier estimates and trends (see, for instance, Stein, Cohen, and Gadon 1976; Elbing, Gadon, and Gordon 1975; and Donahue 1975) have been maintained, the number of companies now using the system is around 10,000. The theory behind FWH is unbelievably simple, yet in practice, it has turned out to be a potent way of improving productivity and the quality of work life. Whereas the other strategies discussed in this book improve the quality of life of the worker, principally within the work setting and only indirectly outside of work, FWH seems to have a direct effect on quality of life both inside and outside work.

The term flexible working hours is adopted here in preference to the many other terms used (for example, flexitime, variable working hours, and flexible time systems). This chapter discusses the theory behind FWH and presents a strategy for implementing it in organizations.

THEORETICAL FOUNDATION

It is something of a misnomer to speak of a theory of FWH. Unlike job restructuring, behavior modification, or the other strategies discussed in this book, there is little if any expressed theory underlying the widespread use of FWH. It would seem that whatever theory underpins this technique, it has been articulated in retrospect, after FWH was shown to be an ingenious solution to a number of organizational problems. For instance, problems arose each day at the headquarters of Messerschmitt-Bolkow-Blohm when employees, arriving simultaneously in their cars, created traffic congestion. There were long lines at the main gate and clocking-in points. Consequently, people tended to ease off working about 15 minutes prior to the official end of the day so that they could get a more favorable position in the line of traffic leaving the plant. Productivity and morale suffered. The solution to this problem was to stagger the starting and finishing times and to give employees a choice regarding the hours they worked. Certain limits were established, and people contracted to work a certain number of hours over an agreed period.

The element of choice or discretion regarding the use of one's time is at the heart of the theoretical basis of FWH. Thus, A. O. Elbing and his colleagues (1975, p. 51) explicitly locate FWH "within the general area of theory known as participative management." These writers make a number of distinctions between FWH and other participative systems that highlight its unique features and help explain its motivational significance. First, FWH appeals to the whole person and not only the individual as a worker. Other participative systems, such as job enrichment, permit additional autonomy only within the boundaries of the work situation, whereas FWH allows some discretion regarding the organization of one's family life, leisure activities, and other personal, nonwork matters. Second, FWH is not imposed on everyone whether they like it or not. The system is simply made available, and people can usually choose to make use of it or not. Employees are thus able to test it gradually and revert to normal working hours if they so wish. Third, as Elbing, Gadon, and Gordon (1975, p. 52) state: FWH "no longer violates or is necessarily in conflict with managerial and organizational value systems. When a system of flexible hours is initiated, management is not required to forego a significant part of its managerial philosophy." In other words, the content of participation is encapsulated or limited and does not impinge on most managerial matters. For this reason, FWH is less likely to be resisted by managers.

A final feature of FWH has to do with its physiological, rather than psychological, implications. Cass-Beggs and Emery (1965) reviewed research on fatigue and showed that there are considerable individual differences in fatigue curves. Furthermore, a particular individual's body rhythms may vary from one day to the next. The conclusions drawn by Cass-Beggs and Emery (1965, p. 258) were that

> workers are likely to perform better if they have facilities
> for getting drinks such as tea or coffee, and snacks or

sweets in-between-times at those intervals when they <u>as</u>
<u>individuals</u> need this "lift." That is to say, so far as re-
freshments are concerned, it can benefit production if each
worker is able to regenerate energies in accordance with
the requirements of his or her particular "fatigue curve."
The essential point is that self-regulation can mean that biologically,
as well as psychologically, a person will be more ready and able to
work. Such, in fact, is the case, as Elbing, Gadon, and Gordon (1975,
p. 53) report:

> Since personal rhythms vary, it is sensible to allow each
> person to decide for himself when he needs rest and change.
> One can also conclude that as a consequence of such an ar-
> rangement people approach work each time more ready for
> it. This proposition was recently confirmed by Wolfgang
> Hildebrandt at the University of Aachen. Taking two varia-
> bles, fixed hours and flexible hours, Hildebrandt found that
> under otherwise constant conditions, workers on a single
> repetitive task had a 17 percent greater physiological readi-
> ness for work when they controlled their own working time
> than when fixed hours were imposed.

In summary, FWH evolved as a solution to a particular problem. Its success can be explained by a number of distinctive features: its impact on the person's whole life, the choice it allows to
either take part in the system or not, its relatively restricted im-
pingement on management matters, and its biological underpinning.
FWH is based on sound motivational theory, both psychological and
biological.

Some writers (Baum and Young 1973, for instance) widen the
theoretical basis of FWH to include both societal and company needs,
as well as the above-mentioned individual needs. They describe several changes in the structure of modern life, such as population drift
toward urban centers; more concentrated locations of employment,
for example, in industrial centers; more use of the private car as a
means of transport; and more general acceptance of the right to attend dentists, doctors, family planners, and various welfare agencies
during working hours. All of these factors contribute to a developing
crisis:

> The situation demands a solution both in terms of society,
> the company and the individual. Society, because it cannot
> afford the resources to cope with the surges of humanity
> which take place at <u>work start</u> and <u>work finish</u> times. The

company, because it does not have the resources to cope
with employees' failure to adjust to the transport problem,
the individual metabolism problem, the workload problem,
and the employees' personal problems. The individual,
because he is an individual, not a cipher denied any discretion in how he should organize his working day to meet his
physiological, sociological and psychological needs, finds
himself in a constant state of tension and stress (Baum and
Young 1973, p. 15).

To understand the effect of FWH on a work force, it seems
necessary to include these wider organizational and societal issues.
The crisis mentioned by Baum and Young (1973) creates a general
readiness to accept the solution inherent in the system of FWH. We
would add, as a matter of interest, that its relevance does not extend
only to urban areas but also to agricultural communities, where FWH
would surely help to provide a structure that would allow small farmers to work their farms in tune with the seasons and, at the same tim
take up part-time employment. The problem of raising the incomes
of farmers with small holdings is a major headache in many countries

A STRATEGY FOR IMPLEMENTING
FLEXIBLE WORKING HOURS

As with other strategies discussed in this book, the relative
newness of FWH means that a fully articulated strategy has not been
produced and agreed upon by practitioners. The wisdom of several
authors is collated here, therefore, to produce a step-by-step strateg
for implementing a system of FWH. There are eight distinguishable
steps: (1) conduct a feasibility study and analyze the contingencies,
(2) appoint a project leader and form a steering committee, (3) define the operational features of the system, (4) choose the time-recording method, (5) inform all concerned, (6) conduct a trial and
evaluate it, (7) extend and standardize FWH or revert to the fixed
working day, and (8) evaluate the total project.

Feasibility Study and Analysis of Contingencies

This first step is suggested by Karen Legge (1974), who notes
that FWH has typically been sold to an organization on the basis of its
apparent success in other companies. She says that the tendency has
been to present (to an interested company) the advantages and disadvantages "as existing irrespective of the context in which the techniqu

is to operate" (p. 267). A contingency approach is advocated here, where each situation is examined systematically to ascertain the extent of constraints on the applicability of FWH.

Legge's analysis of contingencies takes account of four broad groups of variables: technology (with aspects of the product market as it affects work flow and job characteristics), labor markets, disputes and dispute procedures, and structural characteristics. An appropriate and inappropriate profile on these sets of variables is constructed, against which the company may compare itself. For example, under the technology heading, consideration would be given to the relative interdependence of jobs; where the jobs are highly independent, FWH would be more likely to apply, whereas the existence of highly interdependent jobs would obviously require much more standardized arrival at, and departure from, work. Similarly, FWH would tend to be more easily applied in situations where, for example, the work flow and work load are even, where there is no shift work, where there is low labor turnover, where there is a white collar work force, or where the services given to clients do not require the constant presence of a given number of employees. The opposites of each of these and the many other pertinent variables listed by Legge constitute indications against the use of FWH.

In a chapter entitled "Special Problems," Baum and Young (1973) cite numerous factors that ought to be included in an assessment of contingencies. Their discussion is much too detailed to present here, but under five headings—communications and servicing, the administrative function, the production function, occupational groups, and legal constraints—they address practical problems associated with customer relations and opening hours, communications between departments, manning the switchboard, cleaning, canteen facilities, overtime, batch production, resistance of white collar employees to time recording, absences on company business, supervisory cover, and the law regarding rest breaks. These same authors also raise a series of key questions regarding contingencies in a later section of their book (pp. 126-30).

The assessment of contingencies along the lines suggested by Legge (1974) and Baum and Young (1973) will give an indication as to the relative ease or difficulty of establishing the new system in a company. Furthermore, the analysis of contingencies will significantly influence the design of the particular scheme, and once the elements of the scheme and the extent of application have been gauged, the likely costs and benefits can be estimated. Legge (1974, pp. 277-79) offers a number of useful guidelines for the conduct of a cost benefit analysis of FWH.

Appoint Project Leader and Form
Steering Committee

Once top managers have satisfied themselves, by means of a feasibility study, that FWH would have more advantages and fewer disadvantages than other systems of work organization, there is need to appoint someone to act as project leader. This individual will need to have easy access to staff at all levels and will require the full support of management. The project leader should also be provided with a steering committee comprised of management and shop floor (union or nonunion) representatives. Line managers and supervisors from departments where FWH is contemplated should be well represented on the committee. One of the steering committee's functions is to assist the project leader in such matters as overcoming suspicion, ignorance, or resistance to FWH. The project leader will benefit from constant consultation with his committee.

Baum and Young (1973) list a number of tasks to be performed by the project leader and steering committee, including the compilation of information about FWH systems, the fostering of positive trade union involvement in the project, the selection of a time-recording method, and the definition of operational features of the system. The steering committee will continue to play an important role throughout subsequent stages of the project, at least until such time as the company's experiment with FWH has been evaluated and a decision has been taken to revert to the old system or continue with the new one. In some cases, it might well be advisable to assign the feasibility study to the project leader and steering committee.

Define the Operational Features of the System

The operational features of the FWH scheme are formulated with careful reference to the contingencies revealed by the feasibility study in order to arrive at the best system for the particular situation. Thorough consultation with all parties likely to be affected by the new system is strongly recommended. The following essential details must be specified:

1. the bandwidth
2. the flexible time
3. the core time
4. the contracted attendance hours
5. the size of credits and debits that are allowed to be carried over to the next settlement period
6. time off permitted during core time

7. the agreement regarding overtime
8. other absences
9. the time-recording method
10. the length and scope of the project and the arrangements for review

The bandwidth is the period between the earliest starting time and the latest finishing time allowed. It is usually easier to expand the bandwidth as the scheme progresses than to reduce it. To be on the safe side, it seems wise to begin with a relatively narrow bandwidth.

The distinction between a fixed working day and a typical flexible working day would be as follows: the fixed working day would simply run from 9:00 a.m. to 5:00 p.m., with a lunch break from 12:00 p.m. to 1:00 p.m. The flexible working day would allow people to arrive as early as 7:30 a.m. and to depart as late as 6:00 p.m. There might be a certain flexibility of lunch hour, for instance lunch might be taken between 11:30 a.m. and 2:00 p.m. Within such a flexible working day, there would always be a certain specified core time when everyone must be present. Core time would probably be 9:30 a.m. to 11:30 a.m. and 2:00 p.m. to 4:00 p.m. The flexible time periods would then be 7:30 a.m. to 9:30 a.m., 11:30 a.m. to 2:00 p.m., and 4:00 p.m. to 6:00 p.m.

The contracted attendance hours are the hours that a person has contracted to work during a given period—for instance, 8 hours per day, 40 hours per week, or 160 hours per month. Should an individual actually work more than the contracted attendance hours, he will have a credit; similarly, he will have a debit if he works less than the contracted hours. Most FWH systems permit a certain number of credit or debit hours to be carried over from one settlement period to the next—say, from one week to the next. Baum and Young (1973) suggest that a month is the most popular settlement period.

Let us say that a FWH scheme allows a carry-over balance of plus or minus six hours from one settlement period of a month to the next. A decision must then be made as to whether time off can be taken in lieu of credits during the flexible time bands, or during core time, or both. It increases the flexibility of the system to allow people with credits time off during core time or to allow time off during core time even for those individuals still in debit. Both options are considered advisable, providing the work does not suffer, the supervisor's approval is sought, and the total debit at the end of the settlement period is within the agreed limit, that is, six hours in this case. Thus, during the settlement period, an individual might be allowed to reach minus ten hours, or more, provided it is feasible to reduce this figure to minus six by the end of the month.

One of the most sensitive aspects of introducing FWH concerns the agreement regarding overtime, especially in situations where overtime is available on a regular basis. The issues that need to be addressed in detail are the following: (1) the new definition of what will constitute overtime—for example, overtime might be confined to work outside the total bandwidth or to work in excess of the contracted hours; and (2) the methods of paying for overtime—for instance, by a special rate of pay or by special time-increased credits. An employee might be allowed to choose the method of recompense, but clear limits would have to be established.

Absences during core time can occur for a variety of reasons other than those that are considered acceptable within the FWH scheme. For instance, someone may be away on a training course or on a business trip. Such kinds of absence occur quite frequently and need to be taken into account when the operational details of the system are being formulated.

Finally, the project leader, the steering committee, and others, such as trade union officials, should jointly define the scope of the FWH scheme. It is necessary to specify the people who will be affected, the length of the trial period, the methods for evaluating the trial, and the criteria to be used for deciding whether to extend the new system or revert to the fixed working day.

Choose a Method of Time Recording

A critical operational feature of any FWH system is the method of time recording. Accurate recording of hours worked is a basic requirement, and a variety of recording methods are available. Indeed, a number of entrepreneurs have developed special mechanical devices for use in FWH systems. One type consists of a main time clock that has a particular kind of card for recording starting and finishing times. A second type of mechanical recording system consists of a master clock to which individual meters or counters can be plugged in close to the individual's place of work, thus avoiding lining up and other problems associated with clocking in. These counters do not record starting and finishing times but simply the number of hours worked during a given settlement period. Computer-based systems are a third type to have been developed in recent years in response to the need for accurate and speedy time recording. A fourth mechanism, manual recording systems, involves keeping a record on a personal card. This latter method, more than the others, depends on the honesty of the individual employee. The other advantages and disadvantages of each type of recording technology are discussed by Baum and Young (1973) and Wade (1973).

Resistance to rigorous recording of time worked is common, especially among people who earlier have succeeded in having time clocks dispensed with. Once employees see, however, that the time recording is primarily a way of measuring time worked and not a control mechanism to catch latecomers and prevent early leaving, the resistance tends to evaporate. Nevertheless, the introduction of strict recording can be a source of considerable discontent, and the choice of the recording system and its introduction must be handled with great sensitivity.

Inform the Target Group

The people who are to take part in the FWH trial must be informed about the operational details of the new system. Because FWH typically involves a considerable departure from previous practice and perhaps the use of a new method of recording time at work, an opportunity must be provided for the subjects to voice their doubts and have queries answered thoroughly. Wade (1973) cites an example where over a three-week period, workers were invited to see the recording machinery and were told individually the benefits of FWH. Many other approaches could be adopted, such as sending complete details to each individual and then holding small group discussions or seminars to deal with questions and overcome resistance. It is worth stressing that whichever way people are informed, the essential thing is that it be done thoroughly.

Conduct the FWH Trial

Conducting a trial FWH scheme serves many purposes. First, the company or the employees affected by the scheme have the option of reverting to the old system if they find FWH unworkable or otherwise unsatisfactory. A second function served by the trial is that problems can be ironed out while the scheme is still operating on a small scale. Also, the trial period enables people to master the technicalities of the system through practice. Finally, the trial permits the project leader and the steering committee to try out a variety of questionnaires and other methods for measuring the effects of FWH.

The trial scheme, which typically lasts from two to six months, must be evaluated thoroughly to assess its effects on productivity, morale, and related dimensions. Equally important is the process of monitoring throughout the trial by the project leader, steering committee, and line management (see Wade 1973, p. 61). Some trial FWH schemes have involved the use of volunteer subjects, so extension to other areas may not always be as easy as mounting the trial.

Extend and Standardize FWH or Revert to the Fixed Working Day

FWH trials appear to be successful in most cases. In particular, the attitude surveys, which often form part of the trial scheme evaluation, have tended to reveal overwhelming support for FWH among the people affected by it. (See, for instance, Fields 1974.) Usually, therefore, FWH trials lead to the introduction of the system as a permanent feature of work or to its extension to additional departments of the company.

Elbing, Gadon, and Gordon (1975, p. 154) note that at the point of choosing to extend FWH or to go back to the old system, an interesting phenomenon is observable:

> The organization cannot go back. Experimenting with flexible hours is like stepping on a moving sidewalk—the organization just keeps going. In thousands of cases observed in Europe, the vast majority rapidly expanded the system throughout the organization regardless of the evaluation. Some organizations expanded even before the completion of this period.

Before implementation of the FWH program, it may be necessary to modify the scheme in the light of experience gained in the trial Such changes must be communicated fully to all concerned. Since certain departments or jobs may not be amenable to FWH because of technological or other constraints, an explanation as to why the scheme is not being extended to their work must be given.

Evaluate the Total Project

In most publications about FWH, considerable space is devoted to listing the advantages and disadvantages of the system. Legge (197 warns against uncritical use of lists of pros and cons. These lists are useful, however, in suggesting the dimensions that might profitably be monitored to evaluate the effects of FWH. The following list of criterion variables is extracted from a number of sources (Butteriss 1975; Bolton 1971; Swart 1974; Walker, Fletcher, and McLeod 1975; Elbing, Gadon, and Gordon 1975; and Baum and Young 1973).

1. Personal effects: Typical variables under this heading would be employee perceptions of balance between personal life and work, scope for leisure activities, freedom and self-sufficiency, ease/difficulty of traveling, job satisfaction, fairness regarding extra work, stress, safety, earnings, and attitude to the time-recording procedure.

2. Patterns of attendance: Dimensions that might be monitored in this category would be absenteeism, tardiness, turnover, arrival/departure patterns, credit/debit buildup, and presence/absence of staff at peak periods.

3. Attitude to work: Among the items in this grouping are sense of responsibility shown toward one's work, teamwork, grievance rates, honesty in using the system, motivational level, and attitudes of people who would not be included in the new scheme.

4. Boundary management—internal and external: Several of the advantages and disadvantages listed by the various authors consulted suggest this kind of subgrouping of variables. These include communications within the company, attendance at departmental meetings, and security.

5. Performance/productivity: Numerous variables mentioned can be subsumed under this heading, for instance, utilization of capital equipment, costs (for example, cost of time-recording equipment, cost of administering the scheme), quality of maintenance, quality of work, performance, overtime, and ease/difficulty of recruiting staff.

6. Effects on the community: Among the many items that could be evaluated in this subgrouping are leveling of peaks in demand for various services, such as transport, use of leisure facilities, and pattern of usage of health and social services.

It must be stressed that no single FWH scheme has ever been evaluated on even a small proportion of these variables. The list does, however, reveal the focus of attention of those who have attempted to cite the outcomes of FWH projects. The inclusion of community variables is perhaps unique to this particular strategy for improving productivity and the quality of work life.

SUMMARY

Flexible working hours was originally devised as an ingenious solution to a particular organizational problem. Later, its motivational significance was elaborated to include both psychological and physiological aspects. A new technology has been developed to meet the need for accurate and quick methods of time recording in FWH schemes. While the operational features of the system must be listed in detail, the system is essentially simply. Many successes and advantages of FWH have been claimed. A step-by-step strategy of implementation, including analysis of contingencies and thorough evaluation, has been presented here.

18

FLEXIBLE WORKING HOURS:
A REVIEW OF SIX
SELECTED EXPERIMENTS

The spread of flexible working hours throughout the industrialized world is occurring with remarkable speed. Already, there have been thousands of FWH schemes put into operation in Europe, the United States, and elsewhere. The reported evidence on the effects of FWH gives an overwhelming impression of success. In this chapter, the published reports of six FWH experiments are reviewed: (1) to ascertain precisely which organizational variables were changed and what outcomes occurred, (2) to assess the efficacy of FWH, (3) to summarize the contingencies on which the success of FWH depends, and (4) to note the various approaches to the implementation of FWH.

ACTION LEVERS AND THEIR EFFECTS

Table 8 reveals that the action levers manipulated in every case were the same. It would appear that whereas most other strategies adopt an eclectic approach—that is, changing every variable that might contribute to a successful outcome—FWH projects involve change on a clearly defined set of variables. The most striking change is on autonomy; people can choose, within certain boundaries, when to start and finish work. The technical/physical changes reported consisted of changes in the time-recording method and, more important, changes in the time boundaries of the job.

Although the published reports seldom made explicit reference to changes on other variables, such changes could readily be inferred from the texts. Thus, writers on FWH typically make only passing reference to the fact that FWH involves a change in interpersonal/group processes. It seems clear, however, from these writings that an essential feature of FWH is the increased communication and cooperation

TABLE 8

Flexible Working Hours: Contextual Variables and Action Levers and Their Effects

	Authors					
	Bolton, J. H., 1971	Cathey, P. J., 1973	Fields, C. J., 1974	Golembiewski, R., Yeager, S., Hilles, R., 1975	Wade, M., 1973	Willatt, N., 1973
Contextual variables						
Type of work	Scientific/technical, clerical/administrative	Manufacturing employees	Clerical	Scientific, research and development	Service/technology and engineering	Office staff including executives
Sex	Male/female	?	?	?	?	Male/female
Occupational status	White	Blue/white	White	White	White	White
Number treated	4,000	?	22	50	?	2,500
Unionized	Yes	Yes	No	Yes	Yes	Yes
Participation in change	Yes	Yes	?	?	Yes	Yes
Country	Germany	United States	United States	United States	Great Britain	Switzerland
Treatment took effect	Yes	Yes	Yes	Yes	Yes	Yes
Action levers						
Pay/reward systems	x	x	x	x	x	x
Autonomy/discretion	x	x	x	x	x	x
Support						
Training						
Organizational structure						
Technical/physical	x	x	x	x	x	x
Task variety						
Information feedback	x	x	x	x	x	x
Interpersonal/group process	x	x		x	x	x
Effects						
Costs				0		
Productivity	+	+	+	+	+	
Quality				+	+	
Withdrawal	-		-	-		-
Attitudes	+	+	+	+	+	+

Code: blank = not relevant; x = variable manipulated; ? = insufficient data; + = variable increased; - = variable decreased; and 0 = variable static.

Source: Compiled by the authors.

218

among co-workers that is required to ensure adequate manning and continuity. Similarly, FWH schemes necessarily involve continuous information/feedback to the individual regarding hours worked, debits and credits, and other details that enable him to control his subsequent working days. It may be noted that whereas most blue collar workers are used to having at least some of these details regarding their hours worked, white collar workers are not. In this context, one user of FWH has made the following interesting remarks: "Under the traditional arrangement, the boss was the one who could cheat. . . . Some of our managers, especially those who lamented over the hardship of having so often to work late, have been surprised to discover through keeping time sheets, how few hours overall they had been putting in" (Willatt 1973, p. 60). A third variable not expressly noted by the recorders of FWH experiments, and on which change occurred, was the pay/reward system. The modification of working hours involved at least some minor changes in forms of recompense for overtime.

Briefly, then, while the variables most purposely changed are autonomy and technical/physical, FWH also involves changes in other organizational variables. These other changes, such as interpersonal/ group process, have yet to be incorporated into statements of the theory underlying FWH.

The outcomes of FWH were the following: in all cases, an improvement in attitudes; in five out of six cases, an increase in productivity; a reduction in withdrawal (absenteeism or turnover) in four out of six cases; and a quality improvement in one case of the six. Insufficient data were given regarding costs, although most writers acknowledge that certain costs, such as the cost of time-recording machines or of extra light and heat (during the wider working band), were increased. A common experience appears to have been that the costs of administering the scheme were smaller than expected. Golembiewski, Yeager, and Hilles (1975) reported that there was no change in the cost of overtime or support services. Wade (1973) reported that, paradoxically, there was a need for more car parking space. Both Willatt (1973) and Bolton (1971) report some minor negative reaction to FWH from managers, but as the former noted, FWH has meant that bosses have had to become more conscious of the hours they spend actually working. Finally, a number of other outcomes were attributed to FWH in separate studies, including an improved climate in the organization and the fact that employees were in almost constant credit, that is, they tended to work more than the number of hours required in a given period rather than fewer hours.

Validity of the Performance Results

More weight can be attached to the validity of the performance findings than of the attitude results. That part of each study that focused on productivity typically employed a time series design with unobtrusive measures. Hence, the performance findings were subject to relatively few threats to internal validity. The most prevalent source of alternative explanations for the findings was history, which was a threat in all cases except one (Golembiewski, Yeager, and Hilles 1975), a study in which the research design included a comparison group. Instability was a probable threat in most studies, though insufficient information about statistical testing of results precludes a firm judgment about the prevalence of this threat. Mortality was judged to be a definite threat in one study and a probable threat in another. The time span of the experiment and the rate of labor turnover in each study was taken into account in assessing the degree of threat from mortality. This latter factor, turnover, also gave rise to the same frequency of threat from selection. The relationship between labor turnover and threats from mortality and selection is explained by Campbell and Stanley (1966, p. 44). Referring to the time series design, they say:

> Selection as a main source of effects is ruled out in both this design and in Design 2 (i.e., One-Group Pretest—Posttest Design), if the same specific persons are involved in all Os [observations]. If data from a group is basically collected in terms of individual group members, then mortality may be ruled out in this experiment as in Design 2. However, if the observations consist of collective products, then a record of the occurrence of absenteeism, quitting and replacement should be made to insure that coincidences of personal change do not provide plausible rival hypotheses.

Although threats from sources other than history were either nonexistent or at least doubtful, the likelihood of alternative explanations from history was so prevalent that the internal validity of the whole set of performance findings is seriously weakened. The possibility that the outcomes could have been caused by some occurrence other than the manipulation of the action levers represents a serious threat; thus, the reported results must be interpreted cautiously.

Validity of Quality of Work Life Results

Perhaps the weakest of all research designs, the "one-shot case study" (Campbell and Stanley 1966), was employed in five of the six cases reviewed. This form of study consists simply of a measureme after the manipulation of a variable. Thus, attitudes were assessed :

ter the introduction of the scheme, but not beforehand. Clearly, the reported improvements in attitude could have been caused by occurrences other than FWH, so history was a threat to internal validity in the five cases in question. Also, insofar as other threats to validity were relevant, the reported attitude changes were subject to these threats. In the one study (Golembiewski, Yeager, and Hilles 1975) that included a comparison group and took pretests and posttests, the only possible source of threat to internal validity was from selection, because control and experimental groups were not chosen randomly. While the results of this latter, well-designed study are consistent with the quality of work life findings of the other five experiments, the predominance of designs that render the findings subject to numerous threats to internal validity suggests that there is little scientific basis for claiming that FWH improves quality of work life.

CONTINGENCIES

Contingencies are those aspects of the situation, the population, the treatment variables, and measurements, which might limit the applicability of the results or moderate the effects of the action levers. In the previous chapter, the first step of the implementation strategy was defined as a systematic assessment of contingencies. Here, the contingencies revealed by an analysis of the studies' research designs, contextual variables, or noted by practitioners in the course of conducting FWH projects are summarized. Little distinction is made between contingencies that might apply to performance variables and those that might operate on attitudinal variables. None of the reports provide the type of information required for making such a distinction, although they say a good deal about contingencies in general.

Table 8 reveals that FWH has been successful in several different countries, in unionized companies, in both big and small organizations, among white collar workers, and in a wide variety of jobs—scientific, administrative, service, and manufacturing. More evidence is needed before a definite judgment can be offered regarding the suitability of FWH for blue collar employees in manufacturing jobs. Contrary to what many believe about the limited applicability of FWH to blue collar groups, however, Wade (1973) shows evidence of a successful scheme involving such a group in the furniture industry. More information is needed regarding possible differences in reaction to FWH from the two sexes.

Details regarding specific contingencies were contained in some of the reports. Golembiewski, Yeager, and Hilles (1975) show that employees at several levels of the organizational hierarchy respond equally favorably to FWH. Bolton (1971) reports that a higher propor-

tion of college graduates favored FWH than did nongraduates, although
the majority of the latter were in favor of the scheme. Walker, Fletch
and McLeod (1975) report that people of differing marital status and
family composition respond to different aspects and consequences of
FWH. Willatt (1973) found that FWH was not possible in the producti
as opposed to administrative and service areas; that management mu
be prepared to change their own time-keeping habits; that a self-
disciplined work force increases the likelihood of success; that a goo
internal and external climate helps; and that the presence of a neither
strong nor militant trade union made the introduction of the program
easier. There were no indications from the other studies, however,
that the trade unions were a hindrance. In fact, where they can protect their members' interests and, at the same time, influence the
design of FWH, success is apparently assured. Finally, some other
contingencies identified were legislation that prevented full use of FW
(Golembiewski, Yeager, and Hilles 1973) and people who relied on
company transport and could not vary their times who tended to see
no value in the scheme (Bolton 1971).

The assessments of the six studies' research designs throws
extra light on the matter of contingencies. It can be noted that the
achievement of performance improvements does not appear to depend
on prior sensitization by a testing or measurement procedure, becau
nonreactive measures were used. The need to inform people thoroughly about the scheme inevitably creates a threat to external validi
from experimental arrangements. Consequently, the success of FWI
in new situations may well require a deliberate effort to create a
feeling that something very significant or special is happening.

To summarize, experience with FWH has revealed a wide rang
of contingencies that need to be taken into account when designing a
FWH program. In the previous chapter, a comprehensive approach
to contingency assessment was outlined and advocated. The most
serious obstacles to the successful adoption of FWH appear to be tecl
nological and product related (for example, the need to provide a continuous service) rather than psychological or social in nature.

IMPLEMENTATION OF FLEXIBLE WORKING HOURS

In each of the six experiments reviewed, there is mention of
several elements of the implementation strategy described in the
previous chapter. Feasibility studies appear to have been carried
out, but not in the same degree of detail as advocated here. The
formation of a representative committee to supervise the project was
a feature of most cases. Trials or pilot experiments typically preceded full implementation of FWH, and a number of authors expressl

mentioned that the pilot scheme gave rise to certain modifications of subsequent extensions of the scheme. There is a suggestion in several cases, and in Fields (1974) explicit mention, of a strategy that consisted of starting with white collar workers and later extending the program to others. Fields also stresses the importance of close monitoring of the progress of the scheme. The methods used to inform the target group of the operational details of the project were not reported in any detail, but Willatt (1973) mentions a case where each individual was informed by a letter to his home address. Time-recording procedures varied widely, from trust and honor (that is, each individual keeping his own personal record) to varied types of mechanical recording. Finally, evaluation was done poorly. There was little evidence of careful planning of the evaluation at the outset of the experiments, except in one or two cases.

A matter receiving lengthy treatment in several studies is the involvement of trade unions. In general, it seems that after a period of caution, the unions take to the idea with considerable enthusiasm. Thus, for instance, Baum and Young (1973) report that in Germany, initial opposition from some unions gave way to conditional acceptance, partly because of demands from union members who wanted FWH. Baum and Young (1973) and Wade (1973) provide information on the evolution of the British Trade Union Council's attitude to the idea. The council's main concerns were to ensure that FWH did not reduce the take-home pay of members; that workers excluded from FWH, say on technical grounds, did not lose out; and that the introduction of FWH did not become an obstacle to reducing the overall number of working hours and working days. In other words, FWH seems acceptable on ideological grounds, but unions want a significant say in defining the ground rules and other operational details of the program. A detailed example of a company-union agreement is provided by Baum and Young (1973).

In several cases of FWH (for example, Wade 1973), the pilot study has been used in a way not often encountered in the implementation of other strategies. After a trial period, a formal attitude survey is conducted to assess reactions to the scheme and the results made public to generate further support for the project.

It is worth mentioning that a number of authors have discussed in detail how to install FWH. Bolton (1971) lists the topics that need to be covered during the initial discussions with staff representatives. The items for discussion include arguments in favor of FWH, definition of core time and flexible bands, overtime regulations, paid absences, the settlement period, debits and credits, and the method of time recording. Baum and Young (1973) have a particularly helpful chapter (chap. 4) dealing with the advantages and disadvantages of the various time-recording methods and machines that have been tried.

Finally, Wade (1973) provides a useful planning and implementation checklist that identifies the principal activities involved in the installa tion of FWH into a company.

SUMMARY

Flexible working hours involves a conscious effort to change the autonomy and technical/physical action levers. Changes also occur in interpersonal/group process, information/feedback, and, to a less extent, pay/reward systems. Typical effects of these changes are an increase in productivity, more favorable attitudes, reduction of absenteeism and turnover, and an indefinite effect on costs. The efficacy of the performance findings is considerably higher than that of the quality of work life results. A wide range of contingencies have been found to determine the precise nature and feasibility of FWH programs.

19

FLEXIBLE WORKING TIME
INSTALLED BY JOINT COMMITTEE:
PILKINGTON BROTHERS LTD.

Michael Wade

Cooperation and total commitment to the system at all levels from top management down have been the hallmarks of another British flexible working pioneer—Pilkington Brothers. Its scheme stemmed from the staff consultative committee at its research and development laboratories at Lathom in Lancashire.

The Lathom site, some 12 miles from the group's headquarters in St. Helens, is approached only through narrow country roads. So the staff suffered the same irritating traffic congestion problems that stimulated Messerschmitt-Bolkow-Blohm (MBB) to develop Gleitzeit (sliding time). Hearing of MBB's system, Manfred Landau, manager of Pilkington's chemistry department at Lathom, visited MBB and then reported his findings on the system to Lathom's staff consultative committee.

This committee consisted of Landau, plus the head of the services research department and six research workers. Six months after its initial decision to explore flexible working hours, a pilot scheme was implemented, in October 1971, which involved members of the service, technology, and engineering departments.

PILOT SCHEME

A steering committee was set up. The staff were involved from the very beginning. The system was explained to them, and a list of

Originally published in M. Wade, Flexible Working Hours in Practice (Eppings, Essex: Gower Press, 1973).

provisional rules was issued. The next step was a general meeting.
Virtually everyone there who was eligible for the pilot scheme voted
in favor, although individuals were allowed to opt out if they insisted.
    The Pilkington system is a much modified version of MBBs.
First, the rules of the scheme laid down four basic principles:

1. The work of the department must not suffer.
2. The staff concerned should not lose any previously enjoyed privi-
   leges.
3. The scheme should include volunteers only.
4. A department's participation should be contingent on its manager's
   approval.

    The hours of work are quite straightforward: a flexible starting
band between 7:00 a.m. and 9:00 a.m.; fixed hours of 9:00 a.m. to
12:00 p.m.; a flexible lunch break (one-half hour minimum, one and
one-half hours maximum) between 12:00 p.m. and 2:00 p.m.; fixed
hours between 2:00 p.m. and 4:00 p.m.; and a flexible finishing band
between 4:00 p.m. and 7:00 p.m.
    For the pilot scheme, and subsequently, arrangements were
made to provide extended cover for other essential services, such as
keys, library, and copying facilities. Sections were told to ensure
that wherever possible, where service work was concerned, cover
be provided for "normal" hours, that is, 8:30 a.m. to 5:00 p.m.

TIME RECORDING

    Time recording was regarded as essential, and the steering com-
mittee proposed a clock/clock-card system. This was agreed to by the
staff, the clock being seen not in the image of a watchdog but as a
standard, unbiased, and permanent means of time recording. The
clocks were sited as near as possible to the place of work.
    The clock cards, mounted in racks beside the clocks, also
served as in/out indicators (being transferred to the relevant racks
when an employee enters or leaves the building). At the end of each
week, they were collected, inspected for legibility, and passed to the
computer department.
    The subsequent printouts, showing time credits and debits, the
amount of sick leave, holidays taken, and so on, then went directly to
section heads for "display and distribution."

INSTRUCTIONS TO THE STAFF

    The guidelines laid down for the pilot scheme were extremely
comprehensive. They took into account credit leave, work off site,

other absences, overtime, holidays, and even forgetfulness. They can certainly aid other managements in British industry develop their own approach to FWH. They started by setting certain limits to flexibility:

Where the nature of the work done by a section means that cover has to be provided between 8:30 a.m. and 5:00 p.m. to deal with urgent work problems, it is the manager's responsibility to ensure that it is maintained.

Where staff form members of a team or section who depend on one another's presence for working efficiently, the members must agree on the monthly hours to be adopted by the team.

The increased safety risks should be borne in mind. Section heads must ensure that anyone doing work alone is capable of doing it safely, and that potentially dangerous work is only undertaken when others are on hand.

A credit or debit of up to 10 hours could be carried forward each month. The standard working day was seven and one-half hours. Normally any credit time in excess of 10 hours at the end of any four- or five-week accounting period was lost.

Accumulated credit time could be used in half- or one-day units —up to a maximum of six in an accounting period. But credit time could not be used to take off more than two consecutive halfdays (Fridays and Mondays being considered consecutive). When taking credit time in this way, as with holidays, the compulsory half-hour lunch break no longer applied. The halfday could start or finish at any time within the flexible lunch period.

One problem that the steering committee felt would cause some trouble—that of introducing the staff to clocking in and out—never materialized. But it was felt that a means of incorporating handwritten entries on clock cards was necessary to maintain a flexible and efficient scheme.

In line with this, a series of code numbers were drawn up to cover different absence situations. Code numbers were the following:

1. Used when absent for a half-day or longer for any reason other than carried-forward credit leave. Examples are business, conference, etc.

2. Used when taking a half-day from carried-forward credit leave. The code must be repeated if two successive half-days are taken for credit.

3. Used when payment is to be made for authorized overtime before 8:30 a.m., and must be accompanied by the department manager's signature.

4. As 3 above, for authorized overtime after 5:00 p.m.
5. Sickness.
6. Holiday.

Handwritten entries require authorization by the section head or department manager; in most cases, this can be verbal. The guidelines say:

> A handwritten entry may be inserted in the column for manual entries on the card. A time, in 24–hour notation, and a day should be written in under the time column with a brief explanation alongside. When the entry is being used to exclude a time period from the scheme—for example, for overtime for which payment is to be claimed—or to obtain a standard amount of credit time—for example, for holidays, sickness or time in lieu—an appropriate code and a day should be written in under the time column. In the latter case for the first entry a standard half–day (3.75 hours) will be credited during processing and this will be assumed to repeat until the next entry appears.
>
> Handwritten entries need not fit into chronological order as the computer program will be designed to sort the entries.

Work visits, conferences etc.

If the visit occurs within a work period, no action is needed beyond transferring the card from the "in" rack to the "out" rack on leaving and the reverse on returning.

If the visit extends beyond the beginning or end of a period, at the first opportunity the time should be written in, including if appropriate a lunch break.

If the visit extends to more than one day the appropriate code 1, giving credit for standard days of seven and one-half hours, should be written in and a written explanation added.

If the starting or finishing time falls outside the flexibile-hour limits and it can be justified then the full time spent should be entered on the card and that part falling outside the flexible limits, since it does not count towards credit time, will be transferred to a separate store during processing.

Authorized absences

Sickness, doctor, dentist, optician visit etc.

If the absence covers a full work period the appropriate code, 5, should be entered on the card either by the person concerned or his section head.

If the absence only covers part of a period the time 8:30 a.m. or 5:00 p.m., as appropriate, should be inserted in the normal column of the card.

Time in lieu

Where a department manager has authorized time in lieu for work done outside the flexible-hour limits the manual entries of time and day should be entered in the appropriate column. This should be initialed by the authorizing manager.

Overtime

Company regulations govern overtime payment for work done outside normal hours. When such work is specifically requested by a department manager and payment for overtime is being claimed then such time cannot form part of the flexible-hours scheme and the manual entry of the appropriate code 3 or 4, and day code should be used. This insertion must be supported by the authorizing manager's initials.

Holidays

If time is taken from the holiday entitlement the appropriate code 6 and day code should be entered.

Bank holidays

No action will be necessary. These will be allowed for automatically.

Day release

Where day release is given to attend a course the appropriate code 1 and day code should be entered, giving seven and one-half hours credit.

Forgetfulness

It is essential that there should be an even number of time entries on the card for each day for processing. Should one be missing through a lapse of memory it should be added at the first opportunity.

Finally, the guidelines to the pilot project gave all workers who participated the opportunity to opt out. Those who felt unable to participate could opt out, as could those who started the trial and felt unable to continue. In fact, no one did.

In the first week, the lunchtime flexible band was changed from one and one-half hours to two hours.

RESULTS OF THE TRIAL

The steering committee administered and monitored the pilot scheme throughout. It consisted of the manager of the chemistry department, plus the head of group services and some six to eight staff members. During the trial, it met each Monday to examine the previous week's cards for mistakes and inconsistencies, to assess whether modifications were necessary to the system, and to evaluate the administrative capability required.

It determined the effects of the system in three ways. It held informal individual or group discussions to probe the feelings of all workers participating in the pilot project. Next, it conducted an attitude survey (in February 1972). This showed 100 percent in favor of FWH, with 80 percent believing it increased morale, 52 percent that it increased responsible attitude among the staff, and 40 percent that it increased efficiency. Meetings were also held by the committee with section heads and department managers to discuss the effects of the system on work. Finally, statistical information on starting, finishing, and lunchtimes was collated at monthly intervals.

The average of results, October to February, proved to be very interesting. The average times of arrival were as follows:

Some 2 percent of staff clocked in in each 15 minute period between 7:00 a.m. and 7:45 a.m., 4 percent between 7:45 a.m. and 8:00 a.m., 10 percent between 8:00 a.m. and 8:15 a.m., 40 percent between 8:15 a.m. and 8:30 a.m. and another 40 percent between 8:30 a.m. and 8:45 a.m. Finally some 10 percent arrived between 8:45 a.m. and 9:00 a.m.

Departure times showed strange "peaks": 5 percent between 4:45 p.m. and 5:00 p.m.; 50 percent between 5:00 p.m. and 5:15 p.m. and 17.5 percent between 5:15 p.m. and 5:30 p.m.

The result of the "scatter" was that traffic congestion was definitely eased. But parking, perversely, proved more difficult. The committee noted, in an interim report, "the total involvement of Lathom with flexible working hours would increase car-parking requirements by up to 10 per cent."

The lunchtime statistics were also significant. The previous lunch break was one hour. With flexible working, a sizable percentage (54 percent) of staff voluntarily shortened the lunch break to 30 minutes—the minimum allowed. Only some 15 percent took advantage of a lunch break longer than an hour during the period.

With such positive results to productivity (much of Lathom's expensive capital equipment being more productive by being used over a longer period), the "experiment" was slowly extended, in three stages, over a period of six months. Some 365 employees are now included, and a current reappraisal could mean that all of the Lathom employees (another 200) would be working flexibly in the near future.

The steering committee believes the scheme it has developed is one of the most flexible in operation. But it is not imposing it in any department, as it feels that both staff and department managers must be in full agreement before it is installed. It is convinced that individuals are the best judges of how to pace themselves. The man doing the job is the one to say what time is likely to be wasted. Also, the man who is not pressed, rushed into missing breakfast, or subjected to a guilty conscience by being late is far more likely to really contribute to a team's performance.

Finally, it says, "Flexible working is something that will inevitably be adopted in the future, and management have the choice of leading towards a situation which they have helped to create, or being compelled to accept something not to their liking."

VII

THE SCANLON PLAN

20

THE SCANLON PLAN:
THEORY AND CHANGE STRATEGY

The Scanlon Plan takes its name from Joseph Scanlon, a charismatic Irish-American, who at one time or another was a boxer, a cost accountant, a steel worker, a union leader, and a lecturer at the Massachusetts Institute of Technology. As a union leader in a steel mill, Scanlon played a significant part in devising a formula for productivity improvement at a time, in the 1930s, when the company was faced with the prospect of closure. The basic idea was that management and workers should cooperate. Workers would contribute their knowledge of the production processes toward increasing efficiency, while management would share with the workers the financial fruits of any productivity gains. There is no definite Scanlon Plan, but the diverse applications can be identified as instances of the plan by the twin factors of company-wide participative mechanisms and a group bonus paid on the basis of productivity increases.

Unlike many of the other approaches discussed in this book, the Scanlon Plan did not spread rapidly or, after 40 years, very extensively. A recent estimate (Hill 1974) puts the number of companies in the United States using the plan at about 100—most of whom appear to be located in the Midwest. The reason for the relatively limited dissemination of the Scanlon Plan will become apparent in this chapter, as will its importance as a distinctive and fruitful approach to improving productivity and the quality of work life. The chapter is divided into two parts: theoretical formulation and operating features, and implementation process.

THEORETICAL FOUNDATION AND
OPERATING FEATURES

Philosophy and Motivational Basis of the Plan

Writers on the topic speak as much about the philosophy of the Scanlon Plan as they do about any theory. The philosophy can be simply stated: the average person is both able and willing to make important contributions to the solution of problems and to other activities normally considered the preserve of management. The fundamental premise of the Scanlon Plan is that genuine participation by the workers in regard to substantial matters is a good thing. The acceptance of this philosophy, which is quite at odds with traditional management beliefs, is a sine qua non for the success of the Scanlon Plan within a company. The details of the application may vary widely but it is the view of several authorities (for example, Schultz 1951; Lesieur and Puckett 1969) that unless this basic philosophy is accepted within a company, it makes little sense to pursue the plan any further.

As was the case with flexible working hours, the Scanlon Plan evolved initially as a creative and practical solution to a pressing problem, and any underlying theory was articulated only much later, by Smith and Gude (1971), for instance. An examination of the philosophy and of various applications of the plan reveal consistencies with several widely accepted propositions of motivational theory. For example, insofar as there is genuine participation, each worker can use his abilities more fully and experience some control over his work. Second, he can see clearly the outcomes of his contributions in the solution of problems and in concrete monetary terms. Another feature of the plan is that group cohesion and group motivation to achieve are fostered by the allocation of rewards on a group basis and by employee participation in the setting of group objectives. Thus the interpersonal competitiveness that can arise with individual incentive schemes is minimized. Fourth, according to Smith and Gude (1971, p. 917),

> Higher order needs, such as feeling a part of the organization, of being able to exercise a certain amount of control over the environment, and ultimately of seeking self-actualization, are more readily achieved in organizations which have adopted the Scanlon Plan, as supervisors support an atmosphere conducive to satisfaction of these needs.

A fifth motivational feature is that monetary rewards are tied directly to specified achievements—a contingency strongly advocated by beha-

vior modification theorists (Luthans and Kreitner 1975) and by writers
on incentive schemes in general (Fein 1976). Still another connection
between the Scanlon Plan and motivational theory is the fostering of
two-way communication, which, in turn, generates trust among various
groups within a company; also, the sharing of information, say about
costing or profit margins, enhances the competence of people at all
levels. A seventh motivational feature of the plan is the concern with
equity (Frost, Wakeley, and Ruh 1974); workers who see themselves
as sharing the fruits of productivity improvements in proportion to
their contribution feel that they have been treated fairly.

There are probably other points at which motivational theory
and the philosophy and practice of the Scanlon Plan converge. Suffice
it to say, however, that the starting point—namely, a strong belief
that each worker has within him resources that far transcend the immediate requirements of his job—gives rise to organizational practices and a climate that foster commitment and cooperation among
employees.

Participation Mechanisms

The philosophy and theory of participation are implemented by
establishing "production" committees and a "screening" committee.
There is a production committee for each functional unit or department, including staff departments. The members of this committee
are, ideally, the supervisor of the department and several people
from operative levels. Operative representatives are elected periodically by their peers, and the committee meets at least once a month.
The functions of the production committee are to

> process, refine, revise, and personally feed back the
> status of employee suggestions. In some cases, the pro-
> duction committee has the right to put a given suggestion
> into effect if (1) it is not a change which involves other de-
> partments and (2) it costs less than a given dollar amount
> (The National Commission on Productivity and Work Qual-
> ity 1975, p. 33).

Lesieur (1958, p. 46) describes the functions of this committee
as being "to discuss ways and means of eliminating waste, easier and
better ways of doing the job, the departmental schedules for that
month, and anything else that might pertain to the work going through
the department in that month." Where there is disagreement between
the parties regarding a suggestion, the suggestion cannot be thrown
out at this level but must go to the screening committee.

The screening committee usually comprises one-half management and one-half members elected from the production committees. According to a recent authority (the National Commission on Productivity and Work Quality 1975, p. 33): "Depending on the structure of a company, there may be a screening committee for each division rather than a suprascreening committee cutting across many divisions." The screening committee constitutes a higher-level body that has the function of supervising and coordinating the suggestions and activities of the production committees. Suggestions that might involve costs above the production-committee limit or which might have an effect on work outside a given department are analyzed and then accepted or rejected by the screening committee. More specific functions of this committee are cited by Ross and Jones (1972, p. 26) as "analyzing the previous month's bonus calculations, discussing and deciding on the disposition of any larger cost reduction suggestion and discussing any problems relating to the efficient utilization of resources, particularly between departments."

While the two types of committee have considerable power to consult people and make decisions, management always reserves the authority to accept or reject any suggestions. Also, it is not unusual to have formal union representation on both committees.

The distinctive features of the Scanlon suggestion system are worth noting, because it is generally acknowledged that this particular type of suggestion scheme is more effective than many other forms. The characteristics of the Scanlon-type scheme have been summarized as follows:

> 1) the plan focuses on the group rather than the individual, thus recognizing the fact that some suggestions affect many people or departments; 2) it may not create as many undesirable relationships between the suggestor and supervisor; 3) ownership of ideas decreases in importance; 4) there is more face-to-face discussion of the suggestions with the plan; and 5) the benefit credited to the plan is closer to the true value of the suggestion (Ross and Jones 1972, p. 26).

The Productivity Formula and Bonus

The third distinctive feature of the Scanlon Plan is a bonus paid to all participating employees in return for productivity increases. A ratio is established

> which measures in some historical period the relationship between total payroll in a particular productive unit and the

sales value of what was produced by that payroll. Once
this relationship has been established, for any one month
under the Plan when the labor costs are below this norm,
the difference between the norm payroll and the actual
payroll constitutes the bonus pool (Puckett 1968, p. 66).

In other words, a base line is established, and any improvements
above this produce the bonus pool. A simple example of the sales
value of production base ratio would be as follows:

$$\text{Base ratio} = \frac{\sum(\text{sales} - \text{returned goods} \pm \text{changes in inventory})}{\sum(\text{wages} + \text{vacations} + \text{insurance} + \text{pensions})}$$

The main advantage of such a simple formula is that it can be
readily understood by everyone. It may be noted, however, that "as
the members of the organization become aware and sophisticated in
comprehending and influencing those facts of life regarding production and their labor bill, serious consideration should be given to en-
larging the instrument or formula to include materials, supplies and
miscellaneous items such as utilities" (Frost, Wakeley, and Ruh
1974, p. 105). An additional and unavoidable complicating factor is
that the formula must be sufficiently flexible to account for changes
in product mix, market conditions, job design, technology, capital
investments, and other such factors. Clearly, then, there is no one
computational formula to fit every situation; each one must be tailor-
made. Detailed examples of productivity formulas may be found in
Ross and Jones (1972); Frost, Wakeley, and Ruh (1974); and in Chapter 22. Also, a recent article by Fein (1976) discusses the limita-
tions of the more common Scanlon Plan ratios and proposes some alternatives.

Any improvement in productivity within a given period (usually
a month) provides a "bonus pool." Frost, Wakeley, and Ruh (1974,
p. 14) list three conditions for equitable distribution of the bonus
pool:

(1) the company as a company and the employees as a total
group must receive fair share of the bonus pool; (2) part of
the bonus pool must be held in reserve to make up to the
company any deficit (negative bonus) that might occur in a
future month; (3) each individual member of the organization must receive a fair share of the pool.

The split made may vary from 50 to 50 to 0 to 100, favoring the employees. The most common split appears to be 25 percent to the company and 75 percent to the employees.

Normally, the full amount is not distributed at once; rather, a certain percentage is retained to reduce the need for frequent, month-to-month adjustments due to small changes in price, inventory, or some such contingency. Bonus payments, therefore, have some stability. At the end of the "Scanlon year," the reserve pool is split and distributed, according to an agreed procedure, as a year-end bonus. If it happens that at the end of the year there is a small deficit, the company may absorb it. If there is a large deficit, the formula will probably need fundamental examining and adjusting.

A significant aspect of the productivity formula and its use is the deepened understanding and trust that follow from the disclosure of information. Apart from focusing attention on the things that most affect productivity within each person's own area, there is a much greater awareness of other people's contribution to productivity.

To summarize, the breadth of the motivational basis of the plan and the variety of its practical implications for an organization are such that it makes more sense to view it as a form of organizational development or a different way of life in the organization than as another management technique. This conception of the Scanlon Plan is necessary if the implementation strategy described below is to be understood properly. A sequence of distinguishable steps will be specified, but in reality, the plan consists of "an ongoing experiment in trying to improve productivity by involving people in their total job" (Donnelly 1971, p. 10). It is not a once-off intervention but a developmental process involving certain distinctive structures, particularly the production and screening committees. As Frost, Wakeley, and Ruh (1974, p. 16) put it,

> The Equity and Participation mechanisms are ways of trying to implement the Scanlon Philosophy. . . . No two companies need have the same Scanlon Plan. What the companies share is some commitment to the philosophy, theory and broad management principles and some ways of implementing and testing the commitment every day against each day's reality.

IMPLEMENTATION PROCESS

The Scanlon Plan involves such a radically different management philosophy from that which prevails in business in general that it cannot be implemented in a simple step-by-step fashion. The Scanlon Plan implies a special quality of relationship between the company and its employees. It affects the total organization and not just a single department or section. In listing certain steps to implementation, therefore, the reader should remember that these are not discrete stages but rather overlapping and ongoing interventions. A company intending to adopt the Scanlon Plan would need to consider at least the following six stages: (1) creating a suitable climate; (2) conducting a feasibility study; (3) jointly specifying the operational details of the plan; (4) giving formal instruction about the plan; (5) implementing the plan; (6) evaluating the operation of the plan; and (7) further integrating the plan into the company's other organization development (OD) activities.

Create the Right Climate

Experience has shown that the Scanlon Plan cannot be grafted on to an organization where attitudes and practices are inconsistent with Scanlon philosophy. In a detailed study of an unsuccessful attempt to introduce this new form of organization, Gilson and Lefcowitz (1957, p. 296) cite among the factors that contributed to the failure that it was a situation where

> a basically autocratic management did not really want participation, and where the members of a weak union were unwilling to accept the responsibility inherent in participation . . . there was a lack of mutual trust and willingness to focus on production problems rather than each other's motivations. . . . Since most of the workers were primarily oriented to the outside, they had little motivation to participate fully in the operation of the plan or to accept the responsibility of participation (p. 295).

The outside orientation mentioned here was attributed to the many housewives in the work force who apparently focused more on their pay than on such psychological rewards as might derive from participation or worker solidarity.

These negative attitudes to power sharing and lack of trust may require years, rather than days or weeks, to overcome. J. F. Donnelly, whose company, Donnelly Mirrors, Inc., has a fully fledged Scanlon Plan in operation in its plants in Ireland and the United States, has offered a number of concrete suggestions about how a company can prepare the ground. He recommends a mixture of reading in applied behavioral science, team-building exercises, and sensitivity training. Donnelly (1971, p. 13) underlines the importance of starting with top management, saying, "We are not talking about a gimmick that someone can install by himself. The company has to change its relationship to its people. The company has to lead, it has to create the climate of trust. This is hard demanding work that needs the leadership and support of the top people of the company. " Relatively small-scale job restructuring projects, regular problem-solving (as distinct from gripe-handling) meetings, systematic appraisal, more promotions from within the company, and human relations training for supervisors are just some of the concrete interventions that migh usefully predate the formal introduction of a Scanlon Plan. Another precondition is that since the bonus is paid to each individual as a per centage of his salary, a fair salary structure must be in operation before the plan is introduced.

   During the period when an appropriate climate is being fostere the company can be doing its homework on the details of a productivit formula and the establishment of a base line. Ross and Jones (1972, p. 24) indicate that it typically takes a "comprehensive three-to-five year study to determine the most appropriate productivity measure." This analysis will involve the exploration of what Schultz and McKers (1973) refer to as the nature of the inputs and outputs, responsivenes to changes, the process of establishing norms on a monthly basis, and the testing of the use of this measure to reward performance.

   A third preparatory task is to select and train the people who are going to play a leadership role in implementation. The training schemes and other small-scale change projects suggested above will provide suitable experience for the people concerned and an opportuni to test their ability to win the trust of all parties.

Conduct a Feasibility Study

   It is necessary to assess the feasibility of a Scanlon-type participation and reward system. Assuming that the right climate and attitudes exist, certain additional factors need to be examined. In particular, two specified by Schultz and McKersie (1973, p. 142): "(1) It must be possible for employees in a given unit to exercise some control over a unit's performance; and (2) it must be possible to identify appropriate achieving units; in some instances this unit will need to be a very broad one. " The same writers, in an excellent example of a feasibility study, refer to a number of other items that determine the prospects of a payment-achievement-reward (PAR) system. The time lag between people's efforts to improve productivit and the resulting changes in output must not be too long; otherwise, people will have difficulty seeing the connection between the two. The achievements must be measurable in fairly precise terms. A certain degree of interdependence must exist among the various jobs in a given unit; thus, geographical separation might be an obstacle. Similarity of job design across the various groups embraced by the

scheme will help matters. There must be some scope for employees
to actually influence productivity; if productivity were almost entirely
determined by the technology, as in some process industries, for example, this would reduce the feasibility of a Scanlon Plan. The size
of the focal unit is also a limiting factor; Schultz and McKersie (1973)
cite an example of a unit comprising over 8,000 people, but they say
that difficulties can usually be expected once the number exceeds the
1,000 mark. Still another factor mentioned is the availability of alternative work if the plan leads to layoffs. The presence of an individual piece-rate pay system may be a major stumbling block, although Ross and Jones (1972) cite a case where such a system was
successfully embodied in a Scanlon Plan.

These and other such factors will determine the prospects of
participative mechanisms and a group productivity bonus scheme.
Should it be considered feasible to introduce some form of this general
type of scheme, these factors will have varying influences on the
shape of the plan. The number of committees, for instance, and the
type of information to be produced monthly will depend on such factors
as unit size, task interdependence, and responsiveness of productivity
to extra effort.

Jointly Specify the Operational Details of the Plan

The participative mechanisms and productivity bonus formula
must be specified in detail. Clearly, the specifics have to be worked
out in close consultation with all parties. Important items to be decided include: the number of committees, method of election to committees, the powers of committees, the method of computing productivity, and the procedure for distributing the bonus.

Since the proper measurement of performance is basic to the
success of the plan, the measurement system should meet certain
requirements, which are listed by Schultz and McKersie (1973, p.
146):

1. The measurement must be alive [that is, it must focus
on central problems, and ones which people can really in-
fluence]. . . . 2. The measure must cover the entire
achieving unit—and no more. . . . 3. The measurement
must be simple and expressed in units that are commonly
understood. . . . 4. The measure must be responsive
to variations in the quality of the job done. . . . 5. The
measures should be reasonably stable from period to period.

These same writers note that the measures that have been most successful are those that are based on the notion of controllable inputs per unit of output. They further recommend the generally accepted practice of keeping the measurement cycle short—that is, one month if possible. Finally, they note that the measure must embody certain administration safeguards that will ensure that the measurement will be adaptable to changing conditions, such as new technology or wide fluctuations in results from period to period.

The problems and procedures of establishing the mechanisms of participation and the equity system (that is, the productivity formula and method of distributing the bonus) have been specified by Frost, Wakeley, and Ruh (1974). The production and screening committees must be representative in that they must reflect the complexities of structure of the company, which might include, for instance, several shifts or a mixture of very large and very small departments, all of which would seek to have a voice. At committee meetings, difficulties can arise over the distinction between suggestions and grievances; therefore, it is necessary to define very clearly the standard that suggestions must meet for acceptance, namely, "economic merit and feasibility" (Frost, Wakeley, and Ruh 1974, p. 22). The practice to be followed in relation to disclosure of management salaries and the payment of established benefits, like sick pay, Christmas bonuses or holiday pay, needs to be formulated explicitly.

A particularly difficult problem stems from the resistance of some people to the inclusion of senior executives and others, like security people, office staff, or research and development people, whose efforts might appear to have little or no influence on productivity. Newly hired employees create a small problem, which has to do with their eligibility for bonus. Usually, this question is resolved either by specifying a particular period—for example, 30 or 60 days—at which they become eligible or else by granting the bonus on a gradually increasing basis over a similar period. The most difficult aspect of establishing the equity system, according to Frost and his co-authors (1974), is to assess the value of production, especially on a month-to-month basis. If the present accounting procedures and personnel are insufficient to this task, then they require strengthening. Finally there is a group of problems pertaining to the distribution of the gains from productivity improvement; determining factors will include the financial position of the company, investment plans, and the degree of stability in the business cycle of the company.

Briefly, then, this major step toward the introduction of the Scanlon Plan involves detailed specification of the participation mechanisms and the equity system: the technicalities of each raise, considerable operational difficulties pertaining to measurement, representation, flexibility, demonstrable fairness, and economic sense.

Apparently, these problems can be overcome wherever a good climate exists and the other necessary groundwork has been done.

Formal Instruction about the Plan

It can be assumed that if the preparatory work suggested above has been completed, there will be considerable awareness within the company of both the general spirit of the Scanlon Plan and certain of its operational features. This is not sufficient, however, to ensure smooth implementation. Hence, a fourth step is specified, which involves formal instruction regarding the details of the plan to all employees, including managers.

Here again, the unsuccessful case reported by Gilson and Lefcowitz (1957) is enlightening. Among the causes of failure, they specify inadequate explanation of the plan to workers as a contributory factor and they note that "even after several sessions the workers did not have an adequate grasp of the Plan's mechanisms and their role in it" (p. 295). Obviously, to ensure a thorough grasp of the plan by all participants, there must be a series of formal educational sessions. The company accountant will play a central role in these sessions, explaining the various calculations, the method for distributing the bonus pool, the purpose of the reserve pool, and so on.

A second educational task to be accomplished before the plan gets under way and during the early stages of its operation is the training of supervisors and line managers to conduct meetings successfully and, in particular, to handle the insecurity they will probably feel in the face of open and regular consultation on substantive matters. Schultz (1951, p. 209) says that one of the biggest obstacles to the success of the plan is "the initial loss of prestige and consequent opposition of middle and lower management people." For purposes of clarification, it may be useful to distinguish this formal educational phase from the continuing emphasis of the plan on learning and staff development. Several authorities have drawn attention to the educational or developmental spin-off from the operation of the plan.

Implementation

The previous steps constitute preparatory work for the actual implementation of the plan. It is recommended (Frost, Wakeley, and Ruh 1974) that the plan should start for everyone at the same time in order to prevent the formation of an apparent elite and to ensure a sense of fairness among all concerned. Another possible benefit of starting off everyone simultaneously is that the company can more readily cite a specific purpose for inaugurating the plan at that particular time. Such a purpose might be, for instance, "to survive the economic recession," and the hope would be to motivate people to cooperate in achieving this goal.

The production and screening committees should be in operation before, or at least not later than, the bonus scheme. A major defect in the unsuccessful case to which reference has already been made (Gilson and Lefcowitz 1957) was that the committees were not formed until five weeks after other aspects of the plan had been installed. Naturally, in these circumstances, people came to believe that they would receive bonuses without the trouble of the committees.

Several authorities stress that particular care must be taken to ensure that the committees function well in the early stages. The insecurity of management in the face of the openness and wide participation at meetings can result in unnecessary blocking of suggestions, rationalizations as to why suggestions may not work, and other such obstructive behavior. Another pitfall in the initial meetings is their tendency to degenerate into gripe sessions about matters that have little to do with productivity. If these defects in the quality of meetings are not dealt with, the whole plan may collapse; thus, close monitoring of progress and continuous coaching in how to handle meetings is essential. Also, participants can be reminded constantly that their function is confined to dealing with suggestions for improving productivity.

It follows that if complaints and grievances are not to be discussed at committee meetings, then the normal negotiating processes and structures must remain. Thus, the production and screening committees do not displace or replace bargaining between unions and management about wages, working conditions, and other such matters. Here, of course, lies one of the most noteworthy features of successful examples of the Scanlon Plan, namely, the fact that the two parties can cooperate so closely on improving productivity and yet retain their respective identities and stances in other, often contentious matters. The functions of the production and screening committees have already been mentioned, but it is worth emphasizing here the need to keep people closely informed about the progress of their suggestion. The motivational significance of communicating the progress of suggestions cannot be understated. Where suggestions are not going to be followed through, then a thorough explanation must be given. Management cannot let up on giving feedback and encouragement; otherwise, the stream of new ideas will dry up very quickly, as empirical evidence has shown. Ross and Jones (1972, p. 28) write:

A four year analysis of the labor-saving suggestion system also revealed some interesting facts. First, the number

of suggestions was related to the support and encouragement given the system by management. That is, when suggestions are encouraged and carefully followed up, the number of valuable suggestions increased.

Finally, the educational groundwork for the plan continues as
an essential feature of its operation. The structure and functioning
of the plan, per se, facilitates continuous learning about human relations and company operations. The accountant who was so essential
in communicating the intricacies of the productivity formula before
implementation retains a central role in producing and explaining
variations and adjustments.

Evaluation of the Operation of the Scanlon Plan

Most writings on the Scanlon Plan include reference to relatively formal evaluations of its operation. These evaluations are conducted in addition to the ongoing evaluation of suggestions and action
for improving productivity. The main purpose of the type of evaluation seems to be to explicate some aspect of the functioning of the
plan. For instance, the Ross and Jones (1972) study, already cited,
sought to test knowledge of the bonus computation among various types
of employee and to assess the relationship between this knowledge
and levels of productivity in various departments. They were also
able to elucidate some of the reasons for a slowdown in the flow of
suggestions.
    In another formal evaluation of the plan, R. B. Gray (1971)
investigated the effects of managerial style, redeployment of workers,
and nature of the work on the rate of suggestions and other indicators
of participation in the plan. His investigation also sought to determine the relationship between absenteeism and exposure to the plan.
Evaluations such as those mentioned here and the Gilson and Lefcowitz (1957) study, already extensively cited, are most instructive
to the companies in which the investigations were conducted and to
other companies operating the plan or contemplating its installation.
These companies are in the rather unique position of having their own
organization, Scanlon Plan Associates, to stimulate additional research on the topic and to disseminate, at conferences and by other
means, reports on various aspects of the plan. Useful summaries of
the research done to date are contained in the publication of the
National Commission on Productivity and Work Quality (1975) and in
Frost, Wakeley, and Ruh (1974).

Further Integration of the Plan into
the Company's Other OD Activities

In the first part of this chapter, Donnelly (1971) was quoted as saying that the Scanlon Plan constitutes a new way of life for an organization. Later, it was noted that the plan could not be successfully installed in a company that functioned according to values other than those embodied in the plan. It follows then that once a company has introduced this type of participative system, there must be a continui effort to integrate the plan with other OD and training activities. Co panies that operate a Scanlon Plan typically have a continuous progra of projects, like job enrichment, personal skills training, T-group training, training in the discipline of goal setting, survey feedback, team-building exercises, and so on. Obviously, these experiences and the experience of the Scanlon Plan are mutually enriching and sustaining. Together, they help to ensure that people will be sufficiently motivated to continue to devise ways of improving productivit

SUMMARY

The Scanlon Plan may not rank among the most extensively use strategies for improving productivity and quality of work life, but it certainly is one of the most comprehensive. It has more far-reachin implications for organizations than any of the other strategies discussed in this book, and this, perhaps more than any other factor, explains why so few companies have adopted it. There are three main elements to the plan: a philosophy of participation, a two-part participative structure, and a group bonus scheme based on productivity improvements. These cannot be installed in an organization without considerable preparation, in most cases extending over a number of years. Once an organization undertakes to install the plan success will depend chiefly on a deep-seated conviction on the part of management that this new way of life is the best way to conduct a business.

21

THE SCANLON PLAN:
A REVIEW OF EIGHT
SELECTED EXPERIMENTS

The Scanlon Plan consists of a strategy that facilitates organization-wide participation and a group bonus scheme tied to productivity increases. In practice, these two elements of the plan are typically reinforced by a wide range of behavioral interventions also intended to improve productivity and the quality of work life. This overlap, between the Scanlon Plan and other strategies, makes a review of its distinctive effects rather difficult. There is probably no need, however, to attempt sifting out the effects of the committees and bonus scheme from the effects of associated changes. It is more in keeping with the Scanlon philosophy to think of the plan as a new way of life, which can only succeed in an organization where there is commitment to building a climate of mutual respect and cooperation. That the plan has usually involved much more than a mechanical adoption of the participative structures and bonus system will be evident from this review of eight cases, which is divided into three sections: action levers and the validity of their effects, the contingencies upon which successful application of the plan may rest, and the implementation strategies used.

ACTION LEVERS AND THEIR EFFECTS

Such is the nature of the Scanlon Plan that it seems reasonable to assume that its implementation and operation over a period of years would ultimately involve the manipulation of almost all categories of action levers. Compared with the experiments reported in other chapters of this book, the Scanlon Plan projects were of very long duration: 20 years, 17 years, 14 years (two projects), 4 years, 3 years (two projects), and 1 year. The reports on Scanlon plans are, in most cases, very detailed, so no guesswork is required to ascertain precisely which variables were changed. The Lesieur and Puckett (1969) report on three cases is rather brief, however, but as the projects in question were of long duration (that is, 14 to 17 years), common sense dictated that Table 8 should specify the manipulation of certain variables—technical/physical and interpersonal/group process, for instance—not explicitly mentioned in the report. In the absence of the necessary information, no assumptions were made about the manipulation of organizational structure, because changes on this dimension would normally require a formal intervention not necessaril implied by a Scanlon Plan. Table 9 identifies the eight studies by author and lists contextual variables and action levers and their effects.

At the heart of the Scanlon Plan are changes in pay/reward system, autonomy/discretion, and information feedback; hence, these were changed in all eight projects. Apart from the Ross and Jones (1972) case, where a complicated individual productivity bonus was maintained, a group bonus scheme was implemented in all cases. Autonomy/discretion was increased formally through representation on the production and screening committees, and more informally, through day-to-day consultation on a wide variety of matters relating to productivity. Regular feedback on the financial performance of the organization and on the processing of suggestions was an integral feature of each case. One of the most fruitful sources of productivity improvements were modifications, both large and small, in the organization's technology; thus, Table 9 shows manipulation of the technical/physical lever in every instance. Consideration of the training dimension is complicated by the fact that the Scanlon Plan is, in its very operation, highly educational. In addition to this informal training, more formal sessions in the behavioral sciences and other topics were reported. The single instance in Table 9 where training is not cited (Ross and Jones 1972) represents a company that had no formal educational program about the plan. In six of the eight cases, the interpersonal/group process dimension was changed. It tends to follow from the group focus of the productivity bonus that teamwork and interpersonal contact increase, but in the Gilson and Lefcowitz (1957) case, a distinct lack of affiliation with one's fellow workers was reported. The individual piece rate in the Ross and Jones (1972) case presumably implies relatively little change on the interpersonal/group process variable. The action lever of support, which means the avail ability of assistance or backup expertise when required, was manipulated in every instance. Often, it was the company accountant who provided the support service, and in some cases (for example, Gray 1971), workers were shifted to more productive departments from relatively slack units. The shifting of workers to production bottlenecks meant an increase in task variety, which accounts for the citation of this dimension in the Gray (1971) and Gilson and Lefcowitz (1957) cases. This type of increased variety, incidentally, was not generally welcomed, unlike the variety that stemmed more from job enrichment, as in the Donnelly (1971) case. The only explicit reference to changes in organizational structure was in the Donnelly (1971) case, where interlocking work groups were installed. It is possible that similar types of intervention were made in some of the other seven projects but were simply not mentioned in the reports. The same possibility would also seem to apply to task variety.

One of the studies reviewed here was reported explicitly as an unsuccessful case (Gilson and Lefcowitz 1957), and another (Gray 1971) is a record of a Scanlon Plan that was abandoned after three years. On close reading, however, the former case was, in fact, quite successful, even though the group bonus scheme was dropped in favor of a return to an individual incentive scheme. As Gilson and Lefcowitz (1957, p. 296) write, "Nevertheless, the plan was instrumental in bringing the company out of the red and saving the workers' jobs, although the workers were not cognizant of this." The Gray case was unsuccessful in that the Scanlon Plan did not succeed in curing restrictive practices, reducing absenteeism, or improving the industrial relations climate. Furthermore, the strategy of redeploying workers from less to more productive units gave rise to much resentment regarding work loads. Conflicts arose between new groupings, and the increased task variety resulting from redeployment was not welcomed, often because some downgrading of a person's skill resulted from the move. So, while the plan did produce some improvements— in costs, productivity, turnover, and certain attitudes—it simultaneously gave rise to a new set of problems. The deterioration in quality recorded in the Gray case was attributed to faults in the technology. The improvement in withdrawal cited in Table 9 refers to a drop in labor turnover, while the deterioration refers to a slight increase in absenteeism, which, incidentally, was attributed to the switch from individual incentive system to a group bonus.

These relative failures of the Scanlon Plan are more than offset by the success of the other six cases. In all cases, costs were reduced, productivity increased, and attitudes improved. Quality improvements were reported in five of these six studies, and there were no data on withdrawal trends.

Validity of the Performance Findings

It has been indicated in this and the previous chapter that the Scanlon Plan typically consists of an ongoing process of change inter-

TABLE 9

The Scanlon Plan: Contextual Variables and Action Levers and Their Effects

Contextual variables*	Donnelly, J. F., 1971	Gilson, T. Q., Lefcowitz, M. J., 1957	Gray, R. B., 1971	Lesieur, F. G., Puckett, E. S. (a), 1969	Lesieur, F. G., Puckett, E. S. (b), 1969	Lesieur, F. G., Puckett, E. S. (c), 1969	Ross, T. L., Jones, G. M., 1972	The National Commission on Productivity and Work Quality, 1975
Type of work	Assembly/machinists	Making ceramics	Automobile body manufacture	Assembly/machinists	Production of pens	Production of glass/steel	Operatives in manufacturing	Paint manufacture
Sex	Male/female	Male/female	Male	Male	?	?	Male/female	?
Occupational status	Blue	Blue	Blue	Blue	Blue	Blue	Blue	Blue
Number treated	?	80	6,000	2,000	1,000	750	?	500
Unionized	Yes	Yes	Yes	Yes	Yes	Yes	?	Yes
Participation in change	Yes	Yes	Yes	Yes	Yes	Yes	?	Yes
Country	United States	United States	Scotland	United States	United States	United States	United States	United States
Treatment took effect	Yes	Partly	Yes	Yes	Yes	Yes	Yes	Yes

Action levers

	1	2	3	4	5	6	7	8
Pay/reward systems	x	x	x	x	x	x	x	x
Autonomy/discretion	x	x	x	x	x	x	x	x
Support	x	x	x	x	x	x	x	x
Training	x	x	x	x	x	x		x
Organizational Structure	x							
Technical/physical	x	x	x	x	x	x	x	x
Task variety	x	x	x					
Information feedback	x	x	x	x	x	x	x	x
Interpersonal group process	x	x	x	x	x	x	x	x
Effects								
Costs	−	−	−	−	−	−	−	−
Productivity	+	+	+	+	+	+	+	+
Quality	+	−	+	+	+	+	+	+
Withdrawal	0	+−						
Attitudes	+	+−	+	+	+	+	+	+

*As the Scanlon Plan typically embraces all the people, including executives and clerical staff, in a given unit, the contextual variables specified in this table refer to the predominant categories or types involved in each case.

Code: blank = not relevant; x = variable manipulated; ? = insufficient data; + = variable increased; − = variable decreased; 0 = variable static.

Source: Compiled by the authors.

spersed with systematic monitoring of performance. In terms of experimental design, this process can be seen as variation of the "equivalent time samples design" (Campbell and Stanley, 1966, p. 43), that is "a form of the time series experiment with the repeated introduction of the experimental variable." The performance findings of all eight studies were derived from this particular experimental design, and in some cases (that is, Donnelly 1971; Gray 1971; and the National Commission on Productivity and Work Quality 1975), this already "strong" design was further strengthened by the use of comparison groups. The method of measuring performance—namely, company records of productivity, costs, and quality—is typically unobtrusive, but at the same time, it must be noted that the operation of the Scanlon Plan makes people acutely aware of the whole process of measurement. In one sense, therefore, the measurements may have been unobtrusive, but in other important respects, they were not. On balance, especially given that after a year or two people would probably have come to see the constant measurement as an ordinary aspect of their work, it seems reasonable to judge that the results cannot be explained away as being caused by the process of measurement. In other words, there is no threat to internal validity from testing. Nor are there any threats from other sources. For instance history is ruled out because the pattern of improvements over several years could hardly be attributed to some extraneous event. Instability does not constitute a source of plausible rival explanations since it would be unreasonable to assume that the reported findings could be attributed to random fluctuations in measurement. The fact that more or less the same people would have been involved throughout long periods of the plan's operation rules out selection as a source of threat (see Campbell and Stanley 1966, p. 41). While instrumentation might well have changed over the duration of the various studies, the findings can hardly be refuted on this basis. Briefly, then, the claims made in the reports reviewed regarding the effects of the Scanlon Plan on performance seem valid.

Validity of the Quality of Work
Life Results

Six of the eight studies reported unqualified improvements in quality of work life, while the remaining two reported mixed results on this dimension. Throughout this book, the validity of quality of work life results has tended to be weaker than that of performance findings, largely because most of the research designs consisted of subjective or obtrusive attitude measures taken only after the intervention.

Of the studies under review here, two fall into this general category, although they are somewhat more complicated than the typical post hoc designs. The Gilson and Lefcowitz (1957) study and the Gray (1971) project both consist of attempts to explain failures of the Scanlon Plan. In each case, there are references to the state of attitudes before, during, and after the plan's operation, but the fact that this entire analysis took place after the whole event and involved subjective assessments renders the findings subject to as many threats to internal validity as the more simple post hoc designs (Campbell and Stanley 1966).

The research designs of five of the other six studies were, in most respects, similar to the two just mentioned, but with the important differences that they were of much longer duration and involved repeated Scanlon-type interventions over many years. There is no easy way to categorize this type of study, and the absence of a clear-cut design leaves much to one's own judgment. The authors take the view that these five studies (Donnelly 1971; Ross and Jones 1972; and the three of Lesieur and Puckett 1969) can be best thought of as crude examples of the equivalent time samples design referred to above. Presumably, these projects embodied some monitoring of attitudes to the various changes made, and the fact that the plan was successfully maintained over such a long time—from 12 to 20 years—suggests that attitudes toward it were favorable. To attribute these consistently positive attitudes to extraneous events or any of the other threats to internal validity seems hardly justifiable.

The single study to include, from the start, a conscious assessment of quality work life was that reported by the National Commission on Productivity and Work Quality (1975). A number of attitude scales were presented at three points in time, with the first measure being taken shortly before the plan was installed and the others at times during its three years of operation. Even though there were three sets of observations, the main findings appear to refer only to differences between two sets, which weakens the design somewhat. Thus, the internal validity of this particular study is subject to threats from history, instability, testing, and possibly regression.

To summarize, the validity of five of the quality of work life experiments is quite strong, while the conclusions of the other three are open to several rival explanations. Given this pattern of threats to the group of eight studies as a whole, it would seem that there are good, but not conclusive, grounds for claiming that the Scanlon Plan improves quality of work life.

CONTINGENCIES

Most of the studies reviewed contain useful information concerning factors upon which success of the Scanlon Plan may be contingent. The contextual details in Table 9 throw additional light on the matter of contingencies, as does an analysis of the research designs of the studies. Since none of these sources makes a distinction between contingencies pertaining to performance findings and those relating to quality of work life results, the discussion treats contingencies for both sets of results.

Certain characteristics of the work force have been found to inhibit or facilitate application of the Scanlon Plan. In the Gilson and Lefcowitz (1957) case, two groups of people, married women and immigrants, had loose ties with the factory—the former because they were secondary wage earners and the latter because they spoke little English. This absence of a sense of belonging and comradeship at work meant that there was poor attendance at committee meetings, little interest in being elected to committees, and bypassing of the local union when there was a problem. The lack of cohesiveness also meant that workers' representatives could not make even minor decisions on behalf of their fellows without consultation, with the result that there were long delays in processing complaints and suggestions. The same two writers and others, including Gray (1971), specify management attitudes as another contingency factor; the presence of authoritarian management is not conducive to success of the plan. The degree of insecurity among front-line supervisors also tends to be a stumbling block (the National Commission on Productivity and Work Quality 1975). It is clear from Table 9 that both men and women are amenable to the Scanlon Plan; indeed, Ross and Jones (1972) found them to be equally knowledgeable about the operational details. People of longer service and those more frequently elected to the committees tended to produce more productivity suggestions than corresponding groups, according to the same two authors. They also found that knowledge of the Scanlon Plan computations was not significantly related to the rate of suggestions. Other characteristics of the labor force identified as contingency variables were skill level—highly skilled people were more resistant to redeployment resulting from the plan for a variety of reasons, including erosion of pay differentials and downgrading of their skill (Gray 1971); the power of work groups to pursue their own narrow aspirations in the face of authority is another obstacle (Gray 1971); and finally, high labor turnover tends to militate against the success of the Scanlon Plan (Gilson and Lefcowitz 1957).

A second grouping of contingency factors has to do with the technology and organization of work. Again, the Gray (1971) case is most enlightening: changes in technology can create problems for the plan, but at the same time, changes produce scope for additional suggestions; jobs that are less rigidly structured and which give more scope for individual discretion are more conducive to the generation of productivity suggestions than restrictive types of work; and internal movement of staff to cope with bottlenecks can have undesirable side effects, such as resentment at downgrading of one's skill, increased work load, loss of earnings, and breaches of demarcation norms. The technology itself may produce conflicting interests and power blocks, which, of course, are inimical to the Scanlon Plan. As Gray (1971, p. 301) says, "The nature of operations helps decide . . . the degree of cohesion of the group and its ability to lay down and follow rational policies related to the nature and importance of its objectives." Another technical factor identified by Gray was where the technology causes quality problems, which, in turn, lowered the bonus earnings for the whole factory. Quality problems created by constant changing of product, as, for instance, when the company takes on small job lots, produce the same effect on earnings. A final item in this group of contingencies may be geographical separation of units involved in the same bonus scheme; Lesieur and Puckett (1969) cite a case where geographical separation did not, in fact, create any major problems for the plan.

A third grouping of contingencies that can be extracted from the eight reports consists of market and environmental factors. For instance, a steady demand for the company's product—as distinct from wild fluctuations in demand—is a facilitating factor (Gilson and Lefcowitz 1957). According to Donnelly (1971), public resentment toward inflation and foreign competition may help to mobilize workers to greater productivity. Gray (1971, p. 313) is more cautious on this topic: "This study suggests that increased cooperation will only occur if the common interest created by adversity does not contain even stronger elements of conflict, or if the order of worker needs [for job security, for instance] if favorable." Gray does suggest, however, that high unemployment in the surrounding area is conducive to lower labor turnover, which, in turn, helps stabilize work groups. There is more on the relationship between market trends and the functioning of the plan in the following chapter.

A fourth category of contingencies includes various aspects of the formula and pay systems. According to the National Commission on Productivity and Work Quality (1975), the presence of an individual incentive system in the organization represents a considerable obstacle to successful implementation; an equitable measure of performance may be impossible; and the performance norm may be difficult to adjust in response to changing circumstances. Any threat to pay differentials that might result from the plan would constitute a major obstacle to its success, as there must be demonstrable equity or fairness in comparison with other companies (Gray 1971). Gray also suggests that attempts to remove an individual incentive scheme may cause an increase in absenteeism, which reduces productivity automatically.

Table 9 provides additional information regarding contingencies. The footnote to the table makes it clear that all types of worker were embraced by the plan; nevertheless, the range of industries represented is relatively narrow. It remains to be seen whether or not service or process industries, for example, would be amenable to the Scanlon Plan. Schultz and McKersie (1973) have produced an excellent feasibility study for a process industry—an oil refinery—and they conclude that the plan would indeed work in this setting, but this has yet to be proven in practice. The major problem with process industries is that productivity depends less on people's efforts than it does, say, in manufacturing industries. Both men and women seem to take to the plan. Some doubts have been expressed regarding the practicability of committees and a group bonus scheme when the total number participating exceeds 1,000 (Schultz and McKersie 1973). The Gray (1971) case involved 6,000 workers and had to be abandoned, yet Schultz and McKersie (1973) quote a successful case involving 8,000 people. As regards unionization, there is no evidence to indicate whether or not the Scanlon approach is applicable to nonunionized companies, although there is evidence that it will not work properly where there is a weak union (Gilson and Lefcowitz 1957). Only a few countries are represented by the cases depicted in Table 9, but they are sufficiently different to suggest that the Scanlon Plan would work in a fairly wide variety of countries. The very nature of this strategy for improving productivity and the quality of life would seem to demand that people be allowed to participate in its design and implementation.

No experiment can be a success unless the treatment takes effect. In the Gilson and Lefcowitz (1957) case, where the plan had ultimately to be abandoned, the treatment only partly took effect, in the sense that people did not really want to get involved in the committees at any point.

Examination of the research designs of the experiments in the third source of information regarding contingencies. The only patently obtrusive pretest used in either the performance or attitudinal components of the experiments was the attitude questionnaire administered in the National Commission on Productivity and Work Quality (1975) case. Most other measures appear to have been drawn from ordinary company records and, as such, were probably unobtrusive. Subjects in the cases under review were not sensitized to the impending changes by the process of measurement, so prior sensitization is not a contingency factor. Put differently, testing/treatment interaction does not limit generalizability of the results. With regard to a second aspect of external validity, experimental arrangements, there is no way in which the plan could be introduced unobtrusively to a company. In fact, it would be against all the best principles and practice of the plan to attempt to do so; hence, it does not make much sense to consider whether or not experimental arrangements might constitute a contingency. Finally, the interaction of selection and treatment may well constitute a contingency; the organizations in each case were not randomly chosen from a given universe of organizations, so the basis of selection, of which we were told very little, would probably constitute factors on which success with the plan would be contingent.

IMPLEMENTATION OF THE SCANLON PLAN

The implementation strategy outlined in the previous chapter was almost entirely culled from references to strategy in the cases being critiqued here. These reports, which were exceptionally rich in information on contingencies, contained some additional points on implementation that are worth mentioning.

A company should not contemplate getting into the Scanlon Plan as an urgent solution to a problem, according to Gilson and Lefcowitz (1957). There is no quick way to install the plan. The same writers caution against raising too high expectations of bonus payments. There must be some prospect of a bonus but not of a bonanza. If no bonus can be paid during the early months, people will become disillusioned.

The technicalities of the Scanlon Plan are so great that most companies would need the assistance of external consultants during preparation and implementation. A critical preparatory task is to ensure wide support for the plan. Gray (1971) reported that extensive consultation took place until a clear majority agreed to go ahead, and in another case (the National Commission on Productivity and Work Quality 1975), a secret ballot was held after a trial period to assess support for the new system. It is not clear whether trials were conducted in every case.

The procedures for forming committees seemed to vary. In one case, employee members of the committees were appointed directly by the union rather than elected. In another case, the foreman or supervisor of a department was automatically appointed to the production committee of his department. Production committees met for ten minutes to one hour and screening committees for one to two hours per month in the project reported by the National Commission on Productivity and Work Quality (1975). Every effort should be made to ensure that high-caliber people are attracted to seek membership of the committees. It is imperative that committees stick rigidly to their main task of processing suggestions for productivity improvements and that committee meetings should not be used for pep talks or for raising grievances. There is evidence, however, that committees will have to accept the fact that during the first year or so, complaints that are unrelated to productivity may predominate over productivity suggestions.

The bonus formula invariably requires some readjustment, which might be done annually or periodically, depending on the technology, product mix, and other factors. Adjustments should be kept to a minimum, however, because frequent changes can undermine trust in management (the National Commission on Productivity and Work Quality 1975).

According to Ross and Jones (1972), it helps to maintain the flow of suggestions if those already put forward are quickly processed and implemented. There is evidence that the majority of suggestions can be processed within one month of submission.

SUMMARY

The Scanlon Plan is a comprehensive approach to improving productivity and the quality of work life, involving the manipulation of practically all action levers that might conceivably achieve these organizational goals. This review confirms that the plan is indeed efficacious in improving performance and that there are some grounds for accepting the claims made about its positive effects on quality of work life. A variety of contingencies, ranging from characteristics of the work force to environmental factors, were listed, and some points on implementation were added. In the chapter that follows, there is detailed illustration of many features of the plan discussed in general terms in this and the previous chapters.

THE SCANLON PLAN IN DESOTO, INC.

The National Commission on
Productivity and Work Quality

THE SCANLON PLAN: A DESCRIPTION

The plan is a company-wide incentive system made up of three basic elements. These are the philosophy of cooperation, a suggestion system designed to increase efficiency and reduce costs, and a formula to permit a bonus based on increases in productivity. Historically, the plan owes a debt to Joseph Scanlon, who never claimed authorship but became identified with it through his early efforts in union-management cooperation.

The Philosophy

Union-management cooperation is basic to the plan. Teamwork is promoted in the belief that the workers have information of value to share with management and that management, in turn, has information that will be shared with the workers. This sharing of knowledge provides the worker with the means to collaborate. Management leads, but workers actively participate.

The Formula

A base-line measure of productivity is necessary in order to pay bonuses out of any increase in productivity. Basic labor costs

---

Published here by courtesy of the National Commission on Productivity and Work Quality, Washington, D.C.

must be determined before installing the plan so that a ratio of labor costs to sales value of products produced can be formulated. The ratio is the relationship between total labor costs and the market value of goods and services produced as a result of labor.

$$\text{Base ratio} = \frac{\text{total personnel costs of items to be included}}{\text{sales} \pm \text{inventory changes}}$$
(finished and work-in-process inventories)

    The basic formula relates total personnel costs to the sales value of production. This relationship between the human resources cost and the value of production is <u>the normal ratio of labor to productivity</u>. Any increase in the denominator relative to the numerator represents an increase in productivity in excess of the base ratio. This increase is a bonus to be distributed to the participating payroll. Therefore, with the entire organization focusing its attention on this relationship of human resource investment to productivity, the formula encourages learning of more productive behavior in order to improve the base ratio.

The Suggestion System

    A committee structure is superimposed on the organization to facilitate communication, evaluation, and disposition of suggestions. Two kinds of committees are established. The production committees are formed in each working unit or department and consist of elected workers. The screening committees include management and elected members of production committees. The functions and authority of the production and screening committees differ from organization to organization.

PRODUCTIVITY OUTCOMES IN DESOTO PAINTS

    The range of average annual bonus from 1971 to 1974 is from slightly less than 4 percent to almost 11 percent (the average for all plants is 6 percent). This bonus is usually paid as a percent of pay earned in a given month. It should be remembered that it is organization-wide—that is, managers, clerical workers, technicians, and hourly employees are included.

    The monthly bonus range in DeSoto plants was 0 percent to 18 percent. That means that one plant in a highly productive period was able to provide a bonus of 18 percent to everyone based on each person's monthly pay plus overtime.

The many intangible benefits resulting from the plan are impressive and are treated in the body of the report. Tangible benefits in terms of productivity improvement are summarized in Exhibit 1.

Exhibit 1 reflects a cost-accounting analysis that has been performed in most of the plan plants. The figures are disguised, since the absolute values are privileged information. However, the percent increase in gallonage is accurate. Thus, one can readily see that while labor cost has gone up by 15 percent with the bonus, gallonage has increased by 41 percent.

Exhibit 1 presents figures for 1970, the last year of operation before the plan. The "actual" payroll with and without the bonus is shown on lines 1 and 2. The output measure of gallons produced in 1970 (line 3) was 15.9 million (approximate), and in 1973, it had increased to 19.5 million (approximate). No major changes in technology accompanied this increase. Lines 5, 12, and 13 are of critical interest. Labor cost per gallon with bonus was 15 percent greater than without it (line 5). A reduction of 115,646 hours worked is indicated (line 12). The production per hour for 1973 represents a 41 percent increase over 1970, and in 1972, the increase was 28 percent over 1970.

Care must be exercised in any measure of productivity, since output per man-hour can be influenced by many factors. Obviously, the plan is only one factor. Nevertheless, DeSoto management believes that the tangible benefits of the plan are measurable. Unfortunately, productivity also depends on demand. Thus, softening consumer markets, compounded by rapidly rising prices for raw materials, have hurt the productivity picture.

The large and rapid changes in prices for raw materials is a special issue associated with the productivity formula. Equity of the formula is disturbed. Management must adjust the ratio to keep it closely tied to true productivity. However, if the formula is constantly being changed, employee trust will diminish.

Another kind of problem DeSoto overcame is the mix in labor costs. As in many manufacturing concerns, some products are buy-outs—that is, much or all of a product is produced elsewhere and is only handled by DeSoto. Thus, the labor content in buy-outs is lower than produced products. Produced products have higher labor content.

Exhibit 2 illustrates the difference between a one- and two-ratio calculation.

Clearly, if the object of the formula is to reward cooperative efforts and true productivity, then equity for both management and workers is important. The worker must trust management's construction and calculation of the formula. On the other hand, manage-

EXHIBIT 1

Annual Comparison to Base Year for Completed Years, 1972 and 1973

(in dollars)

Line		1973	1972	1970	1970 with Payroll Adjusted to 1973 Rates	1970 with Payroll Adjusted to 1972 Rates
1.	Scanlon payroll without bonus	3,464,368	3,380,320	3,357,389	4,158,252	3,915,491
2.	Scanlon payroll with bonus	3,974,134	3,694,662	3,357,384	—	—
3.	Gallons produced	19,456,870	17,872,806	15,965,951	15,965,951	15,965,951
4.	Cost per gallon without bonus	37.9	40.1	44.7	55.4	51.1
5.	Cost per gallon with bonus	43.5	44.1	44.7	55.5	51.0
6.	Percent increase payroll	(+15)	(+10)			
7.	Budgeted Scanlon payroll without bonus	3,707,842	3,399,906			
8.	Budgeted Scanlon payroll with bonus	4,006,302	3,471,687			
9.	Budgeted gallons produced	19,655,638	14,831,194			
10.	Budgeted cost per gallon without bonus	40.3	48.7			
11.	Budgeted cost per gallon with bonus	43.5	49.8			
12.	Hours worked	676,515	684,845	792,161		
13.	Gallons per hour	57.1	51.8	40.5		
14.	Percent increase productivity	(+41)	(+28)			

Source: The National Commission on Productivity and Work Quality.

EXHIBIT 2

Ratio Calculations
(in dollars)

	Overall	Buy-out	Produced	Buy-out Produced
Production value	49,500,000	9,500,000	40,000,000	49,500,000
Allowed payroll				
Overall = 18%	8,910,000			
Buy-out = 4%		380,000		
Produced = 14%			6,600,000	
Actual payroll	7,000,000	390,000	5,600,000	7,000,000
Bonus	1,910,000	(10,000)	1,010,000	1,000,000

Difference between overall and buy-out plus produced = $910,000

Source: The National Commission on Productivity and Work
Quality.

ment must not feel that the formula is a "giveaway." Indeed, one of
management's concerns about the plan has been the efficacy of the
formula. It proves to be an empirical problem, answerable when
accounting data are assembled. Exhibit 2 demonstrates the accuracy
required in ratio calculation.

The value of production is $49.5 million. If one overall ratio
is used, then when actual payroll is less than the allowed payroll, a
surplus of $1.9 million results. This is the bonus pool. However,
since buy-outs reflect products with labor content already in them
(and paid for), the two-ratio approach separates this out from the
calculation. In fact, Exhibit 2 shows that the actual payroll was
greater than allowed. A deficit of $10,000 occurs. When the two
ratios are combined, the buy-out and the produced ratio provide a
bonus pool of $1 million to be distributed.

The purpose of the formula and its accurate formulation is
equity—a fair share for all. As put by Frost, Wakeley, and Ruh
(1974, p. 108):

If the employees decide favorably and the formula is arrived at from the historical accounting facts, then the
ratio is set at the most representative position consistent
with current market and production demands. The ratio
position is the best judgment for the equity of all employ-

ees. The ratio is subject to continuous study and evaluation to insure the optimal equity of everyone. If the ratio jeopardizes the company's fiscal and competitive position, the deficiency in equity for all is recognized and the ratio is appropriately modified. If the ratio severely disadvantages the employee investors, the inequality is clearly defined and the appropriate change is made.

THE SUGGESTION SYSTEM

Often overlooked and sometimes overstated, the suggestion system is the structure and process of the plan. There are no in-depth studies of this system. Therefore, understanding the characteristics of the system is the objective of this section.

The results of a longitudinal analysis of plants A and B are discussed. The study went beyond the trial period in both plants. Since all of the plants at the end of their first year voted to keep the plan "permanently," the suggestion system was a factor. The acceptance vote percentage was never less than 90 percent in any of the plants.

THE STRUCTURE

In the case of DeSoto, the plan was introduced by a consultant (Frederick G. Lesieur) who was highly skilled in this area. The three components of the plan are presented together, that is, the philosophy, the formula, and the suggestion system. If a secret ballot vote on the entire plan for a trial period is successful, the construction of the productivity formula and the installation of the suggestion system can be instituted for a trial period of one year.

Each department or functional area elects members to its own production committee. The foreman or supervisor of the department or area automatically becomes a member. Suggestions are solicited, reviewed, and evaluated by the production committee. Ground rules are established whereby the production committee can accept suggestions and implement them if they do not cost over a certain amount and do not affect other departments.

The screening committee is made up of 50 percent management and 50 percent elected representatives of the production committees. Its purpose is to deal with those suggestions that are beyond the scope of the production committees. Thus, suggestions involving significant expenditures or changes in methods across two or more departments must be reviewed by the screening committee. Also, when a difference of opinion exists in the production committee, the suggestion is sent to the screening committee for resolution. This is purportedly rare, and none of the DeSoto plants have experienced this to date. Production committees meet at least once a month. The screening committee meets monthly to evaluate suggestions and discuss the goals and progress of the company. As a part of that discussion, the productivity data are reviewed and the bonus (or lack of it) is announced. Minutes are kept for production committees and the screening committee. These minutes document the disposition of each suggestion and the accounting information supporting the productivity formula.

THE PROCESS

Whatever the organizational climate and managerial style, the process of group suggestion making involves the entire organization. It is of interest to note that rates of interaction increase: worker to worker, worker to supervisor, and worker to management. The content of these interactions is assumed to focus on productivity-related suggestions. The literature on the Scanlon Plan cites many outcomes that are held to be the results of this structure and process. In this section, evaluation can go a step further, with an analysis of the results of this process, that is, the behaviors themselves. Without hypothesizing about the various social-psychological processes that may be going on, the suggestions themselves are analyzed, and the reader can draw his own inferences. A management committee (consisting of the plant managers, the controller, and the personnel manager) was established in each plant to evaluate the suggestions. Especially helpful was the participation of the technical director of one plant. At the end of the analyses, the managers themselves were surprised at the results.

Each suggestion falls into one or more categories. The rating system permitted tallying multiple-category suggestions in their primary category. The categories in 1971 (the trial year for Plant A) are as follows: (1) irritants—that is, a suggestion that may have improved working conditions but not necessarily the quality or quantity of the product being manufactured; (2) quantity—the increase of number of units; (3) quality—the increase of the product value so that it will obtain a higher price or draw fewer complaints; and (4) cost reduction—the category most mentioned by plan experts. McKersie (1963) argued that workers would focus mostly on cost reduction, that is, methods to reduce waste, save raw materials, and conserve resources allocated for overhead costs.

The 91 different types of suggestions made during the first three months of 1971 involved the majority of the work force, clearly indicating that the installation of this type of suggestion system increases communication within an organization. The involvement is a result of refining, processing, deciding, and feeding back the disposition of suggestion making. In the first three months, irritations with work conditions dominated the suggestions. This is to be expected for two reasons: suggestion-making is a new activity, and common sources of ideas come from the irritants (the dissatisfiers that exist in the work environment); and time is required for the consultant, management, and the committee system to determine which suggestions can influence the bonus. As production committees can put some suggestions into immediate use, they are required to look at costs. An awareness of the true effect of a given suggestion occurs at this time, and priorities become established. This learning also helps to reduce the flow of suggestions, since productivity-producing suggestions are sought. Production committees become more critical over time. As the irritants were taken care of and as suggestions for quality, quantity, and cost were processed, the ideas appeared to dry up toward the end of 1971. Another factor in the rate of suggestion making is the ability of the organization to put into effect good suggestions. For example, when business conditions are not expanding, management is reluctant to make a capital investment on a worthy suggestion due to a slack economy. Also, economies of scale necessary to make suggestions profitable must exist. Holding up a suggestion feeds back to the suggester the information that future attempts at suggestion making have a reduced probability of being accepted. Thus, the suggestion system itself becomes a source of learning about how productivity works.

Overall, in 1971, 231 suggestions were made by 82 percent of the hourly and salaried personnel in Plant A.

The irritants category was subsequently changed to "NP" (not productivity related). The only reason for this change is that careful analysis indicates that most NP suggestions are related to safety rather than irritations with the work environment. All NP suggestions are accepted into the system as this is the philosophy of the plan. However, "not Scanlon" suggestions are referred to safety committees. Also, "not Scanlon" suggestions that may be grievances are dealt with outside the suggestion system. <u>Thus, whether unionized or not, plants A, B, C, and D do not circumvent grievance procedures with the plan.</u>

The main trend in the pattern of suggestions after the first year of operation is that quantity suggestions lead in 1972 and 1973, continuing the trend from 1971. The amount of productivity-related suggestions ranges from 53 percent to 65 percent. That is, summing quantity, quality, and cost suggestions, productivity-related suggestions are the dominant type of suggestion. NP suggestions are greater than quantity alone but not the sum of productivity-related suggestions. Careful analysis of actual suggestions answers one question raised in the plan literature: namely, periods of favorable economic activity, good markets, and so on co-vary with the type of suggestion made. That is, increased productivity focuses worker attention on how to increase quantity, improve quality, and reduce costs. Slack periods may show high rates of suggestion making, but productivity-related suggestions are harder to make and to implement. Here are two contrasting examples taken from the production committee minutes of Plant B.

Slack Period: "Have a bonus of $3.00 or $4.00 a week if you are not late or absent from work."

Disposition: Rejected. It is the employee's responsibility to work every day and arrive on time.

Busy Period: "Tanks D-61, 62, 67 and 70; install 2" valves on bottom of tanks for draining off materials. Understand this was approved the first year of Scanlon, but never completed."

Disposition: Accepted. S. will see that this is done over a period of time.

Slack period suggestions in mature plan organizations reflect search behavior by well-motivated employees. However, it is often unrealistic to expect useful suggestions. Problem-solving behavior requires problems that are immediate and implementable. Conversely, the busy period suggestion exemplifies the immediacy of this type of problem solving. In slack periods, it does not matter as much how quickly the tanks are turned around. However, when production picks up, the productivity-minded worker sees that a larger valve would increase quantity by speeding up drain time. Thus, one can see the interconnection between outside forces of demand and inside problem solving focused on problems of immediacy. Again, the most common productivity-related suggestion is in the quantity category.

One point raised about the structure of the suggestion system has been the amount of time spent on committee meetings. All four plants spend 1 to 2 hours per month in the screening committee—about 12 to 24 man-hours monthly. Production committees meet formally at least once a month for 10 minutes to 1 hour. They schedule their meetings at slow periods—about 24 man-hours per month for each plant. However, breaks, lunch periods, and even car pools are opportunities used for discussing suggestions. Many suggestions are made by groups. They are the culmination of much "pilot-testing" behavior.

How do group suggestion systems compare with individual suggestion systems? Group suggestion systems, such as the plan, are difficult to cost out. The measure employed is reflected in the productivity bonus formula. On the other hand, a formula of 10 percent of the estimated cost savings of a suggestion is applied to most individual suggestion systems. Firms can then point to an actual dollar amount of estimated money saved. For example, a six-year analysis of one firm's experience shows an estimated savings of $601,739 (Montana 1966). Although this is an attractive saving, plan exponents would expect a higher yield, because they argue that individual suggestion systems encourage withholding information. Short and Moore (1975) performed a multivariate analysis of some 200 U.S. firms with individual suggestion systems. Regardless of type of industry, type of suggestion system administration, or any other of some 70 variables the principal finding was that a strong norm seemed to govern the pay-out for suggestions. This lack of variability of suggestion award pay-outs, combined with low acceptance (less than 30 percent of eligibles ever participate), makes the organization-wide suggestion system stand out in marked contrast to the individual suggestion system.

The Scanlon Plan espouses cooperation, participation, and the sharing of information by both worker and management. Thus, the rates and patterns of suggestion making reported for plants A and B are indicative of plants C and D, as well as many other plan companies. Quality of suggestions is high, because the acceptance rate of productivity-related suggestions is higher than any individual suggestion system. Also, many suggestions are authored by groups of co-workers.

What, then, is the economic impact of the group suggestion system? From the experience with DeSoto, it is clear that many suggestions have modest economic impact. Nevertheless, each plant can point with pride to suggestions that have or may have a very high economic impact. Many of these quality suggestions again are group authored. This type of behavior rarely happens under individual suggestion systems. Again, the economic measure is perceived by all to be reflected in the productivity bonus formula.

INTANGIBLE BENEFITS

Whether the tangible benefits of the plan can be measured to the satisfaction of everyone is debatable. Intangible benefits have been reviewed by management of plants A, B, C, and D. Here is their synopsis after seven years of collective experience.

(1) Probably the most important intangible benefit is the
     feeling all employees have of actively participating in
     the management of their department and the plant.
(2) This gives the employee a mechanism to contribute
     ideas that are documented and receive consideration
     of the production committee within his department.
     Eventually a decision must be made on each sugges-
     tion. It cannot be allowed to die by his foreman or
     supervisor. At the same time, the worth of a sugges-
     tion is evaluated and often turned down by his fellow
     employees.
(3) Because of Scanlon, management receives a greater
     number of suggestions from all levels of employees.
     The Plan encourages employees to be more outspoken
     in advancing ideas.
(4) Many suggestions result in savings to management
     that are not directly related to productivity. Exam-
     ples are:
     (a) Helps develop employees at all levels.
     (b) Identifies employees with potential for work
          leader or supervisor positions.
     (c) Educates employees of the need to justify capital
          budget requests.
     (d) Where suggestions result in the addition of a cap-
          ital item, the employees have a greater interest
          in getting the unit operating faster or overcoming
          start-up difficulties.
     (e) Increase knowledge of total plant operations—not
          just a single department. This can contribute
          to a fresh approach to improving plant safety and
          housekeeping.
     (f) Knowledge of Scanlon teaches the reason for hold-
          ing the total plant labor force to a minimum.
     (g) A means of uniting two or more departments in a
          common project.
     (h) An important addition to the benefit program that
          might allow the firm to attract good employees
          compared to other plants in the area.

According to the plant manager of Plant B:

> Scanlon is an excellent means for management to meet and
> discuss plant problems and future plans with all employees.
> If used correctly it can force lines of communication, up
> and down, to remain open at all times. It is also a means

for management to meet and discuss points with problem employees.

To maintain momentum after the first year, each production committee should be working on a couple of management projects that are more complex than most individual suggestions. This interest by management will most likely continue to encourage the individual suggestions.

Most important to the continued success of the Scanlon Plan at any plant is the active support and participation by the manager and his staff. Leadership from this small group is essential to a worthwhile Scanlon Plan.

FEEDING THE SYSTEM

As already discussed, the number of suggestions can be expected to decline. At least two things are happening: irritations are vented as productivity-related suggestion-making behavior is learned; and the potential for continued suggestion making declines.

The wide use of accounting information plays an interesting role. The controller can visit with production committees and review data where high costs exist. The controller or cost accountant may have no knowledge of how to reduce those costs. By focusing problem-solving employees on that area, suggestions soon follow in the area of cost reduction.

DeSoto has also developed task forces to stimulate thought and suggestion making. This is similar to management by objectives. The task forces are formed at the departmental level and are given assignments. If the assignment is clear, the suggestion-making activity is long range. For example, analysis of downtime on fork lift trucks revealed that a fresh approach to preventive maintenance was needed. The maintenance task force determined, through suggestion making, which approaches were best.

Feeding the system requires good managers to manage better by sharing their concerns, thoughts, and information on which areas of production need attention. Clearly, it is a management style that permits this sort of sharing. However, it should be pointed out that Plant C had a change in plant managers. The plan installation began before the current manager took over. After the trial period, the new manager experienced no unusual problems of transition. Managerial succession and the plan appear to be complementary.

SOCIAL-PSYCHOLOGICAL OUTCOMES OF THE PLAN

These outcomes were studied intensively only in Plant A. The attitudinal data were collected over three different time periods during an 11-month period from October 1971 to August 1972.

At time one, 145 employees were contacted; 98 percent agreed to participate in the before measurement. This group included managers, clerical, and blue collar personnel but not the sales force, as they were outside the domain of the plan.

At time two, each individual was contacted again after the plan was introduced but before any bonus was announced. Three months elapsed between time one and time two. Six individuals declined to participate, and 17 were unavailable due to separation, illness, vacation, or military leave. This left 119 in the experimental group.

Finally, time three measures were intended to assess the amount of learning based on communication and experience with the plan. Uniform questions with standard rating scales were carefully administered in face-to-face interviews. Comparisons of times one, two, and three use each individual's scores as his or her own control. That is, any increase or decrease in learning about the plan or attitude is measured by subtracting each person's score from his previous score on the same variable.

SATISFACTION VERSUS DISSATISFACTION

Overall, the entire population of Plant A reflected high levels of general satisfaction. For example, over 90 percent expressed satisfaction with their employer "compared to most they know of." For the blue collar group (the main population for suggestion making), 77 percent were satisfied with job security and 74 percent were satisfied with their pay. However, at time one, there was some general dissatisfaction in interest in the job, feeling of accomplishment, opportunity for being informed, and opportunity for participation.

Whereas many plan studies reveal initial low levels of satisfaction (including outright dissension—see Schultz 1951), this population apparently reflected little room for improvement. The question at time one seemed to be whether or not a "healthy" organization could derive any benefit from the plan.

At time three, the blue collar group increased their satisfaction scores. Interest in the job was higher, as was the feeling of accomplishment. Both scores for opportunity for being informed and for participation increased at time three.

It has been noted in the Scanlon Plan literature that a specific social and psychological outcome of the plan is the change in cooperation, participation, and communication—in other words, the nonbonus outcomes. Many experts have cited that the plan produces or enhance coordination and teamwork (Scanlon 1949; Lesieur 1958; McKersie 1963; and Frost, Wakeley, and Ruh 1974).

Opinions and attitudes about these social and psychological outcomes were elicited at times two and three. Managers were very optimisitc that participation might increase at time two (some 90 percen At time three, all managers were optimistic that participation had increased.

In the area of communication, 79 percent of the managers believed it might improve. After eight months of the plan (at time three), 93 percent of the managers felt communication had improved. In the area of cooperation, managers were less optimistic. Roughly 75 percent believed it would be better under the plan, and that percentage remained the same at time three.

Blue collar workers were conservative in their belief that participation would increase at time two. After eight months' experience however, 82 percent perceived that participation had increased. Some 65 percent believed that communication (both within departments and between departments) would improve with the plan. This perception increased only slightly at time three, when 72 percent perceived that communication had improved. In the area of cooperation, slightly more than half (53 percent) of the blue collar workers believed that cooperation would be better under the plan. After eight months, 71 percent perceived that cooperation was better.

It is worthwhile to contrast the two groups. Managers were higher in their perceptions that the plan would indeed improve participation, communication, and cooperation. Although the blue collar group may have been more conservative in their opinions about these factors, their net change is in a positive direction. It is significant that across the three measures, better than 70 percent perceived these nonbonus factors as outcomes of the plan.

Thus, net changes, spanning an eight-month experience with the plan, are generally impressive. Could these nonbonus outcomes keep improving? At time three, this question was asked. The majority of the managers and the blue collar workers agreed that participation, communication, and cooperation could continue to increase. The new organizational climate was one of acceptance and optimism. Indeed, overall levels of trust and satisfaction were high. Also, the outcome measures of participation, communication, and cooperation were at high levels. Oftentimes, incentive plans or organizational innovations increased productivity for the short run. One criticism is that increased output was caused by the Hawthorne effect (change caused by creating attention rather than the planned reason for change). Only time will tell; however, Plant A embarks on its fifth year with the plan and enthusiasm is still high.

CONCLUSIONS AND RECOMMENDATIONS

Productivity across four DeSoto plants appears to be enhanced by the plan. The bonus formula, which measures productivity, shows an average payroll bonus of 6 percent. When this result is combined with a careful accounting of units of output, labor cost, and hours worked, the gains to productivity are high—as high as 41 percent.

Construction of the formula raises special problems of employing sufficient techniques to maintain equity and mutual trust. Ross (1975) offered the most comprehensive formula model compared to simple one-ratio formulas. The decision to use a simple rather than a comprehensive formula depends on the complexity of the organization and how important worker understanding of the formula is to management.

The analysis of the suggestion system reveals that irritants with the working environment can be expected as a common source of suggestions. As learning occurs, productivity-related suggestions dominate—especially those focusing on quantity. However, suggestion-making behavior is affected by productivity itself. Slack period suggestions reflect ideas not associated with productivity. Feeding the system with accounting and technical information is especially helpful in overcoming this slack.

Job satisfaction, as measured, increased from already high levels. After nine months' experience with the plan, probably as a function of the bonus, feelings about increased responsibilities and involvement with work increased also. Costs associated with operating the plan, such as time spent in meetings, appear to be outweighed by the benefits, both tangible and intangible.

Indeed, the benefits of the plan appear to be the reason it has remained viable through the years. It could be that the times are catching up to the plan. As the quality of the labor force consistently improves, industrial culture is now more conducive to this form of sharing benefits from productivity improvement.

There are a number of key considerations of which decision makers should be aware in the installation and maintenance of the plan. Based on available knowledge and the results of this multiplant evaluation, the following recommendations are made:

1. Key people in managerial and working ranks who understand the formula act as filters of trust for others in the organization. Key people must be identified and exposed to the mechanics of the formula very early in its formulation or installation. Good distribution and circulation of these individuals enhance acceptance of the plan.

2. Complaints or dissatisfiers (hygiene factors) are the most likely type of suggestion to be received. Managers must anticipate

these nonproductive suggestions in a way to (a) instruct production committees that the nonproductive suggestions will not influence the bonus and (b) deal with the substance of the nonproductive suggestions by encouraging union leadership to handle them. If there is no union, then management must deal with the nonproductive suggestions on a basis that is perceived to be outside the plan. If some of these nonproductive suggestions should be processed as suggestions, that is, accepted and implemented, they should be reviewed later as nonproductive suggestions and be processed (in terms of policy) outside the plan.

3. Another issue is the decline of suggestions over time. All organizational leaders should prepare for this decline. Managers must seek opportunities to "feed the system" and direct efforts toward new areas. One role in the organization most suited for this task is the controller or chief cost accountant. By participating in production committee meetings, he can indicate high-cost services or operations, inform the committee of apparent redundancies in services or operations, or point out cyclical costs with the objective of smoothing the production processes.

4. Front-line supervisors may feel threatened by new types of participation and high rates of suggestions from their departments (including grievances). Managers and consultants must work with the supervisors by counseling and reassuring them. There may be some turnover at this level of supervision. However, the suggestion system also serves to identify promotable individuals and can assist in solving this problem.

5. Information must be provided so that an individual has a clear picture of the relationship between behaviors and rewards. The committee meetings should be utilized to transmit this information.

6. Since individuals differ in the ability to process information about a new reward system, it is often necessary to individualize the communication. That is, the communication must be tailored to the ability of the employee to receive the information. Again, the committee system can facilitate this end.

7. All too frequently, the plan is presented as a structure or formula that will produce greater cooperation and productivity. This emphasis ignores the process of participation in favor of the structure. Basic human values and attitudes about work, co-workers, the organization, and our economic system are at stake. There is no substitute for organizational policies built on trust and mutual dependence. The process of participation can be enhanced by supportive training in interpersonal skills for all members of the organization. This type of training helps smooth the process of group interaction so central to the plan's success.

REFERENCES

Frost, C. F., J. H. Wakeley, and R. A. Ruh. The Scanlon Plan
    for Organization Development: Identity, Participation, and
    Equity. East Lansing: Michigan State University Press, 1974.

Lesieur, F. G., ed. The Scanlon Plan: A Frontier in Labor-Man-
    agement Cooperation. Cambridge, Mass.: MIT Press, 1958.

McKersie, R. B. "Wage Payment Methods of the Future." British
    Journal of Industrial Relations 1 (June 1963): 191–212.

Montana, J. "Managing an Effective Suggestion System." Adminis-
    trative Management 27 (October 1966): 38–45.

Ross, T. L. "Measurement under the Scanlon Plan and Other Produc-
    tivity Incentive Plans." Mimeographed. Bowling Green, Ohio:
    Bowling Green State University, 1975.

Scanlon, J. N. "Talk on Union Management Relations." Proceedings
    on Conference on Productivity. Madison: Industrial Relations
    Center, University of Wisconsin, 1949.

Schultz, G. P. "Worker Participation on Production Problems: A
    Discussion of Experience with the 'Scanlon Plan.'" Personnel
    28 (November 1951): 201–11.

Short, J., and B. E. Moore. "Preliminary Findings of a Multivariate
    Analysis of Suggestion System's Impact on Productivity." Mimeo-
    graphed. Austin: Graduate School of Business, University of
    Texas, 1975.

23

The strategies reviewed in this book represent a variety of approaches for improving work. The different experiments, when taken as a whole, portray a broad array of organizational changes for increasing workers' productivity and quality of work life. Examination of the review's findings leads to three major conclusions. First, different combinations of action levers, when changed according to particular theories and implementation strategies, seem to produce positive results. Although the efficacy of the findings is less than ideal, there is sufficient evidence to attest to the validity of the different approaches. Second, the existence of contingencies, those factors upon which positive outcomes are dependent, appears to be pervasive. This suggests that the organizational setting—its technology, environment, and characteristics of workers—must be taken into account if change programs are to be successful. Finally, the method of implementing the change strategy is critical if the action levers are to be changed as intended. Such factors as organizational climate, managerial and workers' support, and preliminary diagnosis seem to affect the course of the change program. Given these conclusions, what can be said about improving work in a specific organization? In other words, what do the different strategies suggest about managing organizational change to increase both productivity and worker fulfillment?

A primary theme running through most of the experiments is the inherent uncertainty in conducting work-improvement programs. Whether one is concerned with such complex approaches as organization-wide change and Scanlon plans or relatively simple strategies, such as flexible working hours and individual job restructuring, an underlying message is the inability to foresee all possible factors that may affect the change program. Indeed, a cursory examination of contingencies points to a multitude of variables that may limit the most thought-out approaches to organizational change. Given this relative uncertainty, answers to the above questions do not fall within a tightly defined calculus that would inform experimenters precisely what to do in a specific situation. Rather, the body of knowledge reviewed here suggests a more experimental method of work improvement (an appreciation for organizational change as a rational yet unpredictable process). This chapter discusses the need for an experimental approach to work improvement, a strategy appropriate to experimental change, and guidelines for managing change effectively in organizations.

THE NEED FOR AN EXPERIMENTAL
APPROACH TO CHANGE

Application of the strategies discussed in this book raises the issue of how to make general prescriptions for work-improvement responsive to specific situations. The current state of knowledge in this field presents a number of problems for experimenters who want to formulate change programs appropriate to their organizations. Foremost among these difficulties is the fact that there is not a complete and valid set of empirical knowledge needed for strategy development. When the different approaches are assessed in terms of the three kinds of information required for strategy formulation—action levers, contingencies, and change processes—the results suggest that there is sufficient understanding of action levers and their effects. Knowledge of contingencies, however, provides only a preliminary list of those factors limiting the general applicability of results, while information about change processes is at best anecdotal, with few serious attempts to study organizational change systematically. Lack of complete knowledge about contingencies and change processes makes it difficult to specify precisely under what conditions a particular strategy is likely to be successful or to know how to carry out a change program effectively. Without such understanding, it is difficult to devise a work-improvement program assured of success in a particular context.

Another problem raised by the review's findings is the assumption that the strategies are generally applicable across organizations. The results on contingencies, tentative though they may be, argue strongly against this belief. Although many of the approaches to work improvement seem relatively robust in their generalizability, the existence of contingencies makes it impossible to recommend to all organizations the use of a particular strategy. The large number of possible contingent factors, the variety of organizational contexts, and potential changes over time in the relevance of specific contingencies make it highly unlikely that success in one setting will be appropriate to other contexts. This argues against the popular desire to simply transplant carbon copies of the experiments into one's own organization. Rather, the data point to a contingency approach that tailors the strategy to fit the specific context.

A final difficulty in using the review's findings to formulate a change program concerns reporting of work experiments. Most of the studies reviewed here were published research reports. This tends to bias the findings in two important ways. First, there is a serious underreporting of failures. Most academic journals do not publish insignificant results, and the failure of an experiment usually implies that there was no significant change in outcomes. Further, most organizations do not want their failures published. Success, on the other hand, appears more likely to receive widespread dissemination. Severe underreporting of negative results, as evidenced by the predominance of positive outcomes in the experiments under review, may lead organizational members to seriously overestimate the probability that a particular strategy will lead to positive outcomes. The false sense of security that this engenders can blind the most ardent experimenter to implementation problems. Second, published research findings and written reports represent a reconstructed logic of the actual experimental process (Kaplan 1964). This after-the-fact version of the change program invariably reduces the complexity and richness of the events to manageable proportions. Again, the experimenter can be seriously misled by this idealized version of the experimental process.

Given the above-mentioned considerations, it is simply not feasible or wise to implement the strategies reviewed in this book in a mechanical manner. Current knowledge is insufficient to formulate a blueprint for success in most organizations. The existence of contingencies, furthermore, argues against strategies that assume a one-best approach to work improvement. Indeed, the very reporting of experiments may lull the experimenter into false impressions about the complexity of organizational change. Rather than despair over trying to increase productivity and the quality of work life, experimenters can apply a more innovative approach to overcoming the difficulties inherent in applying knowledge in this field: an experimental stance that recognizes the contingencies existing in a given situation and tailors the change program to fit the needs and complexities of the organization.

AN EXPERIMENTAL APPROACH TO WORK
IMPROVEMENT

A major premise underlying an experimental strategy for organizational change is the need to develop work-improvement programs in the settings where they are applied. The review of work experiments points clearly to the inadequacy of implementing carbon copies of the different approaches in one's organization. The uncertainty of organizational change and the presence of expected and unexpected contingencies reduce considerably the probability that standard approaches will be applicable to specific contexts. A promising alternative is to innovate on site. By tailoring the change program to the situation, organizational members can confront the contingencies existing in a given context and respond to them appropriately. This is not to imply that the strategies discussed in this book are not effective and appropriate to particular organizations. What an experimental approach recognizes, however, is the need to fit these strategies to the situation.

An experimental approach to work improvement has two central components: a concern for solving organizational problems rather than demonstrating the efficacy of particular solutions and data gathering as a feedback mechanism to guide the change program.

Commitment to Solving Problems

Theperson typically responsible for a work-improvement program is committed to his chosen strategy. In most instances, he must demonstrate to others in the organization, usually top management, that his innovation is successful. While commitment to a specific strategy is certainly natural, and indeed may be necessary to introduce new ideas into existing organizations, it can easily trap the experimenter into a position of having to succeed with the approach he has championed. "Trapped administrators" as Donald Campbell (1969) has come to refer to such individuals, cannot afford an honest assessment of their programs. Rather, they are forced, both by their own and other's expectations, to demonstrate the efficacy of their solutions. If the solution is correct, trapped administrators have few problems, but if the solution is inappropriate, as is often the case, they do not have the latitude to discontinue the program and try a more promising approach.

For those engaged in work-improvement programs, these circumstances often lead to a situation where a change program is supported for its own sake, regardless of its actual utility to the organization. The person responsible for the program is frequently biased in his interpretation of data about the success of his strategy. Rather than gathering accurate information to help modify or even scrap the program, the tendency is to bend the facts to support the efficacy of the chosen approach. Thus, the individual is no longer committed to solving problems concerned with productivity and human enrichment but is trapped into demonstrating the success of his strategy.

Commitment to solving organizational problems rather than defending specific solutions is especially important to organizations engaged in work improvement. The uncertainty of organizational change and the presence of contingencies make it highly unlikely that specific change programs will be appropriate in all circumstances. These conditions make honest assessment of the change program mandatory if experimenters are to gather the information needed to adjust their programs to fit their organizations. Trapped administrators who follow doggedly a particular approach open themselves to unnecessary failure. By neglecting to collect necessary data, they base the success of their programs on intuition and luck. The risk inherent in this approach is obvious.

A promising approach to resolving the trapped administrator problem is to separate the implementation and evaluation functions in the organization (Notz, Salipante, and Waters 1976). Those who are directly responsible for implementing the change program could use the full strength of their commitment to see that the program is supported and accepted fully in the organization. In effect, they would serve as advocates of the change program. On the other hand, others in the organization could be responsible for evaluating the strategy to see if it is working as intended. These individuals would be committed to the larger goal of solving organizational problems. They would use this commitment to take a hard look at specific solutions, either recommending their continuance, pushing for necessary adjustments, or advocating another approach. While the simplicity of this solution is appealing, it raises a number of difficult issues. The paramount problem concerns the relationship between these two functions. Implementors can readily come to resent external evaluators. Evaluation by others invariably raises doubts about one's competence. Insecurity aroused by this feeling may place unnecessary but real barriers between the two sides. Overcoming this natural separation may require a good deal of intergroup confrontation and problem solving. Differences of opinion and perspective would have to be resolved in the context of a working relationship. Another problem inherent in separating the implementation and evaluation roles is how to keep the evaluative activities from intruding upon and affecting the change program. The very collection of relevant information may itself change the respondents (Brown 1972). One method to overcome this problem is to use unobtrusive or nonreactive evaluative techniques, such as company records, to minimize the effects of evaluation. Of course, awareness that one is being evaluated by others may create special experimental arrangements, thus limiting the general applicability of change programs to those situations where there is an external evaluator. Although these problems appear formidable, there is no reason to suspect that they cannot be overcome in most organizations. If so, separation of the implementation and evaluation functions may allow organizations to commit themselves to specific work-improvement strategies in the context of solving larger organizational problems.

Data Gathering as Feedback for Change

The second component of an experimental approach to work improvement is data gathering as an integral part of the change process. Inherent in the idea of experimentation is uncertainty in producing intended results. Information is needed to guide the change program so that it can be modified if circumstances demand. Without accurate and timely feedback, experimentation is merely a hit-or-miss proposition. Data gathering can reduce considerably the risks of experimentation by providing both long-term and short-term feedback. The former assesses the overall effects of the program, while the latter guides the change process as it evolves.

The problem of gathering long-term information to test the efficacy of a work-improvement program has been discussed at length in this book. Assessment of the work experiments' effects shows that few studies evaluate adequately their overall results. In most cases, improper research design makes interpretation of evaluative information equivocal. Attention to the following guidelines may improve considerably collection of valid, long-term information (Cummings, Molloy, and Glen in press):

1. Assess whether and to what extent the changes were actually implemented: Most work-improvement studies measure only the outcomes or effects of the program, with little attention to whether the action levers were changed as intended. Since it is possible that only parts of the change program were implemented effectively, it is important to know which aspects of the strategy actually produced the observed results. Further, workers' experience of work-related changes may have a greater impact on their behavior than objective assessments of what was changed (Hackman and Lawler 1971). Thus, it appears desirable to elicit workers perceptions of the change program whenever possible.

2. Use multiple measures of variables: Work experiments typically employ single measures for a particular variable, such as job satisfaction. Single measures of a variable make it difficult to determine if the measure represents what it purports to record. Multiple measures, on the other hand, allow the experimenter to triangulate on a common variable—that is, if the measures converge in a common direction, one has some assurance that a specific varia-

ble is being measured. Thus, if several methods of measuring job satisfaction, such as interviews, questionnaires, participant observations, and peer ratings, show similar results, one can be fairly certain that job satisfaction is being measured.

3. Use unobtrusive measures where possible. Unobtrusive measures consist of physical evidence, secondary data, and simple observations rather than direct responses from people. These measures minimize the reactivity of the measurement process by lessening the probability that it will change the respondents or experimental process in some relevant way. Also, unobtrusive measures may be easier to obtain than reactive measures, especially in those organizations that routinely record such data—for example, productivity, costs, absenteeism, and turnover.

4. Avoid changes in instrumentation: A common threat to the validity of evaluative data is changes in the calibration of measurement instruments. A modification in accounting methods, for example, may easily be mistaken for an experimental effect. To reduce this artifact, it seems preferable to retain a specific measuring procedure during the experimental period, even if it may be obsolete in the wider organization.

5. Use control groups where possible: Work-improvement programs are seldom able to randomize individuals to experimental and control group conditions. A weaker yet powerful alternative to randomization is the use of nonequivalent control groups as comparisons to the change program. The addition of a nonequivalent control group reduces greatly the ambiguity of causal inference, especially if the control group is recruited from the same or a similar setting as the experimental group.

6. Avoid extreme bias in the choice of experimental groups: Selection of experimental groups because they manifest some characteristic to an unusual degree may open the results to a regression artifact. Thus, groups that are extremely dissatisfied or unproductive may show improvements merely with the passage of time.

7. Use statistical tests to compare measurements: Since variables may change simply as a matter of chance, it seems wise to use statistical analysis to rule out this possibility.

8. Collect time series data: Repeated measures of a variable, both before and after the experiment, provide the data necessary to test for regression and selection-interaction artifacts. Since most organizations record data over time, this is an especially easy way to improve work experimentation.

9. Protect the experiment: Work experiments are easily affected by a multitude of extraneous conditions that make interpretation of results ambiguous. Union-management conflicts, changes in company policy, and informal contact with others outside the experi-

ment are just a few of the uncontrolled factors that may affect the
project's results. While there is no simple way to protect the change
program from these influences, awareness of the problem may well
determine choice of experimental groups, the timing of measurements,
and planned changes in the wider organization.

10. Record all occurrences that might plausibly qualify the findings: Most work experiments report only information directly related
to the change program. Additional data about situational anomalies,
contextual factors, and organizational and environmental events,
though not central to the program, may render inferences drawn from
it invalid. Reporting such information would greatly improve the precision of interpreting experimental findings.

The guidelines outlined above should improve considerably the
gathering and interpretation of long-term information needed to test
the effects of work-improvement experiments. While such data help
experimenters judge whether their programs are responsible for the
observed results, shorter-term information is also required, to guide
the change project as it evolves. Short-term data tells the experimenter if his strategy is progressing as intended; this knowledge allows
for modifications of the change program during implementation. If
short-term information is to serve this function, it must be gathered
repeatedly and with little delay. This shortens the feedback cycle
by providing individuals with an almost continuous mapping of the
change process. The guidelines for collecting valid, long-term information also apply to short-term data gathering. The major difference,
however, is the need for rapid information. To satisfy this requirement, short-term data gathering must be built into the change strategy
(Notz, Salipante, and Waters 1976). This allows experimenters to
design the feedback process before the experiment is started, thus
taking full advantage of their control over methods of data gathering.

Short-term data collection has two major problems, which may
be overcome in most situations. The first concerns the noise or random error that is likely to be present in short-interval data. Repeated
measures of a single variable are subject to random fluctuations,
caused by innumerable factors inherent in the measurement process.
Productivity, for example, may fluctuate randomly because of changes
in the quality of raw materials, machine speeds, workers' behavior,
and the timing of measurement. This problem is especially prevalent
in data collected at short intervals, where there is insufficient time
to average out such noise. Since random fluctuations may easily be
mistaken for actual changes, it is important to ensure that the measurement process is reliable over time. One way to improve the reliability
of frequent data collection is to create an index that pools different
measures of the same variable, thereby averaging out much of the

random error. Productivity, for instance, could consist of an index comprised of such factors as production costs, product quality, machine utilization, and worker output. Frequent pooling of such data would provide experimenters with a relatively reliable measure of how the change program is affecting productivity.

A second problem associated with short-term data gathering involves reactive or obtrusive measures. Experimenters typically use interviews or questionnaires to collect attitudinal data. Such instruments are particularly effective for obtaining employees' perceptions of the change program. Their use for short-term information collection, however, poses problems: repeated use of interviews or questionnaires is not only time consuming and reactive but is likely to cause changes in workers' attitudes irrespective of the organizational changes. One way to overcome these problems is to employ unobtrusive measures as surrogates for attitudes. Unobtrusive measures are not obtained directly from respondents, but rather consist of observations, company records, and other sources of secondary data (Webb et al. 1966). This form of information is usually easy to collect and relatively nonreactive. The major difficulty is developing unobtrusive measures that are valid reflections of workers' attitudes. Although little effort has gone into developing such measures, there is evidence to suggest that turnover and absenteeism are related to job satisfaction (Brayfield and Crockett 1955). If so, these data, which are typically available in organizations, may serve as proxies of workers' attitudes. With some ingenuity, it should not be difficult to obtain similar information. For example, grievances, requests for transfers, drinking as evidenced by the number of liquor bottles in the employees' parking lot, visits to the company infirmary, cleanliness of the work area and bathrooms, and participation in company-sponsored activities may indicate how workers feel about their jobs and the organization. One could validate such measures by examining how well they relate to standard attitudinal questionnaires. Those unobtrusive measures that relate strongly and are easy to collect could comprise an unobtrusive index of employees' attitudes toward work.

In summary, an experimental approach to work improvement involves commitment to solving organizational problems rather than defending specific solutions. Separation of the implementation and evaluation functions allows organizations to commit themselves to particular work-improvement strategies while remaining open to modifications or other approaches if the initial strategy is not producing desired results. Given the uncertainty of organizational change, data gathering must be built into the program to guide the change process. Long-term information allows experimenters to judge the overall efficacy of their projects, while shorter-term knowledge permits continual modification of the strategy to meet contingencies present in the situation.

MANAGING ORGANIZATIONAL CHANGE

It should be apparent by now that whatever strategy is chosen for work improvement, there is a great deal of skill and artistry involved in organizational change. Although much of this mastery is personalized wisdom gained through on-line experience, certain rules of thumb seem applicable to most settings. This practical knowledge has received little systematic attention in the literature reviewed. In most experiments, it was included almost as an afterthought to the primary focus of study—organizational change and its effects. Given the anecdotal nature of this information, the following guidelines serve primarily as a checklist, sensitizing the experimenter to certain issues that might otherwise be overlooked in planning and implementing a work-improvement strategy (Cummings, Molloy, and Glen 1975).

Choosing a Strategy

The seven theoretical and change orientations presented in this book provide the experimenter with well-tested strategies for increasing productivity and the quality of work life. Although choice of a particular approach may well be a matter of personal preference, examination of the contingencies associated with each orientation informs the experimenter under what conditions positive outcomes are likely to result. Thus, a first step in choosing an appropriate strategy is to compare its contingencies to those in the proposed situation. Where there is a match, one has some assurance that the approach will produce positive results. For example, autonomous work groups seem appropriate whenever tasks are interdependent and form a relatively self-completing whole and when there is a supportive organizational climate where workers can be involved directly in the change process. Job restructuring appears relevant when there are a number of routine and monotonous jobs that are relatively independent of each other. Participative management requires an organizational climate where there is high trust and confidence between workers and management. Organization-wide change is suited to situations where changes in technology, environment, or company policy make existing structures inappropriate. Behavior modification seems relevant when the desired performance is behaviorally determined and measurable. Flexible working hours is suited to organizations where the task does not require continuous manning of the total work force. Finally, Scanlon plans are appropriate to organizations that can measure employees' contribution to costs or output.

Although examination of contingencies helps experimenters choose the most appropriate of the seven orientations, it is equally important to retain the flexibility to incorporate aspects of the other six. There is nothing exclusive or sacred about the different approaches. Successful change may depend on one's ability to graft useful elements from all the strategies on to the change program. The primary orientation may be job restructuring, for instance. Changes in technology and production layout suggested by the autonomo group approach, reduction in the number of managerial levels (organization-wide change), or more flexible working hours may improve considerably the effects of job restructuring. The need to be eclectic runs through most of the experiments reviewed. Few studies employed a single orientation in toto; rather, the situation often demanded modifications suggested by the other strategies. The pertinent point is not to follow any strategy blindly but to remain open to elements from all the orientations.

Planning for Spillover Effects

Most work experiments affect related parts of the organization. These spillover effects are frequently unintended, resulting from inability to isolate or buffer the experiment from the rest of the organization. Although some spillover may be desirable for wider dissemination of experimental results, it is more often an unplanned byproduct of the change process, which can jeopardize its success. Some programs, for instance, have reduced the number of workers needed to do the job. Unless this kind of side effect has been anticipated and planned for, labor relations problems could end the experiment. Analysis of the work experiments reveals that as the unit of change widens from individual jobs, such as job restructuring and organizational behavior modification, to organization-level changes, such as organization-wide change and Scanlon plans, the probability of spillover effects increases. This follows from the greater complexity and uncertainty of larger-scale programs where the time scale of change is longer, the amount of disruption in organizational functioning is greater, and the probability that separate modifications interact unpredictably increases. Awareness of these dynamics forewarns the experimenter that he may encounter a multitude of unintended consequences, especially as the scope of the change program enlarges.

The risk of unintended spillover effects may be reduced through support and protection for the experiment before any changes are made.

This involves a sanctioning process, where members from the highest implicated levels in the organization agree to protect the program and manage its possible side effects. A good example of this approach is the implementation strategy associated with autonomous work groups. Here, the change process is sanctioned and supervised by a joint management and worker committee. These individuals provide the ground rules for the program, the protection needed for experimentation, and the decision-making mechanism for dealing with spillover effects arising during the project. Although such sanction is no guarantee that unexpected consequences will always be resolved, it increases greatly the adaptive capacity of the organization to confront and work through these problems.

Deciding on Worker Participation

Worker participation in the change process appears to be a major contingency in at least four of the strategies renewed: autonomous work groups, participative management, organization-wide change, and Scanlon plans. The remaining approaches seem to require direct participation to a lesser degree. Although the need for worker involvement in the change process may be a function of the theoretical orientation underlying the strategy, there are more practical considerations to be taken into account. First, where participation is likely to be seen as collusion with management, it is unlikely to work. This seems probable in those situations where there is not a strong union or where there is not a cohesive work force. Under these conditions, involvement may divide the employees into pro- and countermanagement groups. Second, where there is low trust and confidence between workers and management, involvement in change may impede the program and reduce it to a traditional bargaining process. Third, if employees have genuinely useful ideas to contribute to the project, their participation is likely to be beneficial. On the other hand, if involvement is merely a ploy to give workers the feeling of participation, the strategy is likely to backfire. Fourth, where involvement is likely to generate expectations that the organization is either unwilling or unable to meet, management is probably better off prescribing the changes. This seems likely in those circumstances where the organization is more committed to a metaphor, such as participative management, than to a concrete plan for change. This is not to suggest that the strategies reviewed are nothing more than metaphors; in some cases, however, organizations try to implement such programs without understanding fully their methods and requirements for change. Finally, worker involvement in the change process is desirable and may be mandatory if workers have had previous experience with participation. Here, it seems beneficial to take full advantage of employees' experience.

Taking an Evolutionary Approach

For organizations just starting in work improvement, it seems reasonable to begin with small pilot projects and to expand the scale of change slowly. This evolutionary strategy recognizes that long-term gains in productivity and human enrichment depend on a gradual process of experimentation and learning. A major element of this process is gaining familiarity with organizational change and establishing trust and confidence among workers and managers. Starting with smaller-scale projects allows organizations to learn how to experiment, with minimal amounts of organizational disruption. Confidence also increases as individuals become experienced with managing change under relatively protected circumstances.

A promising approach to evolutionary change is to integrate several of the theoretical and change orientations into an overall program. Such a strategy might start at the individual job level, where minimal amounts of organizational disruption are likely to occur. If individual job-restructuring experiments were successful, organizational members would have the confidence and experience to expand the scale of change to work groups. This could include experimentation with autonomous work groups or participative management, which entail closer collaboration and trust between workers and management. Group-level modifications would also provide new areas for innovation and change when the expansion of individual jobs had reached its limits. Successful experience with work groups would provide the preconditions to engage in wider organizational change. Organizational members would have the confidence and knowledge to deal with structural changes applicable to related parts of the organization. Further, these changes could consolidate and enhance the gains from earlier experimentation by stimulating more effective ways to design the organization.

An evolutionary approach to work improvement is congruent with workers' tendency to want increased discretion and challenge over time. As employees gain autonomy, they frequently desire, and are able to manage, wider aspects of the workplace. An evolutionary strategy anticipates this trend by expanding the scale of change to meet workers' growing needs and skills. In effect, it paces the scope of change to the needs of the work force.

Being Opportunistic

The final guideline for managing organizational change is the ability to detect and react to events that make an otherwise difficult change program feasible. In several of the experiments reviewed, certain occurrences related indirectly to the program were used to facilitate work improvement. For example, a major technological change may open the possibility to work redesigns and structural modifications in the organization. Organizations contemplating work improvements might attempt to identify such inevitable events so they can plan their change programs around them. Typical changes occurring naturally in organizations that may help work improvements include technical and physical changes, managerial reassignments, product or service innovations, modifications in company policy, new government regulations, and changes in the work force brought about by training, recruitment, or turnover.

CONCLUSION

Strategies for improving productivity and the quality of work life abound in organizations today. This book has presented and critiqued seven of the most tested approaches to work improvement. These orientations provide the organization with both a theoretical base and an implementation strategy for improving work. Their use in a particular organization, however, requires much experimentation and innovation on site. Current knowledge in this field points clearly to the authors' inability to predict precisely how a specific program will work in an organization. Given the contingencies that arise in the situation, it seems highly unlikely that we will ever have all the necessary understanding to guarantee success in a particular setting. Rather, experimenters will always be faced with uncertainties and anomalies that demand unique responses. It is hoped that this book provides innovators with a clearer path toward designing work for greater productivity and human enrichment.

Adam, E. E. "Behavior Modification and Quality Control." Academy of Management Journal 18 (June 1975): 662–79.

Alderfer, C. "Job Enlargement and the Organizational Context." Personnel Psychology 22 (Winter 1969): 418–26.

Anonymous. "Small Team Production." Mimeographed. Columbus, Ohio: R. G. Barry Company.

Bartlett, A. "Changing Behavior as a Means to Increased Efficiency. The Journal of Applied Behavioral Science 3 (May/June 1976): 381–411.

Baum, S., and W. Young. A Practical Guide to Flexible Working Hours. London: Kogan Page, 1973.

Beatty, R., and C. Schneir. "A Case for Positive Reinforcement." Business Horizons 11 (April 1975): 57–66.

Birchall, D., and R. Wild. "Job Restructuring Amongst Blue- Collar Workers." Personnel Review 2 (Spring 1973): 40–56.

Blackler, F., and C. Brown. "The Impending Crisis in Job Redesign. Journal of Occupational Psychology 48 (1975): 185–93.

Blain, I., and J. Keohane. "One Company's Management Structure after a Change." Occupational Psychology 43 (January 1969): 23–38.

Blood, M. "Intergroup Comparison of Intraperson Differences: Rewards from the Job." Personnel Psychology 26 (Spring 1973): 1–9.

Bolton, J. H. Flexible Working Hours. London: Anbar Publications, 1971.

Bowers, D., and S. Seashore. "Changing the Structure and Functioning of an Organization." Mimeographed. Ann Arbor: Survey Research Center, University of Michigan, 1963.

Bragg, J. E., and I. R. Andrews. "Participative Decision Making: An Experimental Study in a Hospital." The Journal of Applied Behavioral Science 9 (November/December 1973): 727-35.

Brayfield, A., and W. Crockett. "Employee Attitudes and Employee Performance." Psychological Bulletin 52 (September 1955): 396-424.

Bregard, A., J. Golowsen, F. Hangen, E. Jolstad, E. Thorsrud, and T. Tyslano. "Norsk Hydro: Experiment in the Fertilizer Factories." Mimeographed. Oslo: Work Research Institutes, 1968.

Brown, D. "Research Action: Organizational Feedback, Understanding, and Change." The Journal of Applied Behavioral Science 8 (November/December 1972): 697-711.

Business Week. "Where Skinner's Theories Work." Business Week, December 2, 1972, pp. 64-65.

Butteriss, M. Techniques and Developments in Management: A Selection. London: Institute of Personnel Management, 1975.

Campbell, D. "Reforms as Experiments." The American Psychologist 24 (April 1969): 409-29.

Campbell, D., and J. Stanley. Experimental and Quasi-Experimental Designs for Research. Chicago: Rand McNally, 1966.

Cass-Beggs, R., and F. Emery. "Food, Drinks and Sweets in the Reduction of Industrial Fatigue." Occupational Psychology 39 (December 1965): 247-59.

Cathey, P. J. "Flexible Hours—An Idea Whose Time Has Come." Iron Age 21 (May 1973): 35-37.

Chase, R. "A Review of Models for Mapping the Socio-Technical System." AHE Transactions 7 (March 1975): 48-55.

Coch, L., and J. French. "Overcoming Resistance to Change." Human Relations 1 (August 1948): 512-32.

Collins, D., and R. Raubolt. "A Study of Employee Resistance to Job Enrichment." Personnel Journal 54 (April 1975): 232-35.

Conant, E., and M. Kilbridge. "An Interdisciplinary Analysis of
Job Enlargement: Technology, Costs, and Behavioral Implications." Industrial and Labor Relations Review 18 (April 1965):
377–95.

Cox, D., and K. Sharp. "Research on the Unit of Work." Occupational Psychology 25 (April 1951): 90–108.

Cumming, E., I. L. W. Clancey, and J. Cumming. "Improving Patient Care Through Organizational Changes in the Mental Hospital." Psychiatry 19 (August 1956): 249–61.

Cummings, T. G. "Socio-Technical Systems: An Intervention Strategy." In New Techniques in Organization Development. Edited
by W. Burke. New York: Basic Books, in press.

_____(a). "The Estimating and Die Engineering Experiment: A Case
Study of White-Collar Department Redesign." In T. G. Cummings and S. Srivastva. Management of Work: A Socio-Technical Systems Approach. Kent, Ohio: Comparative Administration Research Institute, 1976.

_____(b). "The Wheel-Line Experiment: A Case Study of Blue-
Collar Work Design." In T. G. Cummings and S. Srivastva.
Management of Work: A Socio-Technical Systems Approach.
Kent, Ohio: Comparative Administration Research Institute,
1976.

Cummings, T. G., E. S. Molloy, and R. Glen. "Intervention Strategies for Improving Productivity and the Quality of Work Life."
Organizational Dynamics 4 (Summer 1975): 52–68.

_____. "A Methodological Critique of 58 Selected Work Experiments."
Human Relations. In press.

Cummings, T., and S. Srivastra. Management of Work: A Socio-
Technical Systems Approach. Kent, Ohio: Comparative Administration Research Institute and Kent State University Press,
1976.

Davis, L. "Toward a Theory of Job Design." Journal of Industrial
Engineering 8 (1957): 305–15.

Davis, L., and E. Valfer. "Intervening Responses to Changes in
Supervisor Job Designs." Occupational Psychology 39 (July
1965): 171–89.

Davis, L., and R. Werling (a and b). "Job Design Factors." Occupational Psychology 34 (March 1960): 109–32.

Donahue, R. "Flexible Time Systems. Flex Time Systems in New
York." Public Personnel Management 4 (July/August 1975):
212–15.

Donnelly, J. F. "Increasing Productivity by Involving People in Their
Total Job." Personnel Administration 34 (September/October
1971): 8–13.

Duerr, E. "The Effect of Misdirected Incentives on Employee Behavior." Personnel Journal 53 (December 1974): 890–93.

Elbing, A., H. Gadon, and J. Gordon. "Flexible Working Hours:
The Missing Link." California Management Review 17 (Spring
1975): 50–57.

Emery, F. E. "Characteristics of Socio-Technical Systems."
Mimeographed. Document no. T 176. London: Tavistock Institute of Human Relations, 1959.

_____. "The Democratisation of the Workplace." Manpower and Ap-
plied Psychology 1 (1969): 118–29.

_____. "Some Hypotheses About the Way in Which Tasks May Be
More Effectively Put Together to Make Jobs." Mimeographed.
Document no. T 176. London: Tavistock Institute of Human
Relations, 1963.

Emery, F. E., E. Thorsrud, and E. Lange. "Field Experiments at
Christiana Spigerverk." Mimeographed. Document no. T 807.
London: Tavistock Institute of Human Relations, 1970.

Englestad, P. H. "Socio-Technical Approaches to Problems of Process Control." Paper read at Fourth Fundamental Research
Symposium: "Paper-Making Systems and Their Control," 1970,
at Oxford University. Mimeographed.

Fein, M. "Improving Productivity by Improved Productivity Sharing."
The Conference Board Record 13 (July 1976): 44–49.

Fields, C. J. "Variable Work Hours—The MONY Experience." Personnel Journal 53 (September 1974): 675–78.

Ford, R. (a and b). Motivation Through the Work Itself. New York: American Management Association, 1969.

Ford, R., and H. Sheaffer. "Appendix." In R. Ford. Motivation Through the Work Itself. New York: American Management Association, 1969.

Foster, M. "Analytical Model for Socio-Technical Systems." Mimeographed. Document no. 7. London: Tavistock Institute of Human Relations, 1967.

French, J., J. Israel, and D. As. "An Experiment on Participation in a Norwegian Factory." Human Relations 13 (February 1960): 3-20.

Foulkes, F. Creating More Meaningful Work. New York: American Management Association, 1969.

Frost, C. F., J. H. Wakeley, and R. A. Ruh. The Scanlon Plan for Organization Development: Identity, Participation, and Equity. East Lansing: Michigan State University Press, 1974.

Gilson, T. Q., and M. J. Lefcowitz. "A Plant-Wide Productivity Bonus in a Small Factory: Study of an Unsuccessful Case." Industrial and Labor Relations Review 10 (January 1957): 284-96.

Golembiewski, R., S. Yeager, and R. Hilles. "Factor Analysis of Some Flexitime Effects: Attitudinal and Behavior Consequences of a Structural Intervention." Academy of Management Journal 18 (September 1975): 500-09.

Goodall, K. "Shapers at Work." Psychology Today 6 (November 1972): 53-158.

Gorman, L., and E. S. Molloy. People, Jobs and Organizations. Dublin: Irish Productivity Centre, 1972.

_____ (a). "Job Restructuring in the Ledger Department of a Bank." In L. Gorman and E. S. Molloy. People, Jobs and Organizations. Dublin: Irish Productivity Centre, 1972.

_____ (b). "The Process of Job Enrichment." In L. Gorman and E. S. Molloy. People, Jobs and Organizations. Dublin: Irish Productivity Centre, 1972.

_____ (c). "Planned Change in a Computer Punchroom." In L. Gorman and E. S. Molloy. People, Jobs and Organizations. Dublin: Irish Productivity Centre, 1972.

Gray, R. B. "The Scanlon Plan—A Case Study." British Journal of Industrial Relations 9 (November 1971): 291–310.

Gray, R. B., P. Graubard, and H. Rosenberg. "Little Brother Is Changing You." Psychology Today 7 (March 1974): 42–46.

Hackman, J. R. "Is Job Enrichment Just a Fad?" Harvard Business Review 14 (September–October 1975): 129–238.

Hackman, J. R., and E. E. Lawler, III. "Employee Reactions to Job Characteristics." Journal of Applied Psychology 55 (June 1971): 259–86.

Hackman, J., G. Oldham, R. Janson, and K. Purdy. "A New Strategy for Job Enrichment." California Management Review 17 (Summer 1975): 57–71.

Hall, E. "Will Success Spoil Skinner?" Psychology Today 6 (November 1972): 65–130.

Hammer, W., and E. Hammer. "Behavior Modification on the Bottom Line." Organizational Dynamics 5 (Spring 1976): 2–21.

Herbst, P. Autonomous Group Functioning. London: Tavistock Publications, 1962.

_____. "Situation Dynamics and the Theory of Behavior Systems." Behavioral Science 2 (January 1957): 13–29.

_____. "Socio-Technical Unit Design." Document no. 899. Mimeographed. London: Tavistock Institute of Human Relations, 1966.

Herzberg, F. "One More Time: How Do You Motivate Employees?" Harvard Business Review 8 (January–February 1968): 53–62.

_____. Work and the Nature of Man. Cleveland: World Publishing Company, 1966.

Herzberg, F., B. Mausner, and B. Snyderman. The Motivation to Work. New York: Wiley, 1959.

Hill, R. "Working on the Scanlon Plan." International Management (1974): 39–43.

Hulin, C., and M. Blood. "Job Enlargement, Individual Differences and Worker Responses." Psychological Bulletin 69 (January 1968): 41–55.

Johnson, P., and M. Sorcher. "Behavior Modelling Training: Why, How and What Results." Journal of European Training 5 (1976): 62–70.

Kaplan, A. The Conduct of Inquiry. San Francisco: Chandler Publishing Company, 1964.

King–Taylor, L. (a). "Case Study One: Richard Braxendale & Sons." Not for Bread Alone: An Appreciation of Job Enrichment. London: Business Books, 1972.

_____(b). "Case Study Four: Mercury House Group." Not for Bread Alone: An Appreciation of Job Enrichment. London: Business Books, 1972.

_____(c). "Case Study Seven: Swedish State Power Board." Not for Bread Alone: An Appreciation of Job Enrichment. London: Business Books, 1972.

Lawler, E. E., III, and J. R. Hackman. "Impact of Employee Participation in the Development of Pay Incentives." Journal of Applied Psychology 53 (1969): 447–67.

Lawler, E. E., III, J. R. Hackman, and S. Kaufman. "Effects of Job Redesign. A Field Experiment." Journal of Applied Social Psychology 3 (January 1973): 49–62.

Legge, K. "Flexible Working Hours—Panacea or Placebo." Management Decision 12 (1974): 264–80.

Lesieur, F. G., ed. The Scanlon Plan: A Frontier in Labor–Management Cooperation. Cambridge, Mass.: MIT Press, 1958.

Lesieur, F. G., and E. S. Puckett (a, b, and c). "The Scanlon Plan Has Proved Itself." Harvard Business Review 47 (September/October 1969): 109–18.

Lewin, K. "Frontiers in Group Dynamics: Concept, Method and
    Reality in Social Science; Social Equilibria and Social Change."
    Human Relations 1 (January 1947): 5-42.

Lewin, K., and P. Grabbe, eds. "Problems of Re-education."
    Journal of Social Issues 1 (August 1945): 1-66.

Likert, R. New Patterns of Management. New York: McGraw-Hill,
    1961.

Lippitt, R. "An Experimental Study of the Effect of Democratic and
    Authoritarian Group Atmospheres." University of Iowa Studies
    in Child Welfare 16 (1940): 43-195.

Lippitt, R., and R. White. "The Social Climate of Children's Groups."
    In Child Behavior and Development. Edited by R. Barker, J.
    Kounin, and H. Wright, pp. 485-508. New York: McGraw-
    Hill, 1943.

Luthans, F. Organizational Behavior. New York: McGraw-Hill,
    1973.

Luthans, F., and R. Kreitner. Organizational Behavior Modification.
    Glenview, Ill.: Scott, Foresman and Company, 1975.

_____. "The Production Case." In F. Luthans and R. Kreitner.
    Organizational Behavior Modification. Glenview, Ill.: Scott,
    Foresman and Company, 1975.

_____. "The Management of Behavioral Contingencies." Personnel
    51 (July-August 1974): 7-16.

Maher, J., W. Overbagh, G. Palmer, and D. Piersal. "Enriched
    Jobs Mean Better Inspection Performance." Industrial Engi-
    neering 11 (November 1969): 23-26.

Mann, C., and L. Hoffman. Automation and the Worker. New York:
    Henry Holt, 1960.

Marks, A. "An Investigation of Modifications of Job Design in an In-
    dustrial Situation and Their Effects on Some Measures of Eco-
    nomic Productivity." Ph.D. dissertation. University of Cali-
    fornia, Berkeley, 1954.

Marr, D. "A Job Enrichment Project for Customer Contact Resource. Mimeographed. American Airlines, Training and Development Division, 1970.

Meacham, M., and A. Wiesen. Changing Classroom Behavior: A Manual for Precision Teaching. New York: International Textbook Company, 1969.

Miller, E. "Technology, Territory, and Time: The Internal Differentiation of Complex Production Systems." Human Relations 12 (Fall 1959): 243-72.

Miller, E., and A. Rice. Systems of Organization. London: Tavistock Publications, 1967.

Morse, N., and E. Reimer. "The Experimental Change of a Major Organizational Variable." Journal of Abnormal and Social Psychology 52 (January 1956): 120-29.

Mumford, E. "Job Satisfaction: A Method of Analysis." Personnel Review 2 (Summer 1972): 48-57.

_____. "A Strategy for the Redesign of Work." Personnel Review 5 (Spring 1976): 33-39.

The National Commission on Productivity and Work Quality. A Plant-Wide Productivity Plan in Action: Three Years of Experience with the Scanlon Plan. Washington, D.C.: The National Commission on Productivity and Work Quality, 1975.

Nord, W. "Improving Attendance Through Rewards." Personnel Administration 33 (November/December 1970): 37-41.

Notz, W., P. Salipante, and J. Waters. "Quality of Work Life: A New Approach." Proceedings of the Canadian Association of Administrative Science. May 1976.

O'Connell, J. Managing Organizational Innovation. Homewood, Ill.: Irwin, 1968.

Organizational Dynamics. "At Emery Air Freight Positive Reinforcement Boosts Performance." Organizational Dynamics 2 (Winter 1973): 41-50.

_____. "Conversation with B. F. Skinner." Organizational Dynamics 2 (Winter 1973): 31-40.

Paul, W., Jr., K. B. Robertson, and F. Herzberg (a, b, c, d, and e). "Job Enrichment Pays Off." Harvard Business Review 47 (March/April 1969): 61-78.

Pauling, T. "Job Enlargement—An Experience at Philips Telecommunication of Australia Ltd." Personnel Practice Bulletin 24 (September 1968): 194-96.

Pedalino, E., and V. Gamboa. "Behavior Modification and Absenteeism: Intervention in One Industrial Setting." Journal of Applied Psychology 59 (December 1974): 694-98.

Petersen, R. "Swedish Experiments in Job Reform." Business Horizons 19 (June 1976): 13-22.

Porter, L., E. E. Lawler, III, and J. Hackman. Behavior in Organizations. New York: McGraw-Hill, 1975.

Powell, R., and J. Schlacter. "Participative Management: A Panacea." Academy of Management Journal 6 (June 1971): 165-73.

Premack, D. "Reinforcement Theory." Nebraska Symposium on Motivation. Edited by D. Levine, pp. 123-80. Lincoln: University of Nebraska, 1965.

Prestat, C. "Une Experience de Groupes Semi-Autonomes." Mimeographed. Paris: Foundation Internationale des Sciences Humanies, 1971.

Puckett, E. "Measuring Performance Under the Scanlon Plan." The Scanlon Plan: A Frontier in Labor-Management Cooperation. Edited by F. G. Lesieur, chap. 6, pp. 65-79. Cambridge, Mass.: MIT Press, 1968.

Randall, R. "Job Enrichment Insures Savings at Travelers." Management Accounting 21 (January 1973): 68-72.

Reif, W., and R. Tinnell. "A Diagnostic Approach to Job Enrichment." M.S.U. Business Topics (Autumn 1973): 29-37.

Rice, A. K. Productivity and Social Organization: The Ahmedabad Experiment. London: Tavistock Publications, 1958.

_____(a). "The Experimental Reorganization of Automatic Weaving: The Social Reorganization of a Technologically Disturbed Pro-

duction System." In A. K. Rice. Productivity and Social Organization: The Ahmedabad Experiment. London: Tavistock
Publications, 1958.

_____(b). "The Experimental Reorganization of Non-Automatic
Weaving: The Creation of a New Socio-Technical System."
In A. K. Rice. Productivity and Social Organization: The Ah-
medabad Experiment. London: Tavistock Publications, 1958.

Rogers, E. Diffusion of Innovations. New York: The Free Press,
1962.

Rosen, N. "Demand Characteristics in a Field Experiment." Journal of Applied Psychology 54 (April 1970): 163-68.

Rosen, N., and S. Sales. "Behavior in a Non-Experiment: The Effects of Behavioral Field Research on the Work Performance of
Factory Employees." Journal of Applied Psychology 50 (April
1966): 165-71.

Ross, T. L., and G. M. Jones. "An Approach to Increased Productivity: The Scanlon Plan." Financial Executive 40 (February
1972): 23-29.

Sadler, P., and B. Barry. Organizational Development. London:
Longmans, 1970.

Schappe, R. "Twenty-Two Arguments Against Job Enrichment."
Personnel Journal 53 (February 1974): 116-23.

Schultz, G. P. "Worker Participation on Production Problems: A
Discussion of Experience with the 'Scanlon Plan.'" Personnel
28 (November 1951): 201-11.

Schultz, G. P., and R. McKersie. "Participation-Achievement-Re-
ward Systems (PAR)." Journal of Management Studies 10 (May
1973): 141-61.

Shepard, J. "Job Enrichment: Some Problems with Contingency
Models." Personnel Journal 53 (December 1974): 886-89.

Skinner, B. F. Beyond Freedom and Dignity. New York: Bantam
Books, 1971.

_____. Contingencies of Reinforcement: A Theoretical Analysis.
New York: Appleton-Century-Crofts, 1969.

_____. Science and Human Behavior. New York: Macmillan, 1953.

Smith, E., and G. Gude. "Reevaluation of the Scanlon Plan as a
    Motivational Technique." Personnel Journal 50 (December
    1971): 916-23.

Sorcher, M. "Motivation on the Assembly Line." Personnel Admin-
    istration 32 (May/June 1969): 40-48.

Srivastva, S., P. Salipante, T. Cummings, W. Notz, J. Bigelow,
    J. Waters, R. Chisholm, R. Glen, S. Manring, and E. Molloy.
    Job Satisfaction and Productivity. Cleveland: Department of
    Organizational Behavior, Case Western Reserve University,
    1975.

Stein B., A. Cohen, and H. Gadon. "Flextime. Work When You Want
    To." Psychology Today 10 (June 1976): 40-80.

Swart, J. "What Time Shall I Go to Work Today?" Business Hori-
    zons 17 (October 1974): 19-26.

Thorsrud, E. "Industrial Democracy." Mimeographed. Document
    no. T 886. Oslo: Work Research Institutes, 1966.

Trist, E. L., and K. Bamforth. "Some Social and Psychological
    Consequences of the Longwall Method of Coal Getting." Human
    Relations 4 (February 1951): 3-38.

Trist, E. L., G. W. Higgin, H. Murray, and A. B. Pollock. Orga-
    nizational Choice. London: Tavistock Publications, 1963.

_____(a). "Face Team Organization and Maintaining Production."
    In E. L. Trist, G. W. Higgin, H. Murray, and A. B. Pollock.
    Organizational Choice. London: Tavistock Publications, 1963.

_____(b). "Work Load Stress and Cycle Regulation." In E. L. Trist,
    G. W. Higgin, H. Murray, and A. B. Pollock. Organizational
    Choice. London: Tavistock Publications, 1963.

Van Beek, H. "The Influence of Assembly Line Organization on Out-
    put, Quality, Morale." Occupational Psychology 38 (July 1964):
    161-72.

Van Gils, M. R. "Job Design and Work Organization in Industrial
    Democracy in the Netherlands." Personal correspondence from
    author, 1969.

Van Liet, A. "A Work Structuring Experiment in Television Assembly." Mimeographed. T. E. O. Special, no. 5. Holland: Phillips Company, 1970.

Vossen, H. P. "Experiments in the Special Miniature Department of Philips N.V." Mimeographed. Internal report. Netherlands: Philips N.V., 1974.

Wade, M. Flexible Working Hours in Practice. Epping, Essex: Gower Press, 1973.

_____. "Flexible Working Time Installed by Joint Committee: Pilkington Brothers Ltd." In M. Wade. Flexible Working Hours in Practice. Epping, Essex: Gower Press, 1973.

Walker, C. "The Problem of the Repetitive Job." Harvard Business Review 28 (May/June 1950): 54-58.

Walker, C., C. Fletcher, and D. McLeod. "Flexible Working Hours in Two British Government Offices." Public Personnel Management 4 (July/August 1975): 216-22.

Wall, T., and G. Stephenson. "Herzberg's Two-Factor Theory of Job Attitudes: A Critical Evaluation and Some Fresh Evidence." British Journal of Industrial Relations 8 (1970): 41-65.

Walters, R., and Associates. Job Enrichment for Results. Reading, Mass.: Addison-Wesley, 1975.

Walton, R. E. "The Diffusion of New Work Structures: Explaining Why Success Didn't Take." Organizational Dynamics 3 (Winter 1975): 2-22.

_____. "How to Counter Alienation in the Plant." Harvard Business Review 12 (November/December 1972): 70-81.

Webb, E., D. Campbell, R. Schwartz, and L. Sechrest. Unobtrusive Measures: Nonreactive Research in the Social Sciences. Chicago: Rand McNally, 1966.

White, R., and R. Lippitt. Autocracy and Democracy. New York: Harper, 1960.

Whitsett, D. "Where Are Your Unenriched Jobs?" Harvard Business Review 14 (January/February 1975): 74-80.

Wild, R. "Dimensions and Stages of Job Design." Personnel Management 6 (December 1974): 32–37.

Willatt, N. "Flextime at Sandoz." European Business 39 (Autumn
1973): 56–61.

ABOUT THE AUTHORS

THOMAS G. CUMMINGS is Associate Professor of Management at the University of Southern California, Los Angeles. Until 1976 he was Assistant Professor of Organizational Behavior at Case Western Reserve University, Cleveland, Ohio.

Dr. Cummings has consulted and published widely in the area of productivity and quality of work life. His articles have appeared in Journal of Applied Psychology and Organizational Dynamics. He is joint author (with Suresh Srivastva) of Management of Work: A Socio-Technical Systems Approach (1976).

Dr. Cummings holds a B.S. and M.B.A. from Cornell University, Ithaca, New York, and a Ph.D. from the University of California at Los Angeles.

EDMOND S. MOLLOY is Senior Management Specialist in Applied Behavioral Science at the Irish Management Institute, Dublin. His present work consists of training and consulting assignments in Ireland and abroad.

Mr. Molloy is joint author (with Liam Gorman) of People, Jobs and Organizations (1972) and of several articles on need achievement, productivity, and job satisfaction.

Mr. Molloy holds a B.A. in Philosophy from University College, Galway, a degree in Theology from Rome, an M.S. in Psychological Science from University College, Dublin, and an M.S. in Organizational Behavior from Case Western Reserve University.

AUTONOMY AT WORK: A Sociotechnical Analysis of
Participative Management
Gerald I. Susman

*A FULL EMPLOYMENT PROGRAM FOR THE 1970s
edited by Alan Gartner,
William Lynch, Jr., and
Frank Riessman

INTERNATIONAL LABOR AND THE MULTINATIONAL
ENTERPRISE
edited by Duane Kujawa

THE LABOR SUPPLY FOR LOWER-LEVEL OCCUPA-
TIONS
Harold Wool, assisted by
Bruce Dana Phillips

QUALITY OF LIFE INDICATORS IN U.S. METROPOLI-
TAN AREAS: A Statistical Analysis
Ben-Chieh Liu

SMALL-SCALE EMPLOYMENT AND PRODUCTION IN
DEVELOPING COUNTRIES: Evidence from Ghana
William F. Steel

*WORKER MILITANCY AND ITS CONSEQUENCES,
1965-75: New Directions in Western Industrial Relations
edited by Solomon Barkin

*Also available in paperback as a PSS Student Edition.